VILLAGE CHRISTIANS AND HINDU CULTURE

World Studies of Churches in Mission

VILLAGE CHRISTIANS
AND
HINDU CULTURE

Study of a rural church in Andhra Pradesh
South India

by

P. Y. LUKE and JOHN B. CARMAN

LONDON
LUTTERWORTH PRESS

First published 1968

LUTTERWORTH PRESS
4 BOUVERIE STREET, LONDON, E.C.4.

7188 1484 3

Printed in Great Britain
by Billing & Sons Limited
Guildford and London

In Memoriam

PAUL DAVID DEVANANDAN

and

FRANK WHITTAKER

The Rev. Dr. Paul Devanandan, then Director of the Christian Institute for the Study of Religion and Society, took the lead in arranging for several 'Younger Church Studies' to be conducted in South India, and helped greatly in the preparation for this study and the discussion of the first draft of our Report.

The Rt. Rev. Frank Whittaker, then Bishop in the Medak Diocese of the Church of South India, welcomed the idea of holding this study in his Diocese and co-operated fully in the planning, the field investigation and the writing of this Report, giving us much valuable counsel and, even when he did not agree with our conclusions, continuing his unwavering support.

Both Dr. Devanandan and Bishop Whittaker believed in the value of this kind of study, especially as contributing to the self-study of the Church in India.

CONTENTS

vii

MAPS

EDITORIAL FOREWORD

This is a careful and thorough study of one of the main objectives of enquiry in this series, namely, the interrelatedness of a church and its environment in a 'missionary situation'. Though indeed there is no church which does not exist in a missionary situation, the subject is easier to investigate when the Christian mission faces a culture based on another religion, in which length of tradition and overwhelming superiority of numbers give the environment a challenging advantage.

The result of this research provides much food for reflection. At first sight, this honest presentation may seem to suggest very pessimistic conclusions. But further thought may indicate a hidden strength in what appears an obvious weakness. Does the openness of the village congregation to all the influences of a non-Christian culture enhance the possibilities of its changing that culture *from within*? Yet even if so, what is the evidence of such a possibility being actualized? How can the Christian mission be made more effective?

Of course, as with all volumes in this series, the study is not simply one of the particular situation investigated. The observations made, and questions raised, have relevance for countries other than India and for Christian encounters besides that with Hinduism.

This may claim to have been the most successful attempt to combine the objective questioning and skill in presentation of an 'outside' observer with the insights and experience of an 'inside' collaborator. Dr John Carman of the U.S.A. has explained in his preface the essential part in the inquiry played by the Indian investigator and his wife. Too long a time has been spent on the process of rewriting the final draft, and a special debt of gratitude is owed to the Rev. Richard W. Taylor, as well as to the original authors, for his operations as midwife in a difficult birth! We trust our readers will agree that the final product has been worth waiting for.

VICTOR E. W. HAYWARD
Geneva   *C.W.M.E. Research Secretary*
January 1968

PREFACE

THE FIELD work for this study was done by one of the two authors, the Rev. P. Y. Luke, with the assistance of Mrs. Luke, during a period of ten months, March–December 1959. The study was conducted in one section of the Wadiaram Pastorate of the Medak Diocese, Church of South India. Wadiaram is a large village forty-five miles north of Hyderabad, the capital of Andhra Pradesh and of the former Hyderabad State. Wadiaram is located on the main road and rail line to Nizamabad, and is twelve miles from the Taluk headquarters of Medak, which is also the centre of the Diocese. The Wadiaram Pastorate was chosen partly for reasons of convenience, and partly because the Diocesan Advisory Committee for this study felt that it was more or less typical of rural Christian life in the Diocese.

The thirty Christian congregations in the Pastorate are divided administratively into three sections. The Advisory Committee recommended that we concentrate on one section and select a few village congregations in the section for more intensive study. The presbyter in charge of the Pastorate recommended the Jangarai section, composed of nine congregations in villages to the west of Wadiaram and south of the road to Medak. The villages in which these congregations are located are fairly close together and can be reached from the road, even during the monsoon rains; a more important reason in the choice of this section, however, was the feeling that it was a good average part of the Pastorate. We chose five congregations in the midst of which Mr. and Mrs. Luke lived for at least brief periods, trying to cover as much as possible of the range of conditions present in the rural congregations of the Diocese as a whole, including Christians of both Mala and Madiga background, both older and newer congregations, and both more active and relatively neglected congregations.

The first period of the field investigation was done during the hot season, March–May. Mr. and Mrs. Luke spent three weeks each in the villages of Jangarai, Achampet, and Kondapuram, and one week each in Ambojipet and Gowlapalli.

It was not difficult for the Lukes to become acquainted with the villagers, since they followed the general Indian village practice of greeting strangers with a barrage of questions: 'Who are you?', 'Which place do you come from?', 'How many children do you have?', 'Why have you come to stay in our village?' The answers to these questions established a natural point of contact, and the villagers were glad in turn to answer similar questions. During the hot season the villagers do not have much work to do in the fields. In the hottest part of the day they sit leisurely in informal groups under shady trees and gossip on topics of common interest: money, marriages, the prices of various commodities, their own family affairs, other people's affairs, etc. The attentive stranger can glean much from listening to this chatter, and soon becomes familiar with the village people, their common concerns and problems, the particular social structure of the village, and the intricacies of village politics. Long conversations and mutual sharing of secrets are common among Telugu village people, though when friendships break up, the sanctity of earlier secrets is often unprotected by any code of honour! The Lukes used to join in these gossip sessions, mainly listening but occasionally interjecting a question to gain more information. In addition, some individuals from a number of castes in the village came back to the Lukes on their own initiative. In their turn the Lukes went to their homes.

Mr. and Mrs. Luke tried to identify themselves with the village Christians: to live among them as members of their congregation, and to give a sympathetic hearing to all their problems. In the evenings they visited Christian families, taking along the 'Church Roll', so that they could inquire about every member of the family listed on it. At the end of their conversation, they offered a word of prayer. The Christians naturally continued to regard Mr. Luke as presbyter, though they were initially puzzled that what he was doing (and not doing) did not fit their experience of the presbyter's visits. Their visits to families helped the Lukes to establish personal contacts with the members of the congregation and to gain an insight into their family life, their economic condition and their various problems. At week-night services and Sunday worship they sat among the congregation and observed how the evangelists or lay leaders conducted the service and how the Christians participated in the worship.

Mr. and Mrs. Luke did not conduct any interviews with questionnaire in hand, but tried to keep in mind the questions in the preparatory document drawn up for this series of studies. These questions were an aid in trying to learn from their conversations with individuals and groups and from their participation in the collective life of the congregation.

In the three villages where they stayed somewhat longer, the Lukes remained silent observers for about ten days, but after that they helped the evangelist and the congregation by talking to individuals, conducting family prayers, congregational worship, and evangelistic services. These various activities provided opportunities for instructing Christians in the Christian faith, while at the same time becoming better acquainted with the way in which the villagers expressed their faith.

The second period of investigation was during the monsoon (June–August). In 1959 this was unusually severe, bringing about twice the average rainfall. This made it more difficult to reach the villages, or to find a dry place to stay. It was possible, however, to make some briefer return visits to the Jangarai section. Short visits were also made to villages in other sections of the Pastorate in which there was some special feature that we wished to study. Among those visited was the oldest congregation in the Pastorate, a congregation from which a number of families had returned to Hinduism, and one with some very active lay leaders. In addition, the Diocesan Advisory Committee at its meeting in June recommended that we check our data by collecting comparative information from four other rural Pastorates to obtain as representative a sampling as possible. In each of these four Pastorates Mr. and Mrs. Luke had an all-day meeting with the presbyter and the evangelists, and then made a one-day visit to one village in the Pastorate selected by the presbyter. At the end of this period, Mr. Luke also visited another part of the Church of South India in Telengana, Nekonda, in the ex-Anglican area of the Dornakal Diocese, and he and I visited Hanamkonda in the American Baptist area of Telengana. The heavy rains made it impossible to spend time in village congregations of these other areas as planned, but Mr. Luke was able to have long discussions with the catechists and the pastors.

As the second author of this study, while a research student of the Christian Institute for the Study of Religion and Society, at Bangalore, I helped in the original planning, adapting for this particular study the questions in the Aspect Study Questionnaire prepared for the whole series of 'Studies in the Life and Growth of the Younger Churches'. In June and August I made visits to the Wadiaram Pastorate and the Jangarai section. These visits were too brief, and my knowledge of Telugu too rudimentary, for me to make any independent observations, but the visits provided opportunities for me to see something of what Mr. and Mrs. Luke had observed, and for us to discuss Mr. Luke's first tentative conclusions and determine in which areas further investigation was needed.

The last period of time that Mr. Luke could devote entirely to this study before resuming his regular duties as a presbyter of the Medak Diocese extended from September through December 1959. Mr. Luke wrote up the first draft of the report in collaboration with me, and we both discussed this draft with the Diocesan Advisory Committee in Medak and with our Advisory Committee in Bangalore. Since January 1960 I have had the primary responsibility for preparing the final draft, but Mr. Luke and I met several times to discuss the revisions up to the end of 1962. I greatly regret that because of my other work, first in India and then after March 1963 in the United States, this revision took much longer than originally intended, and was not finished until September 1965. For this long delay I am solely responsible. A further delay occurred during the final editing by the Rev. Richard W. Taylor, on behalf of the All India Committee for these studies and the Christian Institute for the Study of Religion and Society.

Chapters 1 to 3 present different important features of the background of the present situation, a situation that we attempt to describe in Chapters 4 to 7 and more analytically in Chapters 8 to 10. The description of village Christian congregations is based primarily on the five congregations intensively studied, though we have tried to indicate where the situation we found is not typical of conditions elsewhere. Since there are only four evangelists and one presbyter concerned with these congregations, we have tried to base some of our observations on the work of a larger number of presbyters and evangelists. We have indicated where we are speaking specifically about the ministry in the area of investigation. Chapter 11 contains our conclusions about the 'signs of life and growth' that we were trying ¡to discover throughout this study.

Our first draft also included a chapter of recommendations to the Diocese. We concur in the judgment of our Advisory Committee that these recommendations should not form a part of the published report, but we sent a copy of them to the Medak Diocese. A number of these suggestions have been adopted in whole or in part, and Mr. Luke has personally attempted to implement several of them.

In looking for 'signs of life and growth', we have tried to keep in mind the general directive for this whole group of studies originally given by the Research Department of the International Missionary Council:

> We have said that the aim of the studies in the Life and Growth of Younger Churches is to try to see the local church as it really is and to understand the distinctive insights which it may be gaining into the meaning of the Gospel and the Will of God. The point at which this distinctiveness of Younger Churches begins to develop is to be found in the Church's *encounter* with its environment. Through the way in which it reacts and responds to the pressures of the older traditional culture of the nation, the new impact of Westernized ways, the strong currents of nationalism and, possibly, communism, the upheaval of rapid social change—through responsible encounter with such things the life of the Church is lived, and that is where it has to be studied. . . . Underlying these studies there must be the faith that somewhere in the local Church the Holy Spirit is working and that, therefore, a real 'response' is being made. . . . It may not always be found where we expect to find it. But the signposts which will lead us to it are the sensitive spots, the anxieties and convictions in the *conscience* of individual Christians and of congregations. Wherever the conscience of God's people in a particular church is saying 'This must be resisted', 'That must be attempted', there is a point of decision and response.

We have, therefore, looked for 'signs' within the various 'encounters' of these village Christians, their response to the pressures of their environment and to the traditions which they have both inherited and in one way or another made their own. This includes responses to the traditions of village Hindu society as well as to the Christian inheritance which they have accepted in becoming Christians. The responses may be indicated by points of tension and costly personal decision, but they may also be present in those less conscious and perhaps hardly perceptible attitudes which are influential in moulding the life of the individual Christian and of the congregation.

It is not, of course, enough to note that there is some response. We cannot finally escape from the necessity of evaluating the responses. Naturally our evaluation is coloured by our own understanding of the Gospel and by our own experience of life in a Christian congregation. The standards which an Indian presbyter applies *tend* unconsciously to be those of most urban congregations, which are composed largely of those who have received a more or less Western education. These standards are, therefore, not so different from those of a Western missionary in India, whose experience of the Church is largely that of the United States and Western Europe. We have tried to guard against these prejudices by taking as sympathetic a view as possible of any responses we have seen to the various challenges confronting these village Christians. There are many points where we have been unable to discover any response; there is no outward indication of anything stirring in their hearts. We have tried to indicate those areas in which we find no growth, or else serious obstacles to growth, bearing in mind that it is ultimately God alone who searches the hearts of men, both Christians and non-Christians. Some signs of life and growth, however, are more openly manifest, and these we have tried to describe.

We should like to express our appreciation to all those who have co-operated in making this study possible. We are grateful to the Medak Diocese for releasing Mr. Luke for ten months in 1959, and we appreciate the co-operation and helpful counsel of the Diocesan Advisory Committee, headed by the late Bishop in Medak, the Rt. Rev. Frank Whittaker. We also thank the present Bishop in Medak, the Rt. Rev. Ebor Priestley. We are grateful to our Advisory Committee, headed by the late Dr. Paul Devanandan, and must further acknowledge the co-operation of the present Director of the Christian Institute for the Study of Religion and Society, Mr. M. M. Thomas. We express warm thanks for the work of the Rev. Richard W. Taylor, who assumed responsibility for further editing and the delivery of the typescript to the Editor of this whole series. Finally, we should mention our appreciation for the original inspiration, financial support, and continuing guidance of these studies by the Research Department of the International Missionary Council, later the Department of Missionary Studies of the World Council of Churches. We are grateful for the leadership given to this entire project by the Directors of this Department, the Rev. Erik Nielsen, followed by the Rev. Victor E. W. Hayward, as also to the Rev. (now Canon) John V. Taylor and the Rev. R. K. Orchard.

Madras   JOHN B. CARMAN
December 1967

CHAPTER 1

The Political and Social Background of the Telengana Village

THE CENTRAL focus of this study of the 'Life and Growth of the Church' is the Jangarai section of the Wadiaram Pastorate, which is in the Medak Diocese of the Church of South India. The Pastorate headquarters is in Wadiaram, a village with a population of some eighteen hundred, situated sixteen miles east of the Taluk headquarters of Medak, which is the centre of the Diocese, and forty-three miles north of Hyderabad, the capital of Andhra Pradesh. Hyderabad is the second largest city in South India, with a population of a million and a half. Wadiaram is on both the railway to Manmad and the highway running north to Nagpur. Wadiaram is in the region of Andhra Pradesh known as Telengana, that part of the Telugu-speaking area which lies on the upland plateau called the Deccan, and part of the former State of Hyderabad, largest of India's princely states.

The History of Telengana

The Andhras are mentioned in ancient Hindu scriptures as fighting against the Aryan tribes from North India, and they were known to the Mauryan Empire as a kingdom defended by thirty forts and a hundred thousand men. Asoka's empire extended south to include part of the Andhra territory, but with the collapse of the Mauryan Empire, an independent Andhra kingdom was re-established in 226 B.C. by Simukha, the first of the Satavahana dynasty. At its height, this kingdom stretched far beyond the Andhras' home country, all the way to the West Coast and north to Vidarbha, the region of modern Nagpur. The Satavahana rule ended in the third century A.D. The next prominent rule was that of the Pallava dynasty (A.D. 550–1185). After a brief reign of the Yadava kings and the first Muslim invasion of the Deccan, the Kakatiya dynasty established a kingdom with the Telengana city of Warangal as its capital. Under Kakatiya patronage, literature and the fine arts, as well as trade, are said to have flourished. The Muslim rulers of Delhi brought this kingdom to an end in A.D. 1323, after which Telengana was under Muslim rule, but the southern part of the Andhra area continued for another two centuries under Hindu rulers: small Reddi kingdoms along the Krishna river and the Vijayanagara Empire farther west, within which Telugu culture experienced a new flowering. The combined Muslim forces of the Deccan defeated the Vijayanagara Empire in 1566 and thereafter gradually conquered the rest of the Andhra territory.[1]

After the Sultan of Delhi returned to the north, the various Muslim governors of the Deccan began to assert their independence. The Bhamini rulers were the first to assume the royal title. They ruled for almost two hundred years (A.D. 1347–1537), with first Gulbarga and later Bidar as their capital. Bidar was also the capital of the Barid Shahi kings (1538–1609), but their rivals and successors, the Kutb-Shahi kings (1512–1687), established their capital at Golconda, five miles west of Hyderabad City. Hyderabad itself was made the capital by the fifth of these kings, Mohammed Kuli, in A.D. 1589. In 1656 the Mogul emperor Aurangzeb took Bidar, and in 1687 he completed his conquest with the capture of the fort at Golconda. Mir Kamaruddin Nizam-ul-Mulk Asaf Jah was appointed viceroy of the Deccan under the Moguls. He remained loyal to the Sultan of Delhi, but his successors, popularly known as the Nizams of Hyderabad, became increasingly independent. The present Nizam, now living in retirement, Mir Osman Ali Khan, is the tenth of this dynasty.

The Nizam's dominions at one time extended over much of southern Andhra, but the growth of French and British power reduced their extent. The fourth Nizam, Salabat Jung (1751–61), ceded four coastal districts known as the Northern Circars to the French, as compensation for the cost of maintaining a French army in Hyderabad which would fight on his behalf. During his reign the French gained much influence in Hyderabad, but the outbreak of war in Europe between the French and British forced the French commander to return to Pondicherry. The British commander Clive took advantage of this turn of events to annex the Circar districts. The next Nizam, Ali Khan (1762–1803), was the first to make a treaty with the British, and the subsequent Nizams continued to be faithful to them. The British rule of the ceded Circar districts was confirmed in return for their maintenance of their troops in the Nizam's Dominions. Three more districts were ceded during the reign of the seventh Nizam, but because of the loyal service of the Nizam to the British during the Indian Mutiny (1857), these districts were restored to the Nizam and he was granted the title of 'Our Faithful Ally'.

After Indian Independence in 1947, the Nizam did not immediately decide whether Hyderabad State would accede to India or Pakistan, or remain independent. A group known as the Razakara formed a private army in order to keep Hyderabad as an independent Muslim state and proceeded to terrorize non-Muslims. In response to appeals from the rest of the population, the Indian Government sent in its army to restore order. In September 1948 a caretaker government was set up, and the absolute rule of the Nizam came to an end. In the meantime, the Communists had organized a counter-movement of terror against Muslims, but after six months the Communist armed bands were suppressed by the Indian army. The first popular election on the basis of universal adult suffrage was held in 1951, and the Congress Party, which had won the majority of seats in the State Legislature, formed the first full-fledged popular government in Hyderabad State in 1952.[2]

From early in the twentieth century there had been proposals for the organization of the provinces on a linguistic basis, and some Telugu leaders had urged the formation of a separate state which would include the Telugu-speaking districts in both Madras Presidency and Hyderabad State. Independence gave fresh impetus to this movement. The popular feeling aroused by the fasting to death of the pan-Andhra leader, Potti Sriramulu, led the Central Government to agree to separate the Telugu-speaking districts of Madras State into a distinct Andhra State, which was inaugurated in 1953. In 1956 all the states in India were reordered in line with linguistic boundaries. Each of the three language areas in Hyderabad State was merged with its adjacent state speaking the same language. The largest of these three parts of Hyderabad was Telengana, the nine districts of which were joined with the eleven districts of Andhra to form the new state of Andhra Pradesh, with Hyderabad as its capital.[3]

The Character of the Village

In Andhra Pradesh there are 26,450 villages with a population of over five hundred, as well as a great many smaller hamlets attached to the nearest large village. Eighty-two per cent of the State's population is rural, and more than half of the rural population lives in villages with less than a thousand inhabitants.[4]

As in most parts of India, houses are grouped closely together in the villages, rather than being spread about on the farm land. Past experience has taught people the advantage of living closely together, so that they may combine to resist outside attack. The unsettled conditions in Hyderabad until about A.D. 1800 are evidenced by the many forts and walled villages which still survive.

Telengana has long been a meeting place of language and cultures, and this has had a broadening effect on its villages. Centuries of Muslim rule have also left their mark. The feudal system which embraced many of these villages had left the people socially and economically more backward than the people in other areas of Andhra Pradesh. The dialect of Telugu spoken in Telengana, especially in the villages, is criticized by the more sophisticated Andhras for its harshness and rustic accent, and for its host of Urdu words taken over from the Muslim rulers.

The ancient village organization was such as to make the villages in normal times an almost entirely independent and self-sufficient community. Each village has its own body of craftsmen and its own informal governing council, called the Panchayat (literally a 'council of five', actually more than five), consisting of the heads of important families. Each village stands apart, surrounded by its own fields, and in many cases the boundary that divides the houses from the fields has not changed for centuries. Some villages in this area, however, moved to a new site almost a hundred years ago.

Normally there is the village proper for the houses and shops of high-caste Hindus and Sudras, and the houses of the outcastes are located in a separate hamlet, though in many villages in the are a studied the outcaste *palem* (section of the village) is separated from the rest of the village only by a cart track and falls within the village proper. If there are Muslim families in the village, they live in the main section of the village, unsegregated from their Hindu neighbours. There are also a number of semi-nomadic groups which live on the outskirts of the village. These include the *Lambadis* (gypsies), *Erukala* (hunters), *Vaddaris* (stone-cutters) and *Dasaris* (originally professional beggars).

Village Houses

Most of the high-class families, and some of the more prosperous families among the outcastes, have tiled-roof houses with mud and stone or brick walls. These houses are normally built in the shape of a quadrangle. The main entrance of the house leads to an inner court, opening on to rooms on three sides. In the centre of the court there is sometimes a well and a cement-lined area used for bathing.

The poorer-caste people and most of the outcastes have houses of flimsy mud wattle and thatched roofs, which are sometimes less substantial than the cattle sheds of the rich landowners. A few rough timbers form the frame of the hut, and the space between timbers is filled in with wattle screen plastered with mud. It generally consists of one room, from which the kitchen is partly partitioned. There is rarely a window in the wall. The gabled roof is made of palmyra leaves or reeds and straw laid on the foundation of twigs. Such huts are always in danger of being blown down in storms or burnt down in the summer. Often two or three families belonging to the same joint family are crowded into the dwelling. Here they cook, eat and sleep. Each house has an open yard, with an enclosure in one corner where its occupants bathe. Many families have their cattle shed close to the hut. The women of the house smear the floor of the hut with a blend of red soil, water and cowdung, which produces a hard plaster surface, and they sprinkle cowdung water on the floor of the open yard, which keeps down the dust. Their belongings consist of a few earthen vessels, one or two sickles, two brass plates and two drinking vessels – wedding gifts from the bride's parents. They may or may not have a bed – an oblong wooden frame set on four short legs, covered tightly by a mat woven with locally made hemp rope. Hanging from the roof is a rope basket containing two or three earthen pots with the left-overs and the household stores. While the rich people use hurricane lanterns, poor families use oil saucer lamps or kerosene chimneys.

The Family

The joint family system predominates in the villages of this part of Telengana. The joint family is governed by the head of the family and the heads of the cast (*kulam*), and its conduct is regulated by a large number of traditional rules and observances. There are elaborate rules for the ceremonies to be performed at the crisis points, such as marriage, which mark the transition from one stage of life to another. There are extensive rules for the whole range of social relationships. All the members of the joint family are expected to attend family festivals and other occasions. Especially in the event of death in the family, the failure to attend is bound to be viewed seriously.

In the joint family, the head of the family and his wife, and their sons, daughters-in-law and grandchildren, all pool their earnings and are maintained out of the common fund. This system binds the members together and gives them a certain economic and social security. The individual's loyalty is therefore first to the family rather than to himself, and all the individual members strive to maintain the family prestige. Any breach of family norms or traditional conventions is viewed with grave concern.

While joint families are regarded as ideal, it is common for sons to separate from their parents after they are married and have children. Sometimes domestic quarrels and arguments in the family are the cause of separation. They are frequently the fault of the mother-in-law, who looks upon her son's wife as a slave that has been bought and paid for. The sons either make a partition in the same house or build a new house or hut in the yard around the father's house. Thus the main family develops into separate family units. They will, however, maintain close connexion with the main family until the parents die and all the sons have their own separate establishments.

Marriage is universally regarded as natural and necessary. An unmarried man or woman is regarded as without usefulness or status in society. He is not consulted on any important subject. When unmarried persons die, their corpses are treated with less than normal respect. However, those who remain unmarried for religious reasons are looked up to and treated with the utmost respect.

Most villagers believe that women are created only to bear children and to please their husbands. All women, therefore, are obliged to marry, and marriages are carefully arranged before they become mature. Experience has taught the villagers that young village girls do not possess sufficient firmness to resist the ardent solicitations of a seducer. Therefore the parents arrange to place their daughters intact in their husbands' hands before they become mature. Moreover, parents do not want to postpone marriage, because they say 'Who knows what happens to us tomorrow? We may die or live. While we are yet alive, we want to see our daughter's marriage performed'. It is considered a sin for parents to keep their daughters at home unmarried after maturity. No parents will come to ask for such girls for marriage to their sons. This custom of marrying girls in their early childhood, though common to all castes, is most strictly observed by the Brahmins and merchants, who have their daughters married when they are between 3 and 9 years old. Among the outcastes, girls are married when they are between 8 and 14. Child marriage is now prohibited by law, which makes

15 the minimum age for girls and 18 for boys. In actual practice, however, child marriages are still going on in the villages.

The clan (*vamsham*) takes interest in marriages, for marriage is regarded as much more the common concern of the community than the private affair of the two individuals who are getting married. The likes and dislikes of the persons about to be married are seldom considered. Even in adult marriages parents do not usually consult the tastes and feelings of the parties concerned. The choice is left entirely to the parents. The boy's parents are highly concerned with the purity of the caste, the character of their future daughter-in-law, and the health and economic condition of the family. Personal attractiveness counts for nothing in their eyes. The girl's parents look more particularly to the wealth of their future son-in-law and to the character of his mother, who after marriage becomes the absolute mistress of the young wife.

Among the higher castes the dowry system is followed. The parents of the girl are expected to pay some thousands of rupees as dowry to the boy's parents. In May 1961 the Government of Inida enacted a law to prohibit this dowry system. Among the lower Sudras and outcastes, however, another system is practised. The parents of the girl demand from the boy's parents a sum of seventy rupees in return for their daughter. This money is used for buying new clothes for the girl's mother and for other expenses on the girl's side.

All village Hindus accept the teaching of the Hindu law-books that the women should be kept in a state of dependence and subjugation all their lives. A woman must obey her parents as long as she is unmarried and her husband and mother-in-law after marriage. In her old age, or when she becomes a widow, she is at the mercy of her son or daughter-in-law. A daughter is considered a liability and a nonpermanent member of the family. A married woman without children is looked upon with scorn.

The husband is supposed to be the head of the family and to rule over his wife and children, but in actual practice it is the wife who usually controls the affairs of the family, even though many women receive harsh and domineering treatment from their husbands. There is a very strong feeling against female education and emancipation on the part of the men and the older women, who are all-powerful in the home.

The women are fond of such ornaments as ear-rings, nose-rings, rings worn on fingers and toes, anklets, and glass bangles on the wrists. To them jewellery is not merely an ornament, it is a woman's bank—for she can sell it in time of need, or run away with it if her husband treats her harshly. Women have their eyelids tinged with antimony and their forehead with red pigment.

Among Brahmins, a widow is expected to have her head shorn after her husband's death. Among all the castes the woman's *tali* (marriage symbol) is cut and her bangles are broken on the day of her husband's death. A widow is no longer permitted to wear her *tali*, her jewels or her bangles. She must not put saffron on her face or put on a *bottu* (mark on the forehead). Her presence at family festivals and marriage ceremonies would be considered an evil omen.

The women in Telengana Village are the inner core of its society and the basis of its resistance to change. Even when a woman consents to her husband's decision to become a Christian and follows him into the Christian Church, she often keeps up the secret practice of Hindu rites, and hands these on to her children. In many of Hindu ceremonies, festivals and weddings, village women play the key role and take a more active part than the men. On the other hand, when truly won, women can also conserve Christian practices and values, while men are succumbing to temptations to fall away from the Church.

The Caste Groups

The one English word 'caste' has long been used to translate two different Indian words. One of these is *varna*, one of the four 'castes' described in the Hindu law-books. The first three of these are called the 'twice-born', because their boys are entitled to undergo the initiation ceremony at which they don the sacred thread which is considered a 'second birth'. They are referred to in this study as 'high-caste' people. These three varnas are the Brahmins, Kshatriyas, and the Vaishyas. Since there are none of the second or warrior caste in these villages, these three higher varnas are represented in the village by at most a few families of Brahmins and Vaishyas (generally merchants). The fourth varna consists of the Sudras. According to the ancient Hindu law-codes, this was the servile group, but in South India it constitutes the majority in the villages, including the landowners. The term 'out-caste' also refers to caste in the sense of varna. The outcastes were renamed Haijrans ('children of God') by Mahatma Gandhi, and are now for the first time in Indian history considered by the high-caste Hindus as definitely belonging to the Hindu community. They are also sometimes referred to as Panchamas, members of the 'fifth' varna.

The other Indian word translated 'caste' is *kūlam*. This is the endogamous social unit usually following one traditional occupation. The kulam is sometimes described as a sub-caste within the varna, but this is a misleading attempt to relate the two terms, for it is the kulam which is the actually functioning social unit, governed by its own 'caste' council, and there may be sub-castes within it. Only in the case of the 'higher castes' (Brahmin and Vaishya) do varna and kulam coincide. However, because traditional Hindu ethics is framed especially with the higher castes in mind, a certain confusion between the concepts of varna and kulam is inevitable.[5]

To a Hindu, the proper observance of social duties and religious ceremonies prescribed for the kulam is a sacred duty and the indispensable prerequisite for spiritual progress towards eternal salvation. According to the Hindu law-books, each varna has its own specific privilege and responsibilites in the community. Brahmins are priests and teachers, Kshatriyas are rulers and warriors, and Vaishyas are to be agricultutists, providing food and clothing and other necessities for the community (the Vaishyas are actually no longer a farming but a trading caste). The Sudras are supposed to serve the three higher castes and perform agricultural labour. In practice, the Sudras in South India embrace a large number of castes, including landowners, artisans and some traders, while menial service and much of the work in the fields is performed by the outcastes.

For the high-caste people in villages, even where there is no temple, the Brahmin is the family priest. No wedding ceremony can take place without his services. All the people consult him about auspicious days, timings of agricultural operations and horoscopes. He does little or no teaching. Some Brahmins continue to live in *Agraharams* or *Maniams* (estates free of land taxation). There is one *Agraharam* in Gowlapalli village. In many villages the Brahmins hold the office of *Patwari* (revenue clerk).

The Vaishyas who are called *Komatis* or *Sahukars* are the moneylenders and petty shopkeepers in the village. They offer loans at high interest to buy grain at the harvest, to buy seeds, manure, tools, and bullocks before the new crop is sown, and to provide wages for agricultural labourers.

Among the Sudras there are a large number of castes (kulams) and sub-castes. The Kapus, Reddis, Deshmukhs, Velamas and Kammas are landowning agriculturists and often the most influential political groups in the village. There are the occupational castes of potters, shepherds, weavers, toddy-tappers, washermen, barbers, and tailors. There is another group of Sudra castes who consider themselves superior even to Brahmins and themselves wear the sacred thread. They are called the Viswa Brahmas or Pancha Brahmas, and they consist of several other artisan castes: carpenters, goldsmiths, blacksmiths, coppersmiths, and image-carvers. There is also a separate caste of exclusive worshippers of Siva, called Baljis, and among their number is the special priest (*jangam*) for Sudras.

The two large outcaste kulams found everywhere in Andhra Pradesh are the Malas and the Madigas. Both castes are equally looked down upon by the caste Hindus as 'untouchables', but their low opinion and jealousy of one another creates a gulf between them as great as that separating them from the rest of the village. Both groups are equally poor and share in most of the same menial toil, but intermarriage between them is strictly prohibited, and they are often quite antagonistic to one another. Members of both groups will accept food from members of all the higher castes, but the Mala, considering himself superior, refuses to take food touched by a Madiga.[6]

The Malas are cultivators or agricultural labourers. Some of them have the traditional duty of watching over village tanks (reservoirs) and sluices, and of sacrificing the pigs offered to a goddess during certain village ceremonies. Others of the Malas are traditionally given the duty of scavengers. They must dispose of dead animals lying in the village, dig graves and prepare biers (a wooden frame in the form of a stretcher) for funerals, and light fires at the village community hall. They are entitled to take the cloth covering the dead body at each funeral. They are obliged to take part in many village ceremonies by virtue of their office. The official, whether Mala or Sudra, who goes on errands for the village gets six rupees per month from the Government for that service.

Some of the Madigas are leather-workers and drum-beaters. They skin the dead cattle and tan the hides in a *landa* (big earthen pot) just outside their houses. The image of goddess Ellamma is carved on each landa. Like the Malas, they eat the meat of the cattle which have died, though many have now given up the practice. They beat drums at the village festivals and at funerals and marriages, and also make public announcements by drum-beating. These Madigas are expected to carry the luggage of touring government officials and to escort them to the next village. On special occasions, such as the performance of dramas or circuses, they have to patrol the village in turns along with the other village officials. They must carry news of deaths from village to village, take the daily report from the police patrol to the nearest police station, and take the fortnightly report of births and deaths in the village to the Taluk headquarters in Medak. The Madigas also have the duty of bringing fuel for the cremation of the corpses of caste people. It is the Madiga headman, or some other Madiga, who sacrifices the buffaloes to the goddesses at all the village rites.

In the area surveyed, the Madigas have now taken to farming and other trades, and only a few families still continue their traditional occupation of leather-work and drum-beating. These families are entitled to one half of the hide of a dead animal and return the other half to the owner, except that the entire hide of dead cattle belonging to the village officials must be returned after tanning. Very few Madigas possess enough land to be independent farmers; they therefore have to secure work on the land of others, either as day labourers or on a long-term basis. Some of the outcastes serve as sweepers or scavengers. For these and other menial services in the village they are given some tax free land and receive a gift of grain from each farmer at harvest. They feel that they must oblige the village people by performing their traditional duties, lest they lose all their traditional perquisites.

The Malas and the Madigas are further divided into endogamous subdivisions. Besides the main body of Malas, there are a number of small sub-castes. The Baindlas are black magicians and priests at the festivals of the village goddesses; the Jangams are priests who travel from village to village, begging from the Malas; the Potarazus are a group of priests in the service of the village deities and demonic spirits; the Mashti are travelling acrobats; and the Dandem are an agricultural group which considers itself a degree higher than the rest of the Malas. Similarly there is a sub-caste of the Madigas called the Bandelas, who are ranked slightly higher than the rest of the caste. The Sindhollu are a sub-caste of Madigas who are itinerant dramatists, and the Dokkali are professional beggars who travel from village to village begging from other Madigas. Both Malas and Madigas have an itinerant priest or guru with hereditary claims to respect over an area containing many villages, each of which he visits once in several years. In the area studied, the Madiga priest has stopped visiting the villages in which the

Madigas have become Christians, but the Sindhollu continue to visit these Christian Madigas and are entertained by them every two or three years. The Dokkali come once a year to beg from the Madigas of these congregations.[7]

The Malas and Madigas each have a hereditary headman, who officiates as priest for marriage in that caste, unless the 'regional' priest happens to be present. These headmen receive a fixed fee for their services at the weddings. They are further expected by the village as a whole to keep their respective caste under control, fulfilling their traditional duties and remaining properly subservient. At the present time, however, the members of their castes, spurred by the new institutions of freedom and democracy, are little inclined to heed them. This weakening of the authority of the caste headmen also affects to some extent the higher castes in the village.

The 'Kula Panchayat' or Caste Council

It is to the caste headman that all difficult questions affecting the caste system are referred. He calls a few elders from the same *palem* in the village, who are versed in the intricacies of the matters in dispute. Two or three elders from other castes in the village are also invited to their council. Some cases brought before the council arise merely from personal hatred or caprice. When without any apparent justification persons refuse to attend the funeral or marriage ceremonies of their relatives or people of the same caste or when they happen not to invite the latter on similar occasions, the individuals thus slighted never fail to appeal to the caste headman for satisfaction for the insult. Cases of breach of caste obligations or rules, of adultery within the caste group or across caste barriers, and of divorce are all taken up by the caste councils. The Panchayat usually imposes a heavy fine or decrees excommunication or expulsion from the caste. This is a kind of social ostracism or boycott, which deprives the unhappy person who suffers it of all intercourse with the people of his own caste. No one dares to eat with him or give him a drop of water, or attend any of his marriage festivities and family ceremonies. He is refused fire, and is not allowed under any conditions to mingle in the marriage festivities of his friends. About twenty years ago a Sudra man who had sexual relations with a Mala woman in Kondapuram village was rigorously expelled from his caste when his offence became known. He built a hut in the Mala *basti* and lived with this Mala woman for the rest of his life, leaving his caste wife and children. If a man loses his caste, he loses not only his relations and friends, but often his wife and children, who would rather leave him to his fate than share his disgrace with him.

In some cases, restoration of caste is possible. If the culprit shows signs of repentance, pays the fine levied, and then serves a feast to the persons present, he will be taken back into his caste. In Jangarai village during 1958 there were three cases of discipline of Mala men who had committed adultery with a Madiga woman. The caste headmen from eighteen or twenty other villages were called for a territorial inter-village caste panchayat held in Rudaram village. The cases were proved and the accused confessed their fault, so they were fined Rs. 130, and were made to bear all the expenses of a meal and toddy for fifty people. Then the Mala jangam (priest) was called from another village to perform purificatory rites: shaving their heads, giving them a bath in a tank, and three times slightly burning their tongues with a piece of heated gold wire. Thus they were restored to their caste. The caste headmen and others who attended the council were paid two rupees each.

Each caste in a village is related to the same caste in the surrounding villages. The same caste in ten to twenty adjacent villages has the same organization, and may call such an inter-village council.

The Village Community

Until not long ago, the village was an almost self-contained economic unit which functioned without the use of money. Each specialized worker received his remuneration in a share of land or its produce. Priest, carpenter, potter, washerman, barber, sweeper—each had his traditional perquisites and privileges. Each group was strictly separate and endogamous, yet each was bound socially and economically to the whole.[8]

Although members of each caste have a certain amount of autonomy in domestic matters, they are very greatly influenced by the various preferences of the majority of villagers. Their decisions are group decisions, and in several matters they consult one another. The village officials—*Patwari* (village accountant), *Mali Patel* (revenue official) and *Kotwal* (village police official)—wield great influence over the village by virtue of their office, and exercise undue authority over the villagers in conjunction with some rich landowners and *Komatis* (merchant money-lenders). These aristocrats of the village vie with one another to gain power, prestige and influence in the village, in order to safeguard their own vested interests. The rest of the villagers associate themselves with one or two of the key men for their own security and social status, thus forming groups and parties within the village community.

In addition to the caste councils, each village community has its own informal council to deal with general disputes and other cases referred to it. Breaches of the norms of the community and its established usages are dealt with by the village elders and officials in a village council. One such case was dealt with in Jangarai village in 1959. One night one of the Madiga men (a Christian) stole toddy from the toddy pots tied to the tree. When he was caught, the village elders called him before the village council. To disgrace the culprit, they slung one toddy pot round his neck, placed another pot in his hand, and paraded him through the village streets. Because of the factions and cliques which exist within the community, the authority of the village panchayat has been slightly weakened. Some defy these panchayats, and those who can afford to spend money in law courts are resorting to litigation. There has deve-

loped a growing fondness for going to law at crushing expense in connexion with all manner of petty village disputes.

The Changing Village

In this chapter we have tried to summarize the historical background
and the traditional social system of the villages in which the Christian
congregations we studied are located. Many important changes are now
taking place in these villages, so that many of the features of the social
background just described are already being altered and some may soon
disappear. However, they are still of sufficient importance to warrant
our notice.

The recent political, social, and religious changes will be described in
Chapter 5, along with their effects on the Christians in these villages.
One other aspect of the traditional background must be examined in
more detail: the religious ideas and practices prevailing in these villages. To that subject we turn in the next chapter, but an account of
recent religious developments will also be left to Chapter 5.

APPENDIX: SPECIAL FORMS OF MARRIAGE AND INHERITANCE

1. Cousin Marriages

Villagers seem to aim at marrying their children into the families which
are already allied to them, and the nearer the relationship the more easily
are the marriages contracted. A man's children may marry his sister's
children, but the children of two brothers or two sisters will not intermarry.
A man may marry his first cousin, the daughter of his maternal aunt.
Persons so related possess a privileged option of intermarrying. If they
choose, they can prevent any other union and enforce their own preferential
right, however old, unsuited, infirm or poor they may be.

2. Remarriage

Among the high castes, particularly the Brahmins, widows are not
allowed to remarry, but among the lower Sudra and untouchable castes
there is no objection to widow-remarriage. If valuable property is left by
the husband, it is in this wife's financial interest to remain a widow for
life. If the widow has children, her husband's property goes to them. It has
been the custom among the high castes to remarry child widows, treating
the previous marriage as a betrothal. Among the lower Sudras and outcastes,
if a husband leaves his wife, she marries another man, even without a legal
divorce certificate. Ordinarily such divorces are effected unofficially in the
caste councils, instead of in the civil courts. These remarriages used to be
celebrated in a much simpler way, i.e. giving a sari and blouse to the
woman. But now men will spend about Rs. 350 for such a remarriage,
which is as much as they spend on first marriages.

3. Bigamy or Polygamy

Monogamy is the ideal marriage among Hindus. However, if a person has lived for a long time after marriage with a wife who is certified to be barren or who has borne only female children, he is allowed to marry another woman. A man knows no misfortune equal to that of not leaving a son or a grandson behind to perform the rites after his death. In such cases, before a man contracts a second marriage, he usually consults his first wife and obtains her consent. The first wife is regarded as the chief wife and retains all her prerogatives. If a person marries two or more wives, only one of them (the first wife) bears the name and title of wife. The property of the father will be divided according to his wish, but usually the sons of the legal wife (if by chance she has any afterwards) have preference over other sons and receive a large share. The second marriage is at the present time celebrated with the same festivities as the first one, and involves giving the bride a sari, a jacket and jewels, and giving a feast to the caste group to which the man belongs. Nowadays among the outcastes, a man sometimes marries two wives in order to increase his family income and to facilitate his farming. There are five Christian men with two wives in Kondapuram village.

4. Concubinage

Those girls who are unable to enter into any legal union for physical disability or other reasons, form a connexion as concubines with their nearest relative or any other person who cares to receive them as such. They call this method 'treading on each other's feet'. The investigator witnessed such a 'marriage' in Achampet village. Since the elder sister could not get a husband because of her physical infirmity, at the time of her younger sister's marriage she was allowed to go through the whole wedding ceremony along with her sister and to tread on the bridegroom's feet, which meant that she was henceforth also married to the same man. If the parents of such a girl bear all the expenses of her marriage dress, tali and silver bracelets, then the marriage is merely nominal without any obligations on either side, and she is allowed to have sexual relations with anybody she likes. If an offer of regular marriage comes later, she will also be given away without any objection from the previous man. On the other hand, if the boy bears all the expenses of this second wife at the marriage, then he has a hold on her and she is permanently bound to him alone. He can cohabit with her along with her sister.

If a woman does not obtain a husband or if she is dedicated to a god or goddess, she will be married to a 'sword'. Then she can bear children by anyone and live in the house of her own parents. This custom is supported by social sanction.

5. Adoption

When a husband has had no children by his wife, but wishes to avoid the unpleasant consequences of a second marriage, he may decide to adopt an heir, usually from among his relatives. The adopted son renounces wholly and for ever his claim to the property and succession of his natural father. He performs the duties of a son for his adopted father, presiding at his funeral, and fulfilling 'the great debt to his ancestors', the generation of children to continue the family in the male line. So important is this function of a son that the Sanskrit word *putra* (son) is explained to mean one who saves from *put*, the hell into which parents without sons are cast.

6. *Illutam*

This is another method for securing a 'son' if parents have no sons. A son-in-law comes to live with his wife's family, reversing the usual arrangement, and he receives all the hereditary rights of a son.

CHAPTER 2

The History of the Church in the Medak Diocese

The Earliest Christian Mission in Hyderabad State

Christianity was brought to the Deccan by the Franciscans in 1535, when Father Louis was sent by Albequerque as the Ambassador to the King of Bijapur. The first converts were shepherds, weavers, and fishermen; they were gathered together and cared for in Mudgal, a small town in Raichur District. The Muslim ruler was so well-disposed towards the Christians that he granted several acres of land for the support of the Mudgal congregation. The subsequent growth of the Roman Catholic Church in this area was slow; a Roman Catholic Diocese of Hyderabad was not formed until 1886. The present Nizam (now retired) gave grants for many Roman Catholic churches, as well as for Catholic educational and medical work. (He also made generous grants for the building of a few Protestant churches, including Dornakal Cathedral, and used to make monthly grants to all the Christian churches in Hyderabad city.) The Roman Catholics have educational institutions, hospitals, and homes for the aged and disabled in the capital, as well as in many of the cities in Andhra Pradesh. They continue to receive converts from a number of Sudra castes, as well as from the outcastes.

The Church Missionary Society began work in the Marathi-speaking District of Aurangabad in 1860. In 1875 the American Baptist Telugu Mission, following some of the mass movement converts northwards, extended its work to Secunderabad and Warangal. The initiative of European laymen was important in beginning several other Protestant Missions. Captain C. Winkle, a civil engineer employed in the construction of the Hyderabad Railway, led the American Methodist Episcopal church to start work in Hyderabad in 1873, among Europeans, Anglo-Indians and Telugus. General A. E. H. Campbell, while in Jalna cantonment, stimulated the founding of the Church of Scotland Mission. After he moved to Secunderabad as the judge of the Nizam's suburban court in Chandirghat, he co-operated with the newly established Wesleyan Mission.

The Beginning of Wesleyan Methodist Work in the Hyderabad District

The work of the Wesleyan Methodist Mission in Hyderabad State was first conceived by another layman, Sir Arthur Cotton, who was an engineer of the Madras Government working on the Godavari river.

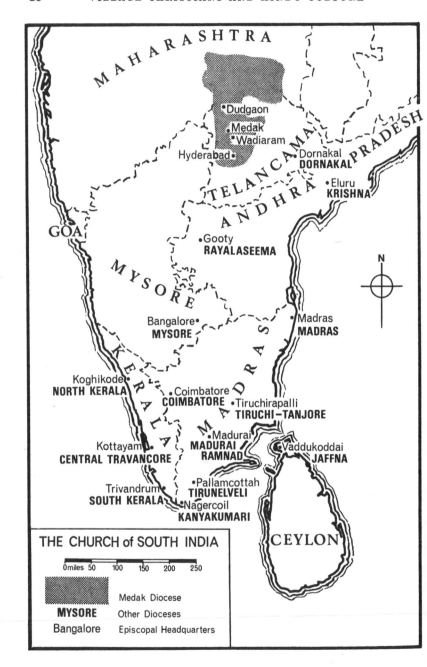

THE CHURCH of SOUTH INDIA

0miles 50 100 150 200 250

Medak Diocese

MYSORE Other Dioceses

Bangalore Episcopal Headquarters

Stirred and aided by him, in 1863 two missionaries, E. E. Jenkins (the chairman of the Madras District) and George Fryar, travelled up the Godavari river for two hundred and twenty miles until they came to Sironcha, a village in Telengana. On their return they recommended to the Madras Synod that a mission be started at Siooncha. The golden jubilee of the Methodist Missionary Society was then being celebrated in England, and £500 from the jubilee fund raised for missionary work was set apart for the 'Godavari Mission', but no further steps were taken to start this mission for fifteen years.

When Mr. Jenkins became a Secretary at the Methodist Mission House in England, this matter was taken up again. In response to a letter sent by Sergeant Goodwin, a British Methodist local preacher, the missionaries Henry Little and William Burgess came up from Madras to Secunderabad in December 1878. Special services were held for the British soldiers in Secunderabad and a Methodist class was formed.

When they returned these two missionaries gave a favourable report, and the Madras Synod gave £500 of its grant for the new mission, and sent to Secunderabad two of its men: the Rev. William Burgess and Benjamin Wesley, an Indian evangelist. The first Methodist Telugu service was held in Ramkote in Hyderabad city in December 1879, in the house of Mr. Joseph Cornelius, a Telugu Christian who had migrated from Madras. This family formed the nucleus around which the Telugu Church gradually grew. Then a building was erected which was used as both a school and a place of worship. By the end of 1880 there were Telugu Christians in Hyderabad city, a Tamil congregation in Secunderabad, turned over by the Church of Scotland Mission, and a Wesleyan group among the British troops in Trimulgherry, a suburb of the Secunderabad cantonment.

In 1881 Mr. Burgess had to take a short trip to Australia because of illness. He returned to the District within six months in renewed health, and brought with him financial help from the Methodists in Australia, at a time when there was no help forthcoming from England. Within two years three churches were built with that money; the present Secunderabad Mission House was purchased, and in 1884 the Girls' Boarding and Normal School was erected in Secunderabad.

The Mass Movement among Malas, Madigas and Caste People

At the very outset of the Wesleyan Mission, the Gospel was preached first to the more educated Muslims and Hindus in the city, through evening evangelistic services and the opening of four schools for their children, but the real response came from the villages, and this leading was unhesitatingly followed. The work in the villages was begun in February 1882 with the long tour made by the three pioneers, Burgess, Wesley and Benjamin Pratt, to Siddipet and Karimnagar, and back to the city via Sircilla and Medak. Thus Siddipet, Karimnagar and Medak were soon marked out as Mission centres. The Gospel was first preached to the caste people in the villages and the first converts were weavers (in (Karimnagar and Siddipet), but on finding that the Malas were equally

B

welcome, the weavers renounced Christianity and were received back into their caste by having their tongues branded. So the missionaries turned to the Malas. After that their policy was 'Go not only to those who want you, but to those who want you most'.[1] They believed that the way to win the caste people was through the untouchables.

After that, the mass movement among the Malas gradually spread and six new stations were started between 1884 and 1891. In 1899 an invitation from the local officials of Nizamabad prompted the founding of a mission station there. In 1911 three new stations were begun, and another was started in 1917. The Malas began to enter the Church in large numbers, especially during the famine years between 1896 and 1900. Along with preaching the Gospel, the missionaries started medical and educational work among the village people. The first rural schools and the boarding schools in circuit centres were intended to provide the District with workers and to build up literate congregations. Hospitals were started to exercise the ministry of compassion in the spirit of Christ and to provide an avenue for evangelism.

Then in 1906, the Rev. H. G. Price, in spite of the misgivings of some of the others, made a venture with the Madigas. He was the missionary who received into the Church the first converts from the Madiga community in Kandi (now called Sangareddy) circuit. After that Christianity spread among the Madiga communities in the villages, but the District faced a great deal of opposition from the older Christians, who were all Malas, and from their non-Christian relatives, because of the wide gulf between those two castes. Objection was raised to the baptism of Madigas, their presence in the same church, their participation in the Lord's Supper and the admission of Madiga children into boarding schools. The objection came to a head when Madiga boys were admitted to the boarding school and the seminary, and later stationed in Mala congregations as evangelists. For some time there was a bitter struggle in the Church, before the discrimination was eventually overcome.

In 1910 the District decided to stop baptizing village groups for a time, because of lack of workers who could look after the new congregations, and to concentrate on winning others in villages which already had Christian congregations. In 1916, however, the baptism of new village groups was resumed. Doubts having been expressed in some quarters about the methods of mass movement work, a Mass Movement Commission was appointed in 1918 which visited the missions of several other denominations in various parts of India and conducted a thorough survey of the Hyderabad District. The report vindicated the methods which had been followed in the mass movement, but also made it clear that there could be no solution of problems in the District without a change in the character and personality of the new convert. It recommended more lay participation and self-government, and urged the formation of a 'panchayat' in each congregation, summer schools for village elders, and more sectional and circuit meetings. It also made a number of recommendations to improve the financial condition of the village congregations: the endowment of pastorates with a few acres of 'glebe land' to support the pastors and evangelists, the founding of agricultural loan and co-operative credit societies, and the starting of normal training and vocational schools.[2]

In 1914 the Methodist Provincial Synod first discussed the creation of an Indian Missionary Society. The Synod was stimulated to act by the report of Dr. Clement, a Telugu layman, who was the only Christian in Nirmal town, working in the government dispensary, and it resolved in 1915 to found such a missionary society. The Rev. P. J. S. Appadurai, a Tamil minister of the Madras Methodist District, was sent to Nirmal in 1920 as its pioneer missionary. The project has been financed entirely by the Indian Methodist Church in South India, and since Church Union by some Dioceses of the Church of South India, without any demand upon the Methodist Home Committee in England, while the Hyderabad District has been responsible for its administration and for the supply of catechists. The development of the work among caste Hindus found its beginning in the evangelization of the Nirmal villages, a movement which gradually spread throughout the whole area, north and south of Godavari, four additional pastorates being later formed out of these Christian congregations. Since Church Union this project has been supervised by the Synod Board of the Missions, and a Junior Missionary Association in each Diocese has sought to enlist the support of young people for this work.

Some Waddaris (stone-cutters) were baptized in Alir in March 1925, and this experience led to a serious discussion of the work among the caste people. A caste summer school was held in Medak in May 1926, which was attended by about 140 caste enquirers. By the time the session ended, many had asked to be baptized, but they were advised to go back to their own villages and be baptized in the presence of their relatives and members of their own caste. Many of them were later baptized in this way. In April 1930 another summer school was held, attended this time by five hundred caste Hindus. Conversions among the lower Sudra castes gradually increased until 1940, decreased until 1947, and have since almost stopped. As the caste people are economically better off than the outcastes, the District hoped that this movement among the caste people would help to solve the problem of self-support in the Church. At present, however, the rate of giving among the Christians of caste background appears to be little or no better than the giving of the poorer Christians of Mala and Madiga congregations.

In 1931 some Gonds (a jungle tribe in the extreme north of the State) were baptized, but after a few years of progress many of them lapsed. Recently the work among the Gonds has been revived, and the lapsed Christians are gradually finding their way back into the Church through the efforts of the faithful Christians.

The early missionaries definitely intended to undertake evangelistic work among Muslims. A school was started for Muslim girls and women, and women missionaries commenced visiting Muslim women in Hyderabad. Muslim converts from North India have been used in this connexion, and a few church workers have been specially trained and set apart for this work. More recently a few individuals in various parts of the District have opened Reading Rooms for Muslims and had informal personal contacts with them. Very few Muslims have become Christians, but some Muslims in the city and a very few in the Medak area and in Toopran (a village in Wadiaram Pastorate) have been baptized.

Taking the Tide at the Flood

There were two periods of famine, one from 1896 to 1899, followed by cholera, and the other from 1918 to 1921, accompanied by epidemics of malaria, plague and influenza; during two World Wars the supply of missionaries dwindled; and there were persecutions and social boycott of the Christians by the local officials and village chiefs. While all these obstacles and trials to some extent impeded the work, yet they also afforded new opportunities for the spread of the Gospel and for the strengthening of churches, and the District 'took the tide at the flood' and made use of these pressures from outside for its own benefit.

After 1883 the income of the Missionary Society began to fall year by year, and from 1888 to 1890 there was widespread dissatisfaction in England about the slow progress of foreign missions in India and about the missionaries' methods and their salaries. The 'Missionary Controversy' swept the Home Church and the Indian Field, and resulted in a sharp decrease of the funds available. One of the results of this controversy was the closing down of the High School in Chandirghat, which was then flourishing. When in 1899 the District again experienced a financial depression, the system of 'private appeal' was begun which enabled the District to seize opportunities without waiting for grants from funds controlled by the Home Committee, but also led to a greater degree of paternalism. Mr. Burgess, and even more markedly Mr. Posnett, appealed directly to the members of the Methodist Church in England for financial aid.

The methods followed for evangelizing new areas by early missionaries and Indian ministers were long tours from the city to the district town, and repeated tours through limited areas with frequent preaching to the same people. Stationary camps of a week's duration were established at certain centres and nearby villages were visited in turn.

There were periods of revival in the District. In 1899 a big convention took place near Karimnagar; in 1900 at the time of the opening of the new 'Theological Institution' at Medak, a District convention was held for the students and all the catechists, and revival followed. Following the famine years, revival services were held in Karimnagar in 1902, after which there was a great spiritual awakening in the whole Karimnagar area. In 1916 a wave of spiritual life in the Nizamabad circuit followed sixteen years of spiritual sterility. After this revival the Christian community increased by three thousand. This in turn created another problem for the District—the supply of enough catechists for the new Christian congregations.

During the famine and war years, particularly in 1919, many of the village Christians migrated to the twin cities of Secunderabad and Hyderabad, to Bombay, and even to Natal and Mesopotamia, in search of work. In 1920 there were more than three thousand so listed in the District statistics. Large numbers left for Bombay, chiefly from the Nizamabad circuit. The District took up town settlement work in the cities, and colonies for Christian settlers were opened. Wesley Bagh and Musheerabad are the settlements which were established in Hyderabad for Christians coming from the villages, especially from the Karimnagar circuit. They are under the pastoral care of an Indian pastor. Wesley Hall is a hostel for young men studying or working in Secunderabad, supervised by a retired evangelist who lives in the hostel. In 1921 a Telugu Christian Church was established in Bombay for over eight hundred Christians.

At the time of the inauguration of the Church of South India, churches had been established with the help of the Methodist Missionary Society in six Districts of Telengana, and the Methodist District was the largest Protestant communion in the Hyderabad State, numbering about 136,000 baptized members. In 1938 there were almost 10,000 baptisms; since then, however, the annual total has dropped considerably.

The Development of Leadership and Organization

The Wesleyan Methodist Missionary Society began to work in Ceylon in 1814 and soon extended the work to South India. The work of this Society in India was organized in three Provincial synods; Ceylon, South India (including the Madras, Trichinopoly, Hyderabad and Mysore Districts) and North India. Provincial synods were constituted by a given number of representatives from each District in the Provincial area, and they were the supreme ecclesiastical authority in the area, subject to the Methodist Conference in Britain.

Secretarial visits from the Mission House in England were paid to the District once in five or eight years, and the Secretaries' reports were presented to the Home Committee and to the Mission Fields for readjustment of Mission policy and for necessary action. Three General Synods for all the provincial areas in India, Burma and Ceylon were also held (in 1903, 1916 and 1946) to discuss matters affecting the general policy of the Methodist Church.

The Hyderabad District was separated from the Madras District in 1885, and the Rev. William Burgess became its first Chairman. His successors were Benjamin Pratt (1896), Frederick Lamb (1908), Charles W. Posnett (1916), F. C. Sackett (1939), and Frank Whittaker (1943). The District owes much to the individual initiative of the pioneer missionaries, and to the leadership of three men: Mr. Burgess in the early formative years, Mr. Posnett in the later years of expansion and consolidation, and Bishop Whittaker in the era of Church Union and independent India. The work grew and developed round these personalities, each of whom built up an organization suited to the new times and conditions. The general policy endorsed by the Madras Synod in 1885 was adopted and continued in later years: the establishment of village schools, the training of more Indian ministers on a par with

Methodist ministers from Britain, and the formation of rural circuits. The Synod set as its goal a trained evangelist for every village with Christians, a house for every evangelist, a place of worship for every congregation, and village schools to secure a supply of workers and Bible-reading homes.

When the mission began in 1879, helpers had to be borrowed from other churches and missions for a short period, and the District secured from the very beginning Indian ministers for the work. The missionaries were soon faced with the task of raising a staff of evangelists and pastors from the ranks of the Christian congregation in the District.

The brightest boys from the boarding schools and the literate young men from the village congregations were sent to the Theological Institution in Medak. The students were divided into four grades: (C) youths from village schools, (B) those who had completed village primary education, (A) those who had studied as far as third form (ninth class) in boarding schools, and (NT) normal training students who had passed third form or matriculation. This fourth group were trained as teachers, so that they could supervise a number of village schools or teach in boarding schools.

In contrast to the Telugu area in British-governed Madras Presidency, the Nizam's dominions were very backward in education, and no government grants were made to Christian schools in the villages. In Madras Presidency, Christian catechists received their full salaries from the Government as teachers, and worked as part-time evangelists. The missions in Hyderabad had to support completely their own village schools. However, this gave them the advantage of determining their own curriculum, which stressed the study of the Bible.

It was never possible to keep pace with the demand for teachers and evangelists, and it was often necessary to place one evangelist in charge of two or more village congregations in order to supply evangelists for new villages, or to call for voluntary service among the literate young men of village congregations. The number of evangelists increased gradually up to a peak of nearly 800 in 1943. Since then their number has steadily decreased.

Theological students were trained for three years at Medak. It was required that all students be married before they were sent out to the village congregations. Their wives also received special training, either before or after marriage, so that they might teach and influence the village woman and help with the village schools.

In 1914 an order of superintending evangelists ('S.E.s') was established. The senior evangelists with some experience and ability were each given charge of ten or twelve village congregations (called a section), in order to supervise and assist the other evangelists in this section and to help the minister with pastoral care.

Because there were so few ordained ministers, the Methodist Conference in Britain agreed to the Provincial Synods appointing as 'licensed lay pastors' some of the superintending evangelists recommended by the District Synod. These men received an annual licence to administer the sacraments and to solemnize marriages under the direction of the minister in charge. This was intended merely as a temporary expedient to meet the special needs of mass movement areas, and it was expected that the District would replace these unordained pastors by ordained ministers. The licences of these lay pastors had to be renewed annually by formal vote in the District and Provincial Synods.

Some picked students from the Wesley Boys' High School in Secunderabad were sent to study for the B.D. in English at the United Theological College in Bangalore. There were few candidates for this level of theological education. The B.D. Course is three years for those coming with a B.A., but most of the students from the Hyderabad Methodist District had three years at the Theological Institution in Medak, two years in the villages for practical training, and then four years at Bangalore, including a preliminary year. After completing the B.D., these ministerial candidates were kept on probation in the field for another four years before they were ordained and made circuit superintendents.

The District Synod met annually in two sessions: the pastoral session, composed of all ordained ministers and licensed pastors, and the representative session, composed of both ministers and laymen. The Chairman of the District Synod presided over these sessions. He was also the 'General Superintendent', and the financial representative of the Missionary Society in Britain. The District Chairman was always a missionary, though the Chairman of the Provincial Synod was sometimes an Indian. After the rules were changed in 1939, it became possible for an Indian minister to be elected as District Chairman, but this did not actually happen, though one served for six months as Acting Chairman.

The Hyderabad Synod was almost always held in Medak immediately after Christmas, and lasted for more than a fortnight. It reviewed the work of the past year, made plans for the future, and considered accounts and estimates. At first the Synod consisted only of ordained ministers. Lay representation began in 1914, and later on the licensed pastors, women missionaries and Indian women working in mission institutions were included. The lay representation thus consisted mainly of lay workers on mission salary. Much of the important business relating to missionaries' appointment and stationing was done at a separate missionaries' meeting.

Because the Hyderabad District was growing very large and had become unwieldy, it was divided into three group committees—those of Medak, Dudgaon and Karimnagar—which met before the Synod and disposed of much routine business, leaving the Synod more time for general matters. The group chairmen were always Indian ministers; they were elected annually by the group committees and served as assistants to the Chairman of the District.

The circuit, consisting of about thirty village congregations, was the unit of administration. Each circuit was divided into three or four 'sections' under the charge of a superintending evangelist. In every circuit there was a regular monthly 'Agents Meeting', at which the evangelists reported about their work and the problems of their congregations, and at which they received their salaries. A senior minister was placed in charge of one or more circuits, with probationary ministers or licensed lay pastors working under his supervisiou.

The need for responsible indigenous leadership led the District to appoint village church elders in each local congregation. B. P. Wesley started the practice in 1903 in Siddipet, and other ministers soon introduced it elsewhere in the District. The first so appointed were already communal leaders. There was no election in the congregation. They were given as their badge of office a silver ring with their name inscribed, and for the first two years an elder was sometimes paid for his services. Most of these men were illiterate. Some proved disappointing, but others showed qualities of Christian leadership. The sending of the most promising boys to boarding school and seminary made it possible for the work to spread rapidly in the District, but deprived the older village congregations of much of the leadership they needed to deepen their own spiritual life. The elders were expected to maintain church discipline. Elders' meetings were held in the circuit headquarters for consultation three or four times during the year. Summer schools for elders were held at the circuit headquarters, where their duties and special problems were discussed and plans for unified action adopted.

The youth who had been through the village schools grew to be leaders in their congregations. They formed youth leagues and helped their evangelists. The young women were organized into a young women's league. Summer schools were also held for young men and women to train them in the elements of the Christian religion and to equip them for lay leadership to their village congregations.

The Church since Union

Conversations for establishing a united Church in South India went on for twenty-eight years between the Church of India, Burma and Ceylon (Anglican), the South India United Church (originally Congregational and Presbyterian), and the Methodist Church in South India, which joined in the negotiations in 1925. The Methodist Church was convinced of the need for a United Church and agreed with most of the plans drawn up in the Joint Committee. However, for a long time many of the Methodists were afraid that the introduction of episcopacy would lead to the absorption of the United Church in Anglicanism. Their doubts were allayed, and the Methodist Church gave its consent in 1943 to the Scheme of Union. In 1947 the Church of South India was inaugurated.

In 1880 the total Christian community in the Methodist church in Hyderabad was only thirty-two; as years went by, it steadily grew with an annual increase of about two thousand up to a total of more than 155,000 in 1946. At the time of Church Union in 1947, about one third of the old Hyderabad District of the Methodist Church (the Karimnagar group) was merged with part of the adjoining former Anglican Diocese of Dornakal to form a new Dornakal Diocese, and the other two thirds of the Hyderabad District joined with some Anglican churches in

Hyderabad and Secunderabad to form the Medak Diocese. On October 3, 1947, the Rt. Rev. Frank Whittaker was installed as its first bishop in the great cathedral in Medak (built by the Rev. C. W. Posnett between 1914 and 1924).

In 1948 the constitution and rules for the Diocese were formed in accordance with the C.S.I. constitution. The progress of the Church in growing together is most visible in the city churches and those in industrial areas, and at the diocesan or area council level. The change brought by church union is least evident in the village congregations. The Medak Diocese supports its bishop, including his office and travel expenses, over and above what it contributes for the general support of its ministry. In 1950 the whole Church set itself to increase its offering for the support of the ministry and there has been some increase.

The constitution of the Church of South India lays more responsibility upon the members of the local congregation and more emphasis on lay participation in the government of the Church at all levels than did the previous organization of the Hyderabad District, which was highly centralized and clerically dominated. In some places in the cities and towns the laymen have eagerly accepted the new opportunities for leadership and service. On their way back from the first C.S.I. Synod in 1948, some of the lay representatives of the Diocese (educated town laymen), fired by the challenge that they had received there, resolved to form a laymen's movement. They began to hold retreats for laymen for the deepening of their own spiritual life, raised an evangelistic fund, and planned to start work in a hitherto unevangelized area in Kamareddi.[3] Thus the Kamareddi Home Mission was started by laymen in 1951, and they have taken the full responsibility of meeting its expenses, chiefly the salary of a presbyter and four evangelists.

Since union, all the licensed lay pastors have been ordained after one year's theological training in Dornakal. From 1954 to 1958 the Diocese sent a group of selected superintending evangelists to Dornakal for a year's training and ordained them as deacons at the end of the course. From 1959 to 1961 this training course was held at Medak.

On account of inflation, the Diocese had to revise the salaries of all paid church workers, and at the beginning of 1950 a composite salary for each grade of workers was fixed, including all the allowances, prizes and other help given to the workers in the previous years. The new salary scales have increased the financial burden on the Diocese, and have necessitated a substantial reduction in the number of evangelists.

The Women's Fellowship, the Order of Sisters in the C.S.I., the Little Flock and the Junior Missionary Association have been introduced and developed in the Diocese since church union.

The Diocesan Council, which meets once in two years, deals with general matters of policy; the details of administration are handled by its Executive, standing committees and boards. The Diocese elects representatives (six presbyters and eight laymen) to the C.S.I. Synod which also meets biennially. Each pastorate has a lay representative (a few pastorates have two) on the Diocesan Council, elected by its pastorate committee. The Diocese is divided into three District Church

Councils, each of which elects one of its presbyters as chairman. Two lay representatives are elected to the D.C.C. from each pastorate. The members of the pastorate committee are elected from among the communicants, and the presbyter in charge of the pastorate is its chairman. The pastorate committee should meet at least three times a year. Each local congregation is expected to be governed by a 'Leaders' Meeting', whose members are nominated by the presbyter and elected by the communicant membership.

The Diocesan Council has a layman as its Honorary Treasurer, elected by the Diocesan Council. All the grants from the Mission House are sent to the Diocesan Treasurer through the Committee Representative, who is also the Assistant Treasurer of the Diocese. (The Diocese is free in the choice of both Treasurer and Assistant Treasurer, but since the forming of the Diocese, the Mission Committee representative has served either as Treasurer or as Assistant Treasurer under an Honorary Treasurer.)

In addition to eight urban Pastorates, there were in 1959 thirty-six rural pastorates, comprising 668 village congregations, which were grouped into ninety-seven sections, manned by 100 superintending evangelists and 216 junior evangelists.[4]

The New Pattern

The Diocesan Council of 1953 adopted and acted upon the report of its Commission on Resources. It re-drew boundaries of the rural pastorates, to provide the greatest measure of pastoral oversight possible with existing staff, decided on the minimum number of paid workers for each section, and redistributed the personnel. Twelve additional pastorates were formed. Under this 'New Pattern of the Church' all the village congregations are supposed to be equally important, and they are all the responsibility of all the evangelists working in the section. It is expected that in addition to receiving regular religious teaching from the team of catechists in the section, the members of the local churches will come together at some central place once a month for more definite training.

One part of the New Pattern is the mobilization of the vast resources of voluntary workers. It envisages the selection and training of a team of consecrated voluntary workers in each local congregation, each of whom is to receive training in his or her own local church, and attend sectional, pastorate and central training courses on the basic subjects of worship, Bible study, Christian doctrine and Christian discipleship, supplemented by additional training according to his gifts and abilities. Provision is made in the scheme for the recruitment of honorary ordained deacons and presbyters. The Diocese aims at having at least one honorary presbyter in each section, in order to ensure regular Sunday worship and regular administration of the Lord's Supper in each local church. The Diocese has prepared and issued courses of study for the voluntary church workers who, after passing the required tests, are given licences by the bishop. Now there are two hundred licensed voluntary workers and a few ordained deacons (town-educated laymen) in the Diocese.

Another aspect of the New Pattern is the more effective mobilization and use of the financial resources of the Diocese. The aim of the Diocese is that every village Christian family should give an average of fifteen rupees per year. It has been estimated that if every village Christian family gave twice that amount (Rs. 30) per year, the total amount now received in overseas support would be met. Village collection books and pledge cards with a picture of Christ on the Cross have been introduced. Below the picture are printed the words, 'This have I done for thee; what hast thou done for me?'

The most important result expected from the New Pattern, through such increase of giving and voluntary service, is the release of funds and personnel for new advances into unevangelized areas. The Diocese feels that the time has come for the congregations which have already been established for one or two generations to stand more on their own feet. The recovery of evangelistic initiative is the main objective of the New Pattern.

Linked with the task of regrouping resources is that of improving the economic condition of village Christians. One presbyter has been given a special responsibility for economic uplift. An Economic Board has been set up to deal with all matters related to the economic welfare of the Church.[5]

APPENDIX: GROWTH OF THE HYDERABAD METHODIST DISTRICT AND PROGRESS OF THE MEDAK DIOCESE, C.S.I.[6]

Year	New Communicants that year	Communicants	Non-communicant Adults ('On trial')	Total of Baptized Christians	Adults Baptized that year	Children Baptized that year
Hyderabad Meth.Dist.						
1880		17	—	32	8	7
1885		147	14	308	15	23
1890		283	448	1,134	224	143
1895		672	2,121	3,866	307	213
1900		1,449	3,036	7,234	1,369	760
1905		2,034	3,844	9,321	399	491
1910		2,862	6,497	14,359	708	708
1915		3,965	9,788	20,464	1,119	930
1920		4,923	21,490	39,242	1,733	1,813
1925		6,695	33,288	56,155	2,593	2,570
1930		8,875	46,110	77,060	3,047	3,310
1935		13,045	54,399	97,167	1,787	4,071
1940		19,429	63,362	123,544	2,200	4,259
1945		23,580	65,648	132,887	1,181	3,681
1947		25,780	68,446	135,143	824	2,781
C.S.I. Medak Diocese						
1948	615	20,033	50,430	93,773	1,215	2,369
1950	1,444	21,881	53,903	99,789	1,810	3,314
1952	1,150	24,393	55,225	100,534	1,316	2,805
1954						
1956	1,310	26,057	54,745	105,474	692	2,509
1957–58	801	27,137	55,464	106,734	466	1,884
1958–59	1,642	28,791	56,322	109,555	932	2,561

CHAPTER 3

Hinduism and Islam in the Village

A. *Types of Hinduism in the Telengana Village*

The 'Hinduism' of these villages is a complex of beliefs and rites concerned with man's relation to the powers thought to underlie both the various patterns of order in society and the cosmos and also the numerous threats or actual events of disorder. In general it is the all-India 'Sanskritic' deities[1] which are considered to support the patterns of order, whereas the 'Dravidian' goddesses and demonic spirits are believed to be responsible for difficulty and disaster. 'Sanskritic' Hinduism itself, however, has several distinct components: (i) the ancient Vedic sacrificial rites; (ii) the orthodox philosophies, especially the sub-schools of the Vedanta; (iii) the sects organized around the more or less exclusive worship of one of the chief Hindu deities, or the joint worship of five of them; and (iv) more popular beliefs and practices, including worship of the images of deities in temples or household shrines, pilgrimages to more famous temples, sacred rivers or other centres, and observance of an annual cycle of feasts and fasts connected with a number of the major deities.

It is especially this fourth component of all-India Hinduism which exerts a strong influence on the religion of villagers in South India. In most villages there are only a few families belonging to the two castes. The Brahmins and the merchants observe much of the Vedic house ritual, but even for them, the influence of Hindu philosophical systems is often limited to a more popular form of certain Hindu concepts. For other Hindus, these philosophical ideas have either less significance or a meaning far removed from that in the original philosophy. In these particular villages in Telegana, the influence of the *bhakti* (sectarian devotional) movements is rather indirect. Some families are formally affiliated with a certain sect because this is part of their ancestral inheritance, but there seems to be little exclusive or enthusiastic devotion to the particular personal god recognized by that sect as the Supreme Lord. All village Hindus acknowledge the 'high gods' celebrated throughout India through their participation in the annual cycle of fasts and feasts, but in many cases the festival or ceremony itself seems more important to the participants than the deity to whom the worship is directed.

The relative importance of the 'Sanskritic' and 'Dravidian' components in village Hinduism varies somewhat in relation to the place in the social structure of the family concerned. The religio-social order of the Hindu community was described in Chapter 1. It consists of three

29

groups of castes (*kulams*). (1) There are the 'high castes' or 'twice-born' (*dvijas*): a few families belonging to the first (Brahmin) and third (Vaishya or Komati) of the three higher *varnas*. (2) The largest group consists of the many occupational kulams which together form the fourth or Sudra varna. (3) A sizeable minority below the four varnas are called 'outcastes' or 'the fifth' (*panchama*) or, since Gandhi's reforms, 'Harijans'. They are themselves divided into the two main kulams of Malas and Madigas, each with its own sub-castes. Within each of these three categories there is a traditional ranking of the castes accepted by the rest of the village, but in the second and third groups many castes hold a higher view of their respective rank than is accepted by other castes, and this leads to much rivalry and acrimonious dispute.

The greater ritual of the Brahmins and Komatis is acknowledged, and the leadership of the Brahmins in the 'Sanskritic' festivals is accepted. From the worship of the village goddesses, however, the Brahmins and Komatis exclude themselves, through their refusal to participate in animal sacrifices, even though they share belief in the 'Dravidian' goddesses and demonic spirits, and sometimes have sacrifices made on their behalf. The priestly functions in these sacrifices are exercised by certain hereditary officials from the lower Sudras and outcastes. On the other hand, since Brahmins consider the outcastes ritually unclean, they are excluded or kept at a distance in many of the ceremonies at which Brahmins officiate. The Brahmin astrologer is consulted by all Hindus, including the outcastes, but the outcaste Mala magicians and priests are also consulted, regarding certain kinds of magic and special sacrifices to the village goddesses, by everyone in the village.

B. *Some Important Religio-ethical Concepts*

The term *dharma* means things for Hindus, but in these villages it signifies primarily the particular social and religious duties of a particular caste. It prescribes not only the legitimate occupations of the members of a particular kulam, but also what special ritual obligations fall upon its members. Some of the morals and mores vary considerably from caste to caste. For example, the Brahmin is forbidden to eat meat of any kind and certain other foods, whereas the Sudra is permitted meat, though there is a strong sentiment against cow slaughter and the eating of beef, and on certain occasions many Sudras are expected to eat the meat of the sacrifices. The outcaste Madiga is expected to dispose of dead cattle and other domestic animals and was traditionally permitted to eat this carrion, though this practice is now disappearing. Some of the ritual observances of a particular caste are considered their duties, while others follow from their choice of a 'favourite deity' (*ishta-devata*); but in these villages this term means 'family god' and therefore reflects not the choice of individuals in the present generation, but an inherited family or group tradition which goes back for many generations. Even when an individual has certain ritual obligations because he was named after a particular deity, these observances, too, are considered to be part of the caste dharma. Some castes, such as the *golla* (shepherds), have quite a number of separate festivals and ceremonies relating to their special caste deities.

Villagers also recognize a *loka-nīti*, 'morality of all the people', which lays down certain ethical prohibitions applicable to all the Hindu castes and even to the Muslims and Christians in the village. Some Hindus in the villages surveyed considered the following as sin (*pāpam*): 'caste pollution, murder, adultery outside the caste, and not performing the prescribed ceremonies.' Some village Christians defined sin as 'adultery, stealing, and lying'. *Loka-nīti* also comprehends generally accepted standards of honesty and fair dealing, but there are certain important qualifications to the general prohibition against lying which are summed up in the saying, 'To save a woman's honour, to secure a marriage partner, to preserve life, money or honour, or to protect Brahmins or cows, it is no sin even to lie.'

Pāpam is frequently uttered as an expression of commiseration, meaning, 'Oh, too bad!' or 'What a shame!' This sense of 'misfortune' gives a clue to the villager's understanding of sin; the misfortune it brings weighs more heavily than the ethical responsibility it entails. For some, especially of the higher castes, papam is any act which brings bad karma and hence tends to diminish the merit or increase the demerit of the soul, thus affecting the soul's status in heaven or hell or in a future birth. Here the opposite of *pāpam* is *punyam* (merit), though there is a difference of opinion as to whether every righteous act brings punyam, or only those done over and above the demands of duty (*dharma*). Hindus recognize that the effects of both papam and punyam may be realized by the individual within his present life, and it is probably the effects of disaster or enhanced prosperity in this life which are uppermost in the minds of most village Hindus.

Sometimes *pāpam* has the connotation of 'what is shameful'. Shame appears to be an even more important regulator of conduct than a sense of moral guilt or ritual impurity. Adultery within the caste, except within the prohibited exogamous groups, is not considered a serious offence unless it is discovered and becomes an open scandal. Some Hindus have a similar attitude towards the prohibitions of lying and stealing. Though they are virtues definitely expected from the ascetic, their absence in the ordinary person becomes serious only when discovered.

The more serious moral infringements are those which place one in a condition of ritual defilement. This is true of murder and of sexual relations across caste lines or within the exogamous group ('incest'). The neglect of ceremonial obligations even more obviously places one in a ritually dangerous position. On the other hand, there are other forms of ritual impurity which are not considered papam: the state of a woman during her menstrual period, the condition of a woman and her family immediately after childbirth, and the state of the dead body, in lessening degree of the deceased's immediate family, clan and caste for a few days after a person's death. A lower degree of ritual impurity is associated with all bodily excretions.[2] For each type of impurity an appropriate ceremonial bath or cleansing is prescribed. These states of impurity are considered dangerous, because in such a state one is particularly subject to dangerous influence from the demonic spirits.

There are two 'opposites' to the state of ritual impurity. One is the state of ritual purity required to carry out certain religious acts, and the same concept denotes the relatively higher purity of a higher caste, which makes it important for its members to avoid polluting contact with members of lower castes. It is however, the second 'opposite' to ritual impurity which is more significant in the lives of most village Hindus. This is the 'auspicious' state. Whereas ritual purity is considered an unusual and temporary condition, exept for ascetics who have placed themselves outside the ordinary structure of society, it is the auspicious state which is the quintessence of normal life in society. It is most fully realized in the state of marriage, and most clearly symbolized in the emblems which the married woman is allowed and expected to wear.[3]

A number of different colours are used for ritual purposes, most regularly for the *bottu or tailka*, the dot on the forehead of a married woman whose husband is living or of a girl eligible for marriage. These colours give some valuable clues to the different shades of meaning contained within the 'auspicious state'. Saffron-coloured marks made with saffron or turmeric paste indicate *śubham*, a general state of wealth and well-being, closely identified with the goddess Lakshmi. The usual *bottu*, however, is vermilion-coloured and is thought to represent and embody the fertility of the goddess Parvati. When a black *bottu* is applied or when a woman dons black beads at marriage, the colour black functions to ward off evil spirits. White signifies purity, both the noblest of the three ingredients of matter (the quality of *sattva*) and as the virtue renunciation of worldly goals. The white ashes which the devotees of the god Siva smear on their foreheads would at first glance seem to indicate the very opposite of the auspicious, for white is the colour which Hindu widows of the higher castes must wear, and it thus signifies not only voluntary asceticism but also the death of worldly hopes and joys. However, Siva is the consort of Parvati, and he himself closely linked to fertility, since the *lingam*, understood by most Hindus as a phallic symbol, is his pre-eminent emblem and is sometimes even regarded as his concrete embodiment. The white ashes of the Saivite bring together the seeming opposites of death and fertility, and the three concepts of ritual impurity (death), ritual purity (asceticism), and auspiciousness (fertility).

Samsāra is a term which has often had a very negative connotation in philosophical and ascetic Hinduism: the ceaseless round of material existence, from which the soul must try to escape. Village Hindus, however, identify *samsāra* especially with marriage, which is conceived as a mixture of pleasure and pain, and is regarded not only as the state which duty requires and desire compels, but also as that which is peculiarly auspicious. *Samsāra* is thus the mixed blessing of life in this world; and the basis as well as the fulfilment of this worldly life is to be found in the auspicious state of marriage, in which human and trans-human well-being consists.

The concept of *karma* ('deeds') means in Sanskritic Hinduism the results ('fruits') of good and bad deeds which are to be enjoyed or suffered in present or future existences. In village Hinduism, this concept is much less a spur to moral action than an explanation of difficulties in life. It is closely linked to a conception of fate. It is believed that the creator god Brahma writes on every child's forehead just after birth and that this 'writing of Brahma' will inevitably be fulfilled during the child's lifetime. This fatalism, though it may help one to accept the distresses of others, usually does not impede a man from trying to improve his own situation. Only when people see no solution to their problems do they make use of the concept of karma, in the sense of fate or of one of the other explanations for disease or disaster mentioned below.

C. *Different Types of Supernatural Powers*

Most villagers have some conception of a single Supreme Being far transcending the lower deities, to whom they refer by the names with which He is addressed in both major sects: Vishnu, Narayana or Bhagavan, and Siva or Paramesvara. Some of the villagers said, 'God is one (*Eko Narayana*) and everything is of God. Before sitting down, getting up, sleeping, or working in the fields, we always say *Swami* ['Lord' or 'God']. Is it not the same Swami that you Christians are worshipping? It is only for our temporary satisfaction that we worship these goddesses, but we all believe in one and the same Swami.' The Supreme Being is not conceived as the impersonal Ultimate, Brahma, but as the transcendent form of one or the other of the two chief gods, Vishnu or Siva. Hindus have sometimes thought of the Supreme Being as a combination of the chief gods, either as the *Trimurti* (Brahma the Creator, Vishnu the Preserver, and Siva the Destroyer), or as Harihara (Sankaranarayana), a composite figure, half Vishnu and half Siva. These conceptions, however, have little significance for these villagers. More important is the idea that the Supreme Deity, whether conceived as Vishnu or Siva, includes His divine consort, who is His own divine energy (*śakti*).

When Siva, Brahma, and Vishnu in his various incarnations are conceived as a plurality of co-equal gods, they constitute a second class of deities, whom the villagers call *devas*. They are considered higher than the third category, which includes the consorts of the three great gods, Saraswati (of Brahma), Lakshmi (of Vishnu), and Parvati or Durga (of Siva), and the associates of the great gods, especially Ganesh, the elephant-headed god who removes obstacles and protects the home, associated with Siva, and Hanuman, the monkey king who helped Vishnu in his incarnation as Rama. Nagendra is also considered in this category. He is the cobra god who protects marriage, and is worshipped at simple shrines under trees or at ant hills thought to be inhabited by cobras. These deities occupy an intermediate position between the great gods and the local village goddesses. The divine consorts, especially those of Siva, are often identified with one or more of the local goddesses. Like the village deities, the conception of these intermediate divine figures is somewhat localized. Though Ganesh remains more universal, the Nagendra of one village is thought to be distinct from the Nagendra of another. The Durga of each village is conceived as a distinct goddess, and the Lakshmi image in a particular home has its own distinct personality. To some extent this is even true of the great gods or lords (*swamis*). The central image of the god in an important shrine or temple is considered to have the status of a distinct incarnation of the deity with a personality of his own.

In spite of the unquestioned pre-eminence of the Sanskritic 'high gods' and their associates, village deities (*grāma-devatalu*) are of more immediate significance to most village Hindus, especially to the lower Sudras and the outcastes; and as elsewhere in South India, they are almost all feminine. They are associated with the well-being of the village as a whole, but they are also believed to cause the epidemic diseases and other village disasters when they are angered. Their names vary considerably even in the same language area, and their own hierarchy in rank varies from village to village. Their authority is restricted to a single village, and even when goddesses of the same name have shrines in adjacent villages, they are regarded as different goddesses. In the villages studied, there are shrines to the following goddesses:

1. Durgamma—considered the most powerful goddess; her shrine visited first in processions; she is responsible for the welfare of the village; the wife of Siva;
2. Black Poshamma—goddess of smallpox;
3. Uradamma—'goddess of the village';
4. Katte-Maisamma—protectress of the village tank bund (dike around the reservoir);
5. Mutyalamma—goddess of chickenpox;
6. Mankāli—another name for Durgamma, but sometimes considered a separate goddess;
7. Bhūlakshmi—the earth goddess, the wife of Vishnu;
8. Mattadi Poshamma—a new goddess, originally the ghost of a murdered woman, whose shrine was installed in these villages in 1954;
9. Bālamma—prayed to for fertility; her wrath is believed to cause sterility in women; also regarded as the protectress of children; her image is often kept in a niche in the outside wall of the house;
10. Wachinamma—literally, 'the woman who has come'; the 'foreign' goddess from another village, who is believed to cause cholera.

There is one male deity, Pota-Lingamiah, the watchman of the village boundaries, who is considered the brother of the divine 'sisters' just named. There are also shrines to a number of deities particularly attached to certain castes but also venerated by others. Lakshmi has no shrine, but her presence within each household is ensured by keeping a special pot containing fermented rice water in the home.

In addition to the all-India and the local deities, village Hindus recognize other kinds of beings and powers. Ghosts and spirits are greatly feared, and they must be propitiated and/or kept away by suitable means. Strange powers are believed to pervade certain objects, which are greatly prized as 'fetishes' and 'amulets'. Finally, there is a universal belief in magical powers which can be acquired and manipulated by knowing certain secret techniques. There are usually three or four people in a village recognized as magicians, as well as some women who are suspected of witchcraft and of casting an 'evil eye'. The spirits may cause any kind of illness; their influence is seen especially in cases of epilepsy, trances or hysteria. The last is regarded as a sure sign of demon possession. The strange behaviour of a mentally defective person is believed to show his peculiar susceptibility to demonic influences. Such troubled spirits as those of men who have met with a sudden or violent death and of women who have died in childbirth are believed to bear a grudge against the world which has treated them so unjustly, and so return to the world as demons to gain satisfaction. A landowner of a village near Kondapuram was murdered while he was returning home. The people of Kondapuram and the adjacent villages feared that this man would return to trouble them as a ghost. When cholera broke out that same year in some of these villages, it was attributed to the murdered man's ghost, and an elaborate ceremony was performed to send the ghost-demon away from the village (see p. 58). In the anti-Christian polemic of the Arya Samaj, Jesus Christ is interpreted as such a demon, because He died a violent death (see p. 205).

Another type of belief in the supernatural is the attitude toward certain animals and trees. All the villagers have a general respect for cattle, including buffaloes, but the majority do not share the special veneration which the high castes give to cows. Any dog may be regarded as belonging to or even embodying one of the special gods of the shepherd caste, and it is therefore regarded as a sin to kill one, but there is no obligation to humane treatment, and dogs, like pigs, roam the village as scavengers. Similarly, a villager will hesitate to kill a cobra, since the cobra 'is' Nagendra, and will definitely not kill a monkey, who embodies the god Hanuman. It is only by higher caste Hindus that certain varieties of trees and plants are considered sacred, but the villagers may consider sacred a particular tree with a peculiar shape, and many frequent shrines under the 'sacred trees'. When a deity appears to someone by a rock, beneath a tree, or in a cave, this place is henceforth considered sacred, which means that in some sense the deity continues to have its dwelling there. Occasionally such a place is regarded as the place where one of the *devas* (high gods) appeared to a devotee, but usually it marks the appearance of a goddess.

D. *Different Patterns of Worship*

Each type of worship is related to the character of the supernatural powers to which it is offered, but these types are often mixed or combined in the actual forms of worship. The ancient Vedic sacrifices consisted of offerings into a sacred fire, accompanied by hymns, spells, and gestures. The worship offered to the major Hindu gods centres around an image of the deity, either a carving representing the god in one of the recognized forms, or a traditional symbol, such as the lingam. After the deity's presence has been invoked in a special ceremony, he is believed to dwell in the idol. The stone or other material is thus not regarded as naturally holy, though there are a few exceptions of idols in which the deity has always dwelt, or has dwelt since a special appearance or descent in the past, without any human act of consecration. Even the priestly consecration, however, is not regarded as an arbitrary act, since it is believed to follow the instructions which the god has given in a vision or dream to a priest or lay devotee about the construction of a new shrine containing his image. The idols of the village deities are crude stone slabs with some marking upon them, and they are enclosed by low 'sheds' of stone slabs open to the front of the idol. A Brahmin priest, who otherwise has no connexion with this type of deity, is brought to utter the efficacious Sanskrit verse (*mantra*) which will bring the life-breath (*prāna*) of the goddess into the image. For a few of the calendar festivals described in the Appendix, there are images which are especially made for the festival and later destroyed as a part of the ceremonies.

The worship of the high gods is organized by the priests of the sub-sects of the major Hindu sects: Vaishnavas or Vishnu-bhaktas (devotees of Vishnu); Saivas or Siva-bhaktas; Saktas, devotees of the consort of Siva conceived as the active (feminine) energy (Sakti) pervading the universe; and Smartas, who worship Surya (the sun god) and Ganesh, in addition to Vishnu, Siva and Sakti. In these villages it is only Vaishnavas and Saivas who have some semblance of sectarian organization. While many village families worship a number of the chief gods, there are other families more or less exclusively devoted to Vishnu or Siva. Many Vaishnavas wear the emblem of the Sri Vaishnava sect on their foreheads. This emblem, called the *nāmam*, consists of three lines in the form of a trident. Vaishnavas belonging to the sect of Bhagavatas paint a single red perpendicular line in the middle of their foreheads, called the *tiruman*. The distinctive mark of the followers of Siva is the *lingam*, a cylindrical black stone rounded at one end, usually understood as a phallic symbol though there are some Saivas who do not accept this interpretation. Most of the Saivas in this area belong to or have been influenced by the Lingayat sect, whose members each wear a tiny *lingam* in a little silver case hung around their necks. All Saivas smear their foreheads (and sometimes other parts of their bodies) horizontally with cowdung ashes called *vibhuti*. Vaishnavas engrave the trident symbol on the doorposts of their houses, while Saivas carve the image of Ganesh, whom they regard as the son of Siva.

The gurus (religious teachers) or priests of the sects are generally Brahmins. They perform the high-caste weddings and are consulted by all castes for drawing up horoscopes and determining auspicious days. The Saivas also have their own non-Brahmin priests, called *jangams*. The jangams are particularly connected with the Balji caste and officiate at their weddings and funerals. The outcastes have their own gurus or priests, but since each caste usually has only one such priest for a large group of villages, the caste headman in the village often officiates at weddings. The headman of the Lambadis (gypsies) is called the Nayak and acts as their priest.

A priest belonging to one caste or sect has no authority over any other priest. Each is assigned by tradition a certain number of villages, and he rarely oversteps his jurisdiction. He visits each of his villages once every three, five, or even ten years, and collects the offerings which are his due (*guru-dakshinam*). He distributes *prasādam* to his followers and gives them his blessing (*asirvadam*). *Prasādam* usually consists of food or flowers which have been offered to one of the deities and are thereby imbued with divine power and grace (the word itself means grace). These gurus do not give any religious instruction on such visits, nor are they regarded as moral examples. Some are married, while others are celibate. Some have indulged in sexual immorality. It is by virtue of his office that they give the guru tokens of respect and even adoration. (In some Hindu sects, the guru is expected to be worshipped as a god.)

There is a different kind of priests, who officiate at the village sacrifices. The *talāri* is the officiating priest of all the village goddesses. He receives as fees all the *devadosillu* (handfuls of rice for the deity) as well as larger offerings of paddy from the landowners. The Potarazu and Baindla priests are outcastes who are called 'the men belonging to the goddesses'. They officiate at the special ceremonies during epidemics or cattle plagues to 'send off' the foreign demons or goddesses who have intruded from other villages. The 'Kolpula woman', who is distinguished by her roll of matted hair, becomes possessed by the spirit of one of the goddesses during these ceremonies, and when she goes into trance she speaks as a mouthpiece of the goddess or demonic spirit that has taken possession of her. She also assists the priests in performing the sacrifices. She is given grain at each threshing floor at the harvest.

Only in the few high-caste families are children taught by a guru or priest. Children learn the traditions from their older relatives; they listen to folklore and folk songs, and observe folk dances and dramas based on the Hindu Epics and Puranas (long cycles of stories about the gods), performed by travelling beggars who make this their profession, or by groups of young men in the village. Hymns are sung composed by the 'saints' of the region, and stories are recited about their lives. Perhaps children learn most by observing and participating in the various ceremonies which make up so much of village Hinduism.

The Appendix to this chapter describes many of the ceremonies in which village Hindus participate, and, in the final section, some festivals celebrated by village Muslims. The household rites are described in the form in which they are observed by the outcastes and lower Sudra castes, but the rites of the higher castes are fairly similar. The Hindu ceremonies are of two main kinds: (i) those marking the significant times in the orderly cycles of existence, and (ii) those performed when minor disorders or major disasters threaten or actually occur. Even ceremonies of the first kind usually take place at the crisis points in the regular patterns of order. Both in the life of the individual and in the annual cycle of the seasons, there are crucial points of transition when it is not certain whether the process will continue normally. It is at such uncertain times that the protection and support of benevolent deities is most necessary and the malevolent influence of demonic spirits or wrathful deities most to be feared. There is, nevertheless, a fairly clear distinction between the two kinds of ceremonies. This is partly because so many of the second kind are animal sacrifices to the village goddesses or spirits, in which the most important roles are taken by priests from the lower Sudras and the outcastes. Certain festivals contain elements of both types. The festival honouring the village goddess Poshamma is an annual event in these villages. It takes place even if there has been no epidemic, but it includes many more animal sacrifices if there has been an outbreak of smallpox or cholera within the previous year. Farmers also have a regular annual festival which includes animal sacrifice, but this is held just before the monsoon rains are supposed to begin, a time when there is the threat of disaster as well as the prospect of great blessing, for the rains may not come at all, they may be too delayed, or too much rain may fall at once.

Two important cycles of Hindu ceremonies have been omitted from the Appendix. The few high-caste families observe the ceremonies of the daily round, and certain elements of such a daily ritual are practised by some other castes. In the larger temples there are different kinds of daily ceremonies: the services rendered to the temple god present in the main idol, at various times from his awakening in the morning to his going to sleep at night. Such ceremonies, however, are generally not performed at the small village shrines. The Appendix includes only a few of the many rites performed at the beginning of various undertakings. Before shaving anyone, the barber worships his razor by putting it to his forehead, and other artisans follow a similar practice. The act of first touching the object and then touching the hand to the forehead is done before many kinds of work: climbing a tree, drawing water from a well, grinding grain, pounding rice, ploughing land, and eating food. This is done so that no accident or misfortune may occur during the work. The touching of the forehead symbolizes prostration before the idol, when in obeisance one's forehead touches the ground or the feet of the image.

E. *Islam in the Village*

Although there are Muslims in only two of the five villages whose congregations were studied, there are a significant number in the area, especially in some of the larger roadside villages, and centuries of Muslim rule have left their impression even on villages where no Muslims are living. The following brief description will concentrate on local features of popular Islam.

During the thirteenth and fourteenth centuries A.D., Muslims carried on missionary work in Telengana and other parts of the Deccan, and the influence of Islam spread after the invasion of the Mogul Emperors and the subsequent establishment of Muslim rule in Hyderabad State. Most notable was the work of Pir Mahavir Khaurdayat, an Arab preacher, who in A.D. 1304 came to Bijapur and started to preach to the villagers.

Muslims are expected to say prayers five times a day and gather for congregational prayer (namāz) on Friday. Fasting during the daylight hours of the month of Rāmzān is undertaken by a number of Muslims, though not all keep the fast to the end. Another 'pillar' of Islam which village Muslims observe is the Witness (Shihadet) or confession of the Faith. The short form of the Muslim creed (Kalimah) reads, 'I testify that there is no God but Allah; I testify that Muhammed is the Apostle of Allah'. The other two 'pillars' are alms-giving and pilgrimage to Mecca. Some alms-giving is done. The pilgrimage (Hajj) is a duty which is theoretically accepted but very rarely taken as a personal obligation. There is also a sixth duty, jihād, which is interpreted as a holy war of Muslims against unbelievers. Considerable appeal was made to this duty by the fanatics who tried to prevent the end of Muslim rule in 1947 and 1948. Muslims feel that warfare against the Hindu majority is now quite impractical, but many still hold the theoretical right and even duty to jihād. Many Muslims in the villages are quite lax about discharging their religious duties, but nevertheless feel very strongly about their membership in the Islamic community.

The Khaji ('priest') of the Muslims in Ambojipet lives in a village with a large number of Muslims four miles from Ambojipet and about eight miles from Kondapuram. He performs minor acts of worship on their behalf and solemnizes their marriages (nikhas). The 'chief priest' or spiritual guide (Murshid) lives in Hyderabad and never visits these villages. Muslims go to him to receive his blessing and prasādam and for instruction in Muslim theology and ethics. Mullahs and fakirs live here and there in the villages; they are recognized by the whole village as having the same status as the travelling Hindu priests. At every harvest the fakir gets his bicham (gift of grain) at each threshing floor along with the various Hindu priests. There is one such fakir in Achampet who is invited by Hindus as well as Muslims to perform the Kanduri ceremony, and is fed and given a fee for this service (see p. 61).

Many mosques in Telengana were built by the Muslim rulers during the last several centuries, but some mosques in the villages have been built by wealthy individuals or the whole Muslim community. There is a small mosque in Kondapuram and a large one in Ambojipet, said to have been built two hundred years ago when the Mogul emperor from Delhi visited Medak, to enable him to stop along the road and perform his namāz. Usually each mosque has an imām, who is put in charge of its upkeep and also has the duty of giving instruction to Muslims and their children. There is often a mosque school (maktab) where the elements of reading and writing in Urdu are taught by the imam, as well as the beginnings of reading the Quran (in Arabic). In Ambojipet there is an imam attached to the mosque, and the Muslims gather in the mosque every Friday for namāz. The Muslims in Kondapuram, however, usually go to Medak (about ten miles away) every Friday to do their *namāz*, as the small mosque there is not now in use.

The Muslim festivals follow an uncorrected lunar calendar, so their date varies from year to year. The principal festivals for village Muslims are described in the Appendix.

Mir Māhaboob (Māhbub) Ali Khan, the father of the last Nizam, was acclaimed as a saint by both Muslims and Hindus. The public held him in high esteem because of his benevolent deeds during his reign in Hyderabad State. When he died in 1911 his son ordered every village to erect a symbolic tomb in his honour. In many villages of Telengana there is still such a 'tomb', called 'Māhaboob Bāsha's Dargah', from which extends a long pole with a white flag flying at the end of it. Both Muslims and Hindus visit the *dargah* in times of difficulty. Incense and incense sticks are burned and a lamp (*chirāg*) is lit at the tomb. A legend is current among the villagers about the power of Māhaboob Bāsha's name. It is said that snake bite will be healed if the victim utters this saint's name and prays to him for relief. These dargahs are to be found in all five of the villages surveyed, but since the Nizam's absolute rule ended in 1948, his father's dargah tends to be neglected.

The devotee believes that the spirit of the saint is actually present in the tomb to hear the petition of the worshipper. It is believed that the saint will intercede with Allah for any worshipper who comes to the tomb, and that the saint has power to heal diseases and grant other requests. Both Muslims and Hindus who suffer from various ills may go to such tombs and live there for some days, weeks, or even months until they get better. No diagnosis is made or medicine administered by any priest. Yet many healings are reported to have occurred. Sometimes temporary booths are erected at dargahs in which devotees may live and worship. Occasionally a Hindu officiates at the dargah. In a village near Nizamabad, a Hindu toddy-tapper is the priest at the Muslim dargah. He goes into periodic trances when he communes with the saint. Some Hindu women come to the dargahs and vow that if they conceive a child they will bring an offering and name the child after the saint. (They make similar vows at Hindu shrines and at the Christian cathedral in Medak.) There is one dargah in Jangarai in honour of a Muslim saint called Madar Sahib and another in Korivipalle for Shaikh Sahib.

There are some Muslims who can be called 'exorcists'. They are usually not professionals, but men with ordinary occupations who possess a power to dispel many ailments. The villagers have great confidence in them and consult them on occasions of sickness or other difficulty. These exorcists use talismans, which contain a paper with the number of a verse from the Quran written on it. These talismans are bought and worn by both Hindus and Muslims. Village Christians also believe in their power.

Muslims do not sing or play musical instruments during their worship at the mosques, but these village Muslims are very fond of music as a mystical technique to elevate the soul. It is now customary to have musical performances on all festival occasions, and sometimes semi-religious congregations assemble to hear songs of divine love sung by professional singers known as *qawwāls*. The tunes they sing, called *qawwāli*, are at present very popular.

Many village Muslims still maintain the custom of keeping their women in seclusion or having them veiled when they go out, but the *purdah* (veil) system is gradually weakening, as an increasing number of educated Muslim women are coming out of seclusion. Muslim men are allowed to have up to four wives and to keep concubines. Muslim men have acquired a bad reputation in the village because they sometimes have illegal connexions with non-Muslim women of the lower castes. Two Christian women in one of the five villages have become concubines of Muslims.

During Islam's many centuries in India, it has both influenced and been influenced by its Hindu environment. In Telengana there have been few conversions to Islam by conviction, but many additions through the marriage of Hindu women to Muslim men. Many Hindus have appreciated the privilege of brotherhood which Muslims enjoy and extend to their Hindu neighbours. Though certain aspects of the caste system are to be found among Indian Muslims, they have no 'outcastes'.

Because Urdu was the official language of Hyderabad State during centuries of Muslim rule, many Hindus in Telegana speak Urdu quite fluently and use many Urdu words even when speaking Telugu. Conversely, almost all Muslims in the village speak Telugu, though with an Urdu accent. In addition to the cultural influence of the language Muslims use, there are some other influences which may be more distinctly religious. Some names in common use by village Hindus and Christians have a Muslim origin. If a Mala or Madiga woman practises divination, the words she utters in her trance will be in Urdu. However, this may be less a Muslim influence than the use of an 'alien' or 'superior' language to express the supernatural reality which is seen in the trance.

Many Muslims share the belief of village Hindus in demonic spirits and join with Hindus in some of their festivals, especially Dasara, Deepavali and Holi. Among the *Dudekulas* ('cotton cleaners' of mixed Hindu–Muslim parentage), tools are worshipped in the same way as Hindus practise at Dasara. Saint worship is common among village Muslims. Evil spirits are avoided by the use of charms, amulets, and talismans tied to the neck. The use of magic is widespread. In times of epidemics or other illness, village Muslims (especially women) go to Hindu shrines to secure healing or immunity from disease.

Even poor village Muslims have a strong sense of belonging to what had so long been the ruling class. The Muslim rulers in Hyderabad State exercised their authority with the air of conquerors. To some extent village Muslims shared this attitude and exploited the poorer Hindus. Moreover, the village Muslims tended to copy the habits of their overlord, the *nawāb*. Traces of this nawāb mentality remain in a certain pomp and ostentatious luxury, and some carelessness in spending money. This attitude affects not only the Muslims but also the better situated Hindus and Christians.

F. *The Nature of Village Religion*

Dube gives the following characterization of the religion of Shamirpet, a village only fifty miles from the Wadiaram pastorate:

> . . . festivals and ceremonies are observed with unfailing regularity. Otherwise the gods are remembered only at times of disease or difficulty. As a rule, only some of the elderly people devote themselves to 'the daily duty of remembering the creator'. . . . The tasks of remembrance and repentance are postponed for old age. . . . In the everyday thought and speech of the younger generation there is very little of religion; and little conscious effort of seeking any deep religious experience or thrill is to be found among them.[4]

The two exceptions Dube notes are an *Urs* (semi-religious fair) commemorating a local Muslim saint, and the annual village worship of a village goddess:

> On both these occasions, several people are temporarily possessed by the spirit of the Muslim saint or by one of the goddesses. Going into a trance these people speak for the spirit which possesses them. The other people who are present there make offerings to them, seek solutions of their pressing problems and difficulties, and request them to remedy their ills and worries. Considerable enthusiasm is evidenced among them at this time. With these exceptions there is very little religious thought, talk, or worship in normal life.[5]

While it is true that Shamirpet is closer to Hyderabad and more subject to urban influence than the villages included in our survey, we believe that the differences between Dube's conclusions and ours do not stem primarily from the different degrees of secularization in the respective villages, but on our somewhat different understandings of the meaning of 'religion' in these villages. Dube characterizes 'Hinduism as it is practised in the village' as 'a religion of fasts, feasts, and festivals, in which prescribed rituals cover all the major crises of life'. But the three marks of religion which Dube looks for and finds lacking in most village Hindus are 'remembrance' (meditation on God or the gods), 'repentance for sins committed', and 'enthusiasm' ('seeking any deep religious experience or thrill').[6] 'All three are marks of *bhakti* Hinduism, which is not at all influential in these villages. The one instance of enthusiasm on which Dube remarks should furnish a clue as to where the villagers' religious interest lies. People are fascinated in watching a spirit-possessed person, because the spirit or village deity is powerful enough and near enough to take possession of a person and thus make its will known, or do something else directly affecting the villagers' material welfare. In relation to these supernatural beings, there is little meaning in the kind of meditation, devotion, or repentance directed to Vishnu or Siva, conceived as the creator of the universe and the bestower of eternal salvation. Dube reports that 'Youth brings in its wake a more worldly and materialistic outlook towards life and its pleasures. Thoughts are turned to religion when the evening of life approaches.' In the context of village religion, however, concern for material welfare is not the opposite of 'turning to religion' but one of its main foundations. The ascetic understanding of religion is respected by villagers as an ideal for the extraordinary man, but does not seem to play an important role in their own religion, whether they are young or old. The complaint of older people against the younger generation which we noted was not that they were too materialistic, but that they were losing their respect for their elders and for the traditional observances.

The ceremonies which punctuate the life of the village indicate an important feature of village religion: the sense of a sacred aspect in every activity or event, a sacredness which must be appropriately recognized in ritual which will minimize the threat in this sacredness and maximize its beneficial effect. It is not true, however, that a sense of the sacred pervades the entire existence of village Hindus. Quite apart from modern secular influences, there is much *tamāsha* ('joking', 'amusement', or 'good time') in the villagers' observance of many of the calendar festivals. One reason for this is that what Srinivas calls 'Sanskritization'[7] has stopped in these villages less than halfway. The all-India festivals connected with 'Sanskritic' deities were presumably introduced many centuries ago with the prestige of North Indian Hindu culture and the authority of the Brahmins, but the official or orthodox significance of many of these festivals has never become thoroughly understood or appreciated by most villagers. The festivals celebrated only by the Brahmins and Komatis are not included in the Appendix, but many of the generally recognized are regarded by most of the village as occasions for feasting. The festival of *Toli Ekadasi* is observed by the high castes as a fast in honour of Vishnu. For the lower Sudra castes and the outcastes, however, it is celebrated as a feast with meat and the drinking of toddy (palm wine).

There is a kind of *tamāsha* which has a religious significance of its own, such as the petty stealing, bad language, rough-housing, and even promiscuity which marks the spring festival of *Holi*, for this is designed to enhance fertility. The highlight of the festival is the nocturnal bonfire of Kāma, the god of erotic love. At a feast in the woods after the sacrifices, relief at the departure of the demons contributes to the festive mood.

The calendar festivals are based on a more northern climate and are directed to deities which have remained rather vague and far away for most of the villagers. Consequently there is little religious core, either of awe or of fitness, in the feasts which are held on these occasions. The agricultural festivals in the yearly cycle have a more deeply felt significance for the whole village. The precedent of joining in the festivals for the sake of the *tamāsha* is already being used by young men who come back after a period in the cities with their belief in the spirits and local goddesses considerably weakened, if not completely destroyed. Unless they have accepted some rationalistic philosophy which repudiates or ridicules village beliefs and customs, they tend to join in the festivals to the goddesses in the same way they were accustomed to participating in the festivals to the 'Sanskritic' gods; largely 'for the fun of it'.

APPENDIX A: HINDU VILLAGE CEREMONIES

A. *The Life Cycle*

1. *Birth and Early Childhood*

In order to secure children, women worship Nagendra (the snake god), offering milk, sugar and coconut at an ant hill (often inhabited by snakes). If a woman remains barren, she goes to various *jatras*, the festival connected with a particular god, held at the most sacred shrine of that god in the region. She prays to the deity of the jatra for a child. If she afterwards becomes pregnant, the child will be named after that deity.

The first confinement usually takes place in the house of the girl's mother, subsequent confinements in the house of her mother-in-law. When the girl is taken to her mother's house in the seventh or ninth month of pregnancy, she drops five small stones before reaching the boundary of her husband's village, and when she returns from her mother's house after the confinement, she does the same in her mother's village, so that no evil spirit will follow her into the village to which she is going.

If the delivery is easy, there is no special ceremony, but if it is difficult, a goat is tied to the mother's bed so that one of the village goddesses will not devour the baby or kill the mother, but be satisfied with the goat, which is afterwards sacrificed to the goddess.

As soon as the child is born, it is washed and put in a winnowing fan containing paddy or millets covered by a piece of cloth, and *kali* is sprinkled over the child's face to symbolize its entry into *kaliyuga* (the degenerate present age). Then all those present turn away, so that the God Brahma may come down and write the child's destiny (*karma*) on its forehead. The lines discovered on the skull after are said to be this 'writing of Brahma'.

A small pit is dug and filled with water, called a *kolanu* ('pond'), in which the new baby must be bathed for the first twenty-one days, each day for the first five days and then on alternate days.

If two or more children in a family die at birth or soon afterwards, or if the mother has several abortions (miscarriage), it is believed that the evil spirits (*dayyamulu*) are responsible. When the mother is again pregnant, a goat and a chicken are slaughtered under a small pandal near the house so that no spirit will seize the embryo.

If a child survives after three or four miscarriages or deaths in the family, it is placed on the ground immediately after birth, so that no goddess or evil spirit will desire it, and it is named 'Earth', which may mean one who is dedicated to the earth goddess and bears her name, but has here the connotation of being one who is cast away on to the ground and is considered useless and practically dead.

Purudu, the purification and naming ceremony, takes place on the twenty-first day after the child's birth. On that day the baby is given a bath and dressed for the first time in a shirt and cap. The mother is bathed and given a new blouse. A string of black or black and red beads, called 'evil eye beads', is tied around the baby's wrist, so that if anyone should cast an 'evil eye' on the child, there will be no ill effects. In order to ward off the evil spirits, an anklet of entwined silver or copper wire is put on the baby. This is called 'anklet of Bhima' (a hero of the Hindu Epic). Strings of hair are similarly tied to the baby's wrists and ankles. The mother receives one blouse from her own parents and one from her husband's parents. If it is the first child, her parents will give her a sari and blouse, and give a shirt and turban to her husband. They also give a feast, including toddy, to the whole kulam.

On the same day, the baby is placed in the cradle for the first time, and the mother is allowed to go to the well and draw water. Two small idols made of turmeric, one male and one female, are then placed on either side of the well. On each of the four side walls of the well balls of turmeric and cotton seeds are placed, and a fifth one is put into the inside wall of the well. The mother must draw five buckets of water from the well, and pour back the same water into the well. Then she must fill five pots with water, and she and four other married women who are not widows must carry the five water pots to her house.

Relatives are invited and ask the parents what name the child is to be given. If the parents have already made a vow to some god or goddess, they will give the name of the deity to the baby. Otherwise the parents may give any name which they like.

The *first haircut* takes place sometime within the first two years. When the hair has grown quite long, the child is taken to the shrine of a goddess, where its hair is cut and offered to the goddess. If the child's mother is pregnant again, the haircut is postponed until after the next baby is born. Only a little of the hair is left at the shrine; the rest is taken home and kept for remembrance.

If the baby is beautiful, it is disfigured by tattooing the bridge of the nose, so that the evil spirits will not be attracted. On the eighth day after birth, the baby is branded on the stomach with a red-hot needle, so that it may digest milk easily. After *Purudu*, a string is tied around the child's neck to which is attached a tiny silver sword, a round thin piece of silver on which charms are inscribed, and a small rectangular copper box containing more charms, with the figure of the monkey god engraved on top. These are to prevent the baby from getting fits. If the child becomes sick at any time, one of the goddesses is invoked and worshipped. If the child recovers, a silver anklet (*bedi*) dedicated to that goddess is put on its left ankle. This is enlarged as the child grows and is worn throughout life. Whenever the anklet is removed and enlarged, it is put back after a coconut has been broken.

2. *The Wedding and Other Related Ceremonies*

When the boy's father learns of a suitable girl, he consults a Brahmin, who fixes an auspicious day for a journey. On the appointed day, the boy's parents, accompanied by some relatives, take along some other members of the kulam from their own village, journey to the other village, where they make their official visit to the girl's parents and ask them if they will give their daughter to their son. The girl's parents ask whether the boy's parents have lands, cattle, a tiled roof house, and other kinds of wealth. If the girl's parents are satisfied, they say, 'We shall come and see your house'.

On the day fixed by the Brahmin and agreed upon by both parties, this visit takes place, and it is not before seeing the home of the boy's parents that the girl's parents, who also bring some relatives with them, give their final consent. Only after this is given do the boy's parents begin to cook a meal. While the food is being cooked, both parties go to a Brahmin and ask him whether the boy's and girl's horoscopes agree. Sometimes the Brahmin says that the girl's name should be changed to fit the boy's horoscope, and he gives the girl another name, which will from that time on be used in her father-in-law's house. Then the Brahmin fixes the date and time for the marriage. For lower caste marriages, the Brahmin invariably sets a time during the night as the auspicious moment for the climax of the marriage proper. Both the parties then return to the boy's home for the evening meal, to which the entire kulam in that village is invited. After the evening meal, they all sit together and discuss what the two parties should contribute in clothes, ornaments and other forms of wealth. Usually the bride's parents will give the bridegroom two brass cooking vessels, two brass plates, and one large brass serving-plate. If the girl's parents are rich, they will give the bridegroom a cow with its calf, and also a silver thread to wear around his waist. The boy's parents are expected to give the girl's mother a sari and the girl's father one turban and a shirt.

The night before the wedding day, the bridegroom's party goes to the bride's village to bring the girl home to their village, where the wedding is to take place. They take the new clothes and ornaments of the bride and bridegroom in a basket and place them before the goddess Poshamma. After various other ceremonies, they slaughter a goat in front of her image, and offer the goddess some specially prepared rice and the goat's liver. Her blessing is a protection against illness, especially smallpox. The bridegroom's party then goes to the bride's village, with drums beating. They stop at a crossroads in the bride's village before entering the girl's home. The girl's parents come to meet this party at the crossroads, also with drums beating, and give them water to wash their feet, water to drink, a mat to sit down on and tobacco. The bride's party also takes a porridge pot, which should be carried by a married woman. The girl's relatives spread the mat on the ground, make a heap of rice on the mat, and put the pot of porridge on the rice. The bridegroom's relatives tie a piece of cotton thread dipped in saffron water round the neck of the porridge pot and stick some flowers into the hairlock of the girl who carried the pot. Then the women of the two parties sing songs to exchange greetings, and they all go to the girl's home.

The same night before the evening meal, the betrothal ceremony is performed in the girl's home. The bride is dressed in a silk blouse and a new sari, and silver bracelets are put on her wrists and a bronze engagement ring on the fourth finger of her right hand. A new mat is spread on the floor, a low stool or a mango plank put on the mat on which the young couple sit, and saffron rice is sprinkled over them. Then they all have their dinner and sleep that night in that village. The following morning the bridegroom's party takes the girl with them to their village. The bride's party follows later the same day, with drums beating, along with other members of their kulam, and they wait at the crossroads in the middle of the bridegroom's village or near the community hall of the village. In a way similar to the previous night, the bridegroom's party meets and takes home the bride's party.

Two further ceremonies take place later the same day in the boy's village. The barber comes and cuts the nails of the bride and groom, and they are both smeared with turmeric paste, sprinkled with saffron rice, and separately given ceremonial baths before being dressed in their wedding clothes. The other ceremony is the bringing of new pots from the potter for the wedding feast, including two large decorated pots known as *aireni* pots. A traditional ceremony of exchange takes place.

The actual wedding ceremony (*lagnam*) usually takes place during the night, but is occasionally performed early in the morning, and is then known as a 'cow-marriage'. Four small pots are placed in four corners and symbolic diagrams (*yantras* or *polu*) are made with rice joining the four pots. The corner pots are also connected with five rounds of cotton string. Then the bride and groom, wearing new clothes and with *bashingalu* tied to their foreheads, each holding a brass plate containing saucer lamps, walk around the *polu* five times.

The bride and groom are then made to sit on a stool near the *polu*; the former on the bridegroom's knees. The feet of both are placed in a brass plate brought by the bride's parents. The bride's hands, palm upwards, are then placed over the groom's hands, and ten copper coins are placed in the girl's hands. The bride's father should wash their feet three times, while his wife pours water, and the bride's mother should wash their feet twice while her husband pours water. The bride's parents then do reverence to them, touching their feet, and put ten copper coins in the brass plate. After this the bride and groom are seated within the *polu*. The ornaments are then presented and placed on the bride, after being examined by the bride's parents. (If they are not satisfied, a quarrel will ensue.) While the bridegroom puts his hand on the neck of the bride, the caste headman ties the *tali* (marriage emblem) around her neck. The caste headman also puts rings on the second toe of the girl. Then jaggery (crude brown sugar) and cummin are put in their hair, as a symbol of the combination of joy and sorrow which awaits them in their married life. The bride and groom hold the brass plate with their right hands, and all the other married women also hold it; thus they swing around and sing the *mangalam* (wedding song).

While the bride holds out her hands, the groom pours rice into them three times, and then the bride does likewise twice to him. Then a small basket full of uncooked rice is put on a low stool and the bride's feet are placed on that rice. The bridegroom should tread on her feet three times, and the bride twice on his feet, after which they both stand up. Some millet mixed with turmeric is put in a cloth and the foot of Nandi (the bull of Siva) is drawn, after which milk and ghee are mixed with millet and rice. This mixture is distributed to the people present and sprinkled three times on the bride and the bridegroom where they stand. After this they are again seated on the stools inside the *polu*, and a clay plate is placed in the hands of each. First the parents put their gifts in the clay plates, one rupee in each plate, after which the other relatives and friends add theirs. This concludes the wedding ceremony; the meal of dahl, curry and rice follows, after which all retire for the night.

The next morning four ceremonies take place, which we shall here only summarize. At dawn there is *surya namaskaram*, worship of the sun. The bride and groom stand facing east, both holding mango leaves in their hands. Five times a mixture of lime and saffron is poured over the leaves, and after each libation, the couple raise their hands in the posture of *namaskaram* (folded hands brought to the forehead) in worship of the sun. Later in the morning is the ceremony of *nagavalli*, a symbolic representation of married life, during which the bride and groom first lie down together on a bed, and later a doll is produced representing the first baby. The caste headman has a prominent part in these rites. While he cries like a baby, the women sing lullabies and a wedding song.

There then follow the symbolic 'games'. One is called 'searching for gold', in which the bride and groom have to search for a copper ring in one of the *aireni* pots. The other is called 'stealing', in which the couple are supposed to 'steal' some pancakes, which lie on a bed under a cloth, without being detected by the caste headman or the five married women who take part in the ceremony. After this the entire wedding party has a feast at noon with mutton curry and toddy, and then disperse.

Most of these ceremonies connected with the marriage are performed by women—who are also behind the quarrels which often develop during the festivities, when one party accuses the other of not preparing good food, of delaying the meal, of not bringing the proper ornaments, or of not supplying sufficient toddy, or else takes up old quarrels. Previously these ceremonies used to occupy four days, but they now go through them in one night and the following morning. It has become too expensive to feed all the relatives for four days.

Weddings are usually held between December and May. The month of Sravana in the Hindu calendar falls in July–August. At any time during this month the boy's parents come to take the bride to live with them. The ceremony performed at that time is called *'Sravana katnalu'* (gifts in the month of Sravana). Five people come from the boy's village, bringing a sari and two blouses for the bride, two dry coconuts, five seers of rice and also blouses for the girl's mother and sisters. They bring some light refreshments in a bamboo basket, covering the food with a *dhoti*. Then they put ten copper coins, ten betel nuts, two dry coconuts, ten dates, and some rice in the girl's sari and tie it round her waist. Before she leaves her mother's house, *bottlu* are put on the door-steps, after the posts have been washed. The girl also has a *bottu* on her forehead. She worships the door-post and then leaves the house. While they are going through the village, they should not come across an ass, firewood, baskets, a new pot, an empty pot, a cat, a snake, or an empty brass vessel. Brass vessels full of water or porridge pots, on the other hand, are good omens. After this the girl lives with her husband's parents and goes home only for festivals and other special family occasions. When she goes home on visits, she is accompanied by her father until she becomes mature, after that by her husband.

3. *Coming of Age (Rajaswala) and Consummation of Marriage*

When a girl is considered mature, soon after her first menstrual period, she is isolated from other people and seated in a corner of the house for ten days, during which time no one will touch her. At the beginning of the period of isolation, five coconuts and some sweet oil are brought, and the sweet oil is poured into half a coconut, which is broken above her so that the oil falls on her head. The girl has to eat the meat of the coconut. Another coconut is broken and mixed with saffron rice, which is then distributed to other members of the family. The other three coconuts are tied into a fold of her sari around her waist. On the first day of isolation, all the girl's clothes and her body are smeared with saffron (or turmeric paste). She should not go outside with saffron on, lest the saffron attract evil spirits.

During the next ten days the girl is not supposed to see a man's face. She is given a separate plate and tumbler, and food and water are served to her from a distance. She is fed rich food, rice and dahl mixed with sweet oil. On the third, fifth, seventh and eleventh days, she is given a bath.

On the eleventh day the girl may rejoin the other members of the family and a special ceremony takes place called *barsala* (abbreviation of the Urdu for 'twelve years of age'). If the girl's father-in-law is rich, he will slaughter a goat on that day, and invite relatives from other places for a feast, at which much toddy is drunk. The girl's mother must buy various gifts of clothes for her daughter and the girl's husband. On the eleventh night, just before the feast, the girl and her husband are seated on two low stools, after they have put on the new clothes, and the relatives place gifts (*katnalu*) before them. After this, they all eat and drink.

Soon after this, the boy's parents consult a Brahmin regarding an auspicious day for the consummation of the marriage. The boy's parents and some elderly women prepare the bed for the couple, and put them in a separate room for one night. Until this night they are not supposed to be alone together at night, or even speak to each other during the day in the presence of others. Even after this it is not good manners for a wife to speak to her husband in the presence of others. A special feast is sometimes given for the whole *kulam*, and red *bottlu* are put on the foreheads of the couple.

4. *The Funeral and Related Ceremonies*

When a person is at the point of death, he is removed from the cot and put on the ground, sometimes on a heap of hay, so that he will not die in the world of the spirits between sky and earth. Then the relatives run to the potter, set a pot with a lid, and in this pot bring water from a tank. They boil water on a fire of cowdung cakes, and bathe the dead body with half of this water and with the other half cook some rice. Then they construct a bier, on which they carry the corpse to the grave.

The son, adopted son or some male member of the family has his head shorn. He carries in one hand a pot of fire and in the other a pot of cooked rice, and walks in front of the bier. The relatives follow the bier, beating their chests, wailing and weeping, while the Madigas beat the drum and dance in front of the bier. Puffed rice is thrown now and then over the bier as it is being carried to the grave, and also some copper coins which are picked up by the Madigas beating the drum.

When more than half the distance has been covered, the rite of 'lowering' is performed. A woman's ornaments are pulled off, and the cord round his waist which a man has worn since *purudu* is removed. One or two bronze beads are put into a woman's mouth and also a betel leaf, so that the yearning to chew betel may not cause her to return to the living in the form of a ghost. Yellow rice from the pot carried by the son or some other male member of the family is put on the four corners of the bier. If the husband had died, one bead is removed from his wife's necklace and put in his mouth. Until now, the Madigas have performed a marriage beat on their drums, but after this they beat the death beat. Up to this point, they still believe that the corpse might come to life again. Stories are told of bodies which sat up alive some time before this point of 'lowering'.

The dead body is then carried to the grave. The relatives walk with the body five times round the grave, and then place it inside with the head pointing south. The male member of the family who carries the pot places dots of rice here and there round the grave. He fills the pot containing rice with water and stands on the north side of the grave, putting it on his left shoulder. The *begari* breaks a hole in the pot with an axe after the grave has been filled with earth, and the one carrying the pot goes around the grave five times while the water comes out of the hole in the pot. At the end he drops the pot at the point from which he started, and goes home without looking back towards the grave.

Then the hay in which the dead body was carried is burned with fire from the fire pot, and also the bier which was prepared by the *begari*. Since all these people are ritually polluted, they go to the tank, wash their clothes and bathe. The pot which was dropped on the ground is broken into small pieces at the grave by the *begari*. These pieces must be so small that no rain water can be collected in them, for it is believed that if a bird were to drink such water and fly over any person, that person would die.

Then the family goes to the Brahmin to consult him about the date for

C

observing *dinalu*, and also to ask whether they should leave the house or not. If he tells them to leave the house for a certain time, they must live somewhere else in a hut for that period. At *dinalu*, usually on the fourth day after death, a goat is killed and a good feast is held, to which all relatives and friends are invited. After dinner they have a *bhajana*, a song recitation or epic or puranic stories by some priest. This is done, they say, so that they may forget their sorrow, and the drinking of toddy is said to be for the same reason. The shedding of blood in the killing of a goat or chicken for a feast has a religious significance, being said to satisfy the village goddesses or some evil spirits.

If a husband has died, the widow goes to the tank, takes a bath, and then places five stones on which she pours lime water and marks saffron and vermilion *bottlu*. This she must do in secret. She must cover herself with a blanket while going to and returning from the tank. Near those stones, she breaks her bangles, removes her rings and black beads, takes off her old sari and blouse and puts on new ones, and then leaves all the things she has taken off at the tank. From then on she is called a widow.

Only high-caste and educated Hindus observe *taddinams*, or death anniversaries. Most village people do not remember the exact date on which a person died, but at each festival, before they eat, they put two leaf plates in one corner of the house and put some rice and curry on the plates, and place tumblers of water at the side, for the ancestors. They hope that the ancestors will come and eat the food and leave without troubling them. After waiting outside for some time, they go back in and take back the food and eat it along with the rest of the meal. This custom is followed at all the festivals.

If a pregnant woman dies, she should be cremated, or else her abdomen should be opened with a knife and shown to witnesses. If the relatives do not do this, it is thought that the rains will fail. A few years ago, a Christian woman died in Jangari while with her parents for her confinement. After she died, one of the elders of the Christian congregation opened her abdomen with a knife, after which she was buried. That year there was no rain, so they exhumed the body, cut her abdomen again, and after showing the body to all the people, buried it again.

B. *The Calendar Festivals*

For all the calendar and agricultural festivals, the villagers clean their houses and hang up mango leaves in the doorways; and they bring their married daughters home from their husbands' villages. If a girl is mature, her husband takes and fetches her, but does not stay for the festival (with one or two exceptions). New Moon day, Full Moon day, Sunday, Wednesday and Friday are inauspicious days for sending girls back to their husbands.

1. *Ugadi*, Telugu New Year's day, usually comes sometime in March, the first day of the month *Chaitra*. People take baths and wear new clothes, and they prepare *purnam*, a beverage of boiled dahl mixed with jaggery, and a chutney, consisting of pieces of mangoes, margosa flowers and jaggery. The village people put up a pandal over the Hanuman shrine, and lead a procession of carts round the village in the evening, with beating of drums. The procession starts from the shrine of Durgamma, the most important goddess in the village, then goes to the shrine of Poshamma, the goddess of smallpox and then to the shrine of all the other goddesses. The procession then returns to the shrine of Durgamma and starts again, making a total of five rounds. Afterwards all the village women walk in a similar procession visiting all the shrines of the goddesses carrying *bonalu*

(special clay pots containing saffron rice). Then they eat in their own houses. After that there is a drama of the stories in Bhagavata Purana (especially those connected with the childhood and youth of Krishna), which goes on throughout the night. The Brahmin priest comes in the evening, goes to the shrine of Hanuman and decorates it with red colouring, lime and vermilion (prepared by the low-caste Sudra village priest), then worships by uttering some mantras. The Brahmin is seated in some central place, and reads the *panchangam* to the people. This is a sort of almanac which predicts the events of the coming year, such as the rains, harvests, cattle diseases, epidemics, and other events. The main item of food on this day is *polelu*, a kind of sweet bread.

2. *Toli Ekadasi*, the eleventh day of Ashada (June–July), is observed by a few high-caste families as a feast in honour of Vishnu, but for the lower castes its only special feature is a feast with meat (preferably mutton, otherwise chicken) and the drinking of toddy.

3. *Nagula Panchami* is the festival of the cobra god, and falls on the fifth day of Sravana (July–August). Only very few among the Malas and Madigas observe it. Jaggery rice and puffed millet are prepared. In the families observing the festival, one member fasts on that day, takes a bath, wears clean clothes, and pours a mixture of milk and ghee into the ant hill which the cobra god inhabits.

4. *Ganesh Chaturti* or *Vinayaka Chaviti*, the fourth day of Bhadrapada, is the festival in honour of Ganesh, the elephant-headed god who is especially popular in South India, and is considered to be a son of Siva. This is a 'sweet festival', at which no meat is eaten, The special food served is *payasam*, a sweet pudding containing milk and ghee. Artisans and cultivators wash their tools and implements, put red colouring on them, and make offerings (*naivedyam*) to these tools.

5. *Krishna Jayanti*, the 'birthday' of Krishna, is celebrated on the New Moon day in Sravana, but is not much observed by Malas and Madigas.

6. *Peddala Amavasya*, 'New Moon for the Ancestors', comes two months later, at the end of Bhadrapada or the beginning of Asvini (September–October). Each family kills a goat or chicken, and makes a big feast on this day. Their priest visits them—a Brahmin in the case of many caste people, the Mala Jangam for Malas and Mitra Ayyavaru for Madigas. He visits each house in the kulam; in the name of their ancestors, they give him some rice, chillies, salt and vegetables, and they fall at his feet and do him reverence.

7. *Saddula Batkamma*, the 'Flower Festival', is celebrated for nine days. Gauramma, the goddess of this festival, is said to be one of the two wives of Siva. Every day during that week women collect different kinds of flowers from the forest or from their gardens, make a big heap of them and put the image of Gauramma in it. In the evenings all the women in the village, in different groups according to their kulam, dance round these piles of flowers, singing and clapping their hands. After this they take the flowers to the tank and throw them in, and there eat some refreshments. On the last day, they celebrate this on a grand scale with much larger heaps of flowers. That day the women wear their best saris and all their jewellery, making a colourful sight. The Madiga men bring their drums, and all the women go in procession. There will be quarrels if anyone does not observe his proper rank. They first go to the police corps' shed and dance there, singing some songs based on stories from Ramayana and Mahabharata about the lives of women. Then they go to the Durgamma shrine, circle it four times, put *naivedyam* and a saucer lamp before the goddess, break a coconut and go to the tank. On the tank bund they dance twice around

the flowers, then throw them all in the water. They eat chapaties, curd rice and pumpkin curry after this before returning to the village. All the remnants are given to the Madigas. This festival is celebrated only by caste people. Mala and Madiga women do not have the piles of flowers, but simply dance and sing.

8. The very next day is the festival of *Dasara*, the 'tenth' day of this month of Asvini (September–October). This is the festival of men, the day after the flower festival of women. On this day everybody is supposed to wear new clothes, no matter how poor he may be. The villagers have a feast at noon of mutton, chicken, pork or beef, and drink toddy at night.

Before Independence a pole was put upright into the ground and the Nizam's flag was hoisted. First the Brahmin did *puja*, and then the Muslim mullah did *namas*. Then several animals, chiefly goats, were slaughtered and eaten. Since Independence, however, the villagers no longer kill any goats or pigs at Dasara. They simply smear the flag post with red colouring; a Brahmin recites some mantras near the flag, and a coconut is broken into small pieces and distributed to all.

In the evening all the village people go to the jambi tree. The Brahmin writes some mantras in the sand under the tree. Vermilion rice and jambi leaves are distributed to those present and to others in the village, according to their rank. These are preserved throughout the year, to bring a blessing. This is a form of celebration of Ayudha Puja, which commemorates the years in which the Pandava brothers were exiles in the forest, and kept their weapons under a jambi tree.

Early the next morning, the villagers bathe and put on new clothes. After the midday meal they go out into the woods, for they must see a bluejay that day, in order to be assured of good fortune in the coming year. When they finally find one, they clap their hands and return home. On their way back, they collect tassels of paddy, ragi or maize, which they tie to the door-frame after their return.

On Dasara day, some villagers believe that they should steal something from the fields, such as a pumpkin or gourd. If they are not found out when they steal it, they will not be found out throughout the year. Therefore some young men attempt a burglary on this day!

9. *Bhogi* and *Deepavali*. Deepavali is the festival of lights and is observed, on the following New Moon day. The village people call the previous day Bhogi. On this 'eve' of the festival, they clean the house with cowdung water, and put five cowdung cakes on to the wall of the cattle shed, marking saffron and vermilion *bottlu*, five of each colour, on each of the cowdung cakes. They smear the bullocks with red colouring, tie bells around their necks, and send them out for grazing. On that day they do not use them for any work, so the bullocks also have a holiday.

For this festival parents bring home not only their daughters but also their sons-in-law, no matter how poor they may be. If a daughter has been married that year, her parents give presents to the son-in-law. On Deepavali morning they give a bath to both the daughter and the son-in-law. This is done by the girl's sisters, or if there are no sisters, by her brothers. Then they dress them in new clothes bought by the girl's parents. Vermilion *bottlu* are put on the couple, and on the others present when they all eat. At succeeding celebrations of Deepavali, the girl's parents simply feed them and send them back home after the festival, without giving any gifts. Nowadays many older sons-in-law do not go to their wife's parents for this festival. If only the daughter comes, the parents give her a blouse, bangles, and rings and send her back to her husband after the festival.

The same evening, broomsticks are tied into a bundle and saucer lamps are fastened to them. This 'lamp' is placed in a dung heap, and expected to burn throughout the night. Near the lamp some children set off fire crackers. The outside of the house is also decorated with saucer lamps. Since this is considered a 'sweet festival', no meat is eaten on this day.

Merchants close their accounts on the night of Deepavali, and affix saffron *bottlu* in their books opposite the names of customers who have paid the money they owed. These merchants worship their cashbook and also offer worship to Lakshmi, the goddess of wealth, so that they may have good business in the coming year.

10. *Sankranti* is the festival of the winter solstice—the return of the sun. It is celebrated on the 24th day of the month Pushya (in January). A month before this festival, each family cleans its house and courtyard, and burns a saucer lamp for twenty-four hours in the main room of the house. For a week before Sankranti the family is busy with preparations: whitewashing the house, bringing daughters home, decorating the walls with red paint, and decorating the courtyard with drawings of lime powder.

Fine rice is kept for this day. The girls pour some milk into a small clay pot, and put the pot on three cowdung balls, which act as a tiny fireplace. The milk is boiled while a drum is being beaten. They watch to see on which side of the pot the milk boils over first. If it is on the side towards the river Ganges (north), it is a good omen.

All bathe in the morning, wear clean clothes and have a feast at noon consisting of *biriyani* or, if they cannot afford meat, saffron rice. Usually the Malas and the Madigas go to the caste people's houses, and beg cooked rice from door to door, as they do at every festival.

When a girl returns to her husband's village, people ask her 'What did your parents give?', and blame her if she has received nothing. In order to avoid such embarrassment, she may buy things for herself, with the proceeds of grain robbed from her husband's house, or sometimes with money earned through adultery.

11. *Maghama Amavasya* is the new moon in the month of Maghama (January–February). The villagers clean their houses. sprinkling cowdung water on the courtyards, and smear the floor of the house with red mud, as on every new moon day. Sometime between this day and Maha Sivaratri, the whole village goes out for a picnic. Each family eats separately, but distributes sweets and light refreshments to other families in the same kulam. A meat curry is eaten and toddy is drunk. Some of the curry and rice is put on a leaf near the fire, in worship of the god of fire, Agni.

12. *Maha Sivaratri* is the night of the dark of the moon in the month Phalguna (February–March), sacred to the god Siva. The previous night. the villagers eat well and sleep long, for the following day they are to fast and stay up through the night of Sivaratri. On the night of Sivaratri, couples must refrain from sexual intercourse. Only certain members of the family keep the complete fast. Those who are not fasting may eat sweet chapaties or rice, but not meat. During the night the villagers enact the Bhagavatam, and tell ballad stories to keep people awake. Early in the morning those who have fasted go the the tank, bathe and wash their clothes, and come back home and eat rice cooked with jaggery. They believe that if they manage to keep awake the whole night they will obtain blessing.

13. The festival of Holi comes two weeks later, on the full moon day of Phalguna. For the seven days prior to Holi, the young men perform *kolatum*, and go from house to house begging. They break pots in one another's houses, sprinkle ashes in the houses, and do all sorts of mischief. On the morning of Holi itself, the potter distributes clay pots to each house. A Madiga collects five cowdung cakes from each house, and the

begari collects one seer of millet, paddy, ragi, or black gram from each house. Dry coconut, boiled black gram and the image of Kama are put into the heap of cowdung cakes and a bonfire is made. The begari and the talari go in the middle of the night to each landlord's house, with the Madigas beating drums, and bring the landlords to the fire. The landlords have their servants pour water round the heap several times, and all the women of the village sing songs. Then the village servants go to the Mala and Madiga *bastis*, and burn other images of Kama on the bonfires there. Early in the morning, after the ashes of the fire have cooled off, the villagers collect them. They preserve those ashes in their houses throughout the year, and use them as medicine.

The following day a big feast is held at noon. The villagers go round from house to house, dancing and singing obscene songs. Every night during the previous week (when there has been moonlight) the women have gone about dancing, singing and joking with the men in a way which is not allowed during the rest of the year. Everyone is expected to tolerate this activity, and even promiscuity is permitted. It is thought that all the jokes, obscenity, and abuse are borne by Kama, and thus do not reflect on those who are ridiculed or insulted.

C. *The Agricultural Festivals*

1. The first agricultural festival is *Krotta Cheyuta* ('Making New'), eating the new crop for the first time. This comes about the middle of April, after the second harvest. For this festival, all must be new: the winnowing fan, the clay pot, and the rice. They cook rice mixed with dahl, saffron and salt, and prepare five different dishes. They decorate the pots in which these dishes are prepared with lime and vermilion. They offer curd-rice on a small leaf plate to the image of Balamma in their house, along with a saucer lamp, and they also offer this to Ellamma. They must all eat off leaf plates. Each house keeps a pot containing some rice-water which has fermented, and this is called *kali*. It represents both *kali yuga* and the goddess Lakshmi. When the married daughter leaves the house after the festival is over, to return to her husband's village, she dips her hand into the rice water in the kali pot.

2. *Mirgam Panduga* the festival of the fortnight when the rains begin, comes at the beginning of June, just before the rains start. On this day families owning cattle put lime and red paint round the niche in the wall of the cattle shed, a saucer lamp inside the niche, and saffron and vermilion *bottlu* around it. All the members of the family gather at the niche and worship the goddesses. They kill a chicken or goat in the cattle shed and invite other members of the kulam for a meal. A pit is dug in the cattle shed, and after they have eaten in the shed, they put their leaf plates, with all the remnants of the meal in the pit, wash their hands over the pit, and then cover it with earth. That night the members of the family must eat fish curry. This festival is observed every year, a new pit being dug each time in the cattle shed. It is observed by all families who own cattle and lands. This is done in order that their cattle and they themselves may be protected by the goddesses.

3. *Prayers for rain*. When the rains are delayed, villagers sing songs to the rain god. Children catch a frog, wrap it in a piece of cloth and tie it to a yoke. Two children will carry the yoke and they go round shouting from house to house. Each house will give them some rice and some flour for *ambali* porridge. After they finish going round the houses, they go to the tank bund, cook the rice which they collected and prepare *ambali*. The

children eat the rice, and pour the *ambali* porridge on |a rock and lick it with their tongues, so that the rain god may have pity on them and give them rain. A group of women dance around in a circle, clapping their hands and singing songs containing the following story. Some hundreds of years ago the rain god went to the palace of Papamma. He lived with her for seven years and forgot about the world, and there was thus no rain, because the rain god was engrossed in his amorous pursuits. So women sang songs pleading with Papamma to release the rain god and send him. When the rain god was leaving Papamma, he asked her what gift she would like him to send her. She replied, 'You can send me anything you like'. Then the rain god said 'Although you have all kinds of ornaments, you still are missing one. This I shall send to you.' The rain god's four brothers (Wind, Dust, Lightning, Thunder) came to know about this. They presented a box to Papamma, saying that their brother, the rain god, had sent this to her as a present. She took it gladly, but when she opened it she found snakes and scorpions inside. She was dismayed and angry, and when the rain god went to her, she would not speak to him. After learning about the trick played by his brothers, he sent the special ornament which he had promised.

4. *Muhurtam* ('auspicious hour') marks the beginning of ploughing in June or July. Each cultivator consults a Brahmin for an auspicious day and hour to start ploughing, and also asks him which direction he should first plough, north–south or east–west, and who in the family should start ploughing. On the day set, the plough and the horns of the bulls are smeared with lime powder. The man who starts ploughing should have a bath, wear clean clothes and, carrying the yoke on his shoulder, go to the field with the bullocks at the appointed hour. On his way no one should cross his path with empty vessels. He takes the plough round the field five times in the direction shown by the Brahmin. After finishing these five rounds, he comes back home. He must eat before the other members of the family may eat. That day they all must drink *ambali* (porridge) and eat rice.

5. *Edla Polamula Amavasya*, 'New Moon of the Cattle and Fields', is four days before *Ganesh Chaturti* (in August). The farmers wash the bullocks in the morning and feed and decorate them. They take them round to the shrines of all the village goddesses, and then give the cattle some re-freshments.

6. *Harvest Festivals and Ceremonies*: At harvest time there is a festival called *Poli Chevuta* ('Making increase'). The crop is reaped and stored in bundles on the threshing floor. A place is cleaned near the paddy field, on which diagrams are drawn with lime powder, and here they slaughter a goat or, if they are poor, a chicken. They invite their friends and relatives and have a feast at the threshing floor. Instead of celebrating Poli, some people perform *Kanduri*, which is really a Muslim custom. They buy the foodstuffs for Kanduri, then bathe, clean their houses and inform the Muslim priest. The Muslims prepare the meal, killing a goat near the threshing floor. They make five balls of chapaties, jaggery and ghee. They also bring incense sticks. They light a lamp near the Muslim place of worship, and the fakir does *namas* there. The fakir's fee is two of the sweet balls. Five Muslims must be fed from the food prepared, and must be given some cooked rice to take home, as well as five copper coins. The remaining rice is eaten by the members of the family and their relatives and friends. That same night they start threshing the grain.

Immediately after Poli comes another custom called *Puli Goliga*. When they start threshing the grain, they shout three times the words, 'Puli

Go-o-o-liga', and likewise three times when they finish threshing. This is said so that the grain may ncrease and evil spirits may not devour the crops.

Another custom immediately following that is *Potti Tirugudu*, 'Going round the heap of paddy', after threshing. When the heap is ready, a Madiga comes, takes two handfuls of grain and goes round the heap of the threshing floor five times, shouting 'Puli Goliga, Sare Puli Goliga'. While they are measuring the grain, the Madiga takes one measure of grain as his appointed share, and puts cowdung on it so that no one else will touch it. The Madiga then takes a winnowing fan, and collects grain in it. He is also given one big bundle of hay. These are all gifts to the Madiga from the landlord for whom he has been working. Then comes the *Potarazu* (literally 'buffalo king', who is the Mala or Baindla priest of the village). He wears a special anklet for the occasion and holds a whip in his hand. He goes round the heap of grain once, shouting 'Puli Goliga'. Then he takes some grain and puts his whip round it to show that it belongs to him and no one else should touch it. He goes to every threshing floor and takes his share in this way. This is the payment for his services as chief priest in the worship of the cholera goddess. Then the Madiga 'Kolpula woman', who assists the Potarazu in the cholera rites, comes and takes her share. The Muslim fakir next receives his share. Then the village menials (some of whom have duties in the religious ceremonies of the village) come for their share. After them come the artisans. The evangelist sometimes comes and receives a small amount, not as his 'right' (*hakku*), as in the case of all the others, but as a free gift (*danam*).

D. *Sacrifices to the Village Goddesses*

1. *Cholera Worship*

The priestess who becomes possessed by the cholera goddess and speaks as her medium is called the 'Kolpula woman', 'jogu' or 'Velpula woman'. She is usually a Madiga. She is set apart for this purpose by her parents, who in worshipping one of the goddesses receive a message from the goddess that they are to devote a daughter as priestess. She has her induction ceremony on an appointed day, conducted by the *Baindlas*, the 'devil priests'. They draw a diagram on the floor, around which the head toddy-tapper leads her, holding the little finger of her right hand. They go together to the shrine of the goddess and stand there, where she is presented with the gifts of a sari, a silver belt and a *tali* (provided by the girl's parents). The Baindla priest sings songs, beating his special drum to finish this induction or 'marriage ceremony', after which she may live with any man. Usually such women live with the Baindla men and bear them children. If daughters are born to the priestess, they also are set apart as priestesses, but some are brought up to do agricultural work and are considered to belong to her parents' family.

As soon as cholera breaks out in a village, the village people take a coconut and a piece of cactus, wrap them in a piece of cloth, and tie the bundle with a knot to the beam of the veranda. These are given to the Baindla priest after the ceremonies.

Two posts are put up at each of the main entrances to the village at such a width that a bullock cart may pass between. A rope is tied between the two poles, and margosa and mango branches are put on both sides. Then a small wooden image of the foreign goddess who has entered the village is suspended in the middle of this rope, after which milk, curds, and buttermilk are poured out on the ground directly beneath this image. In the middle of the village, four poles are put in the ground in an oblong shape and covered with cloth. Inside this 'tent' a small pit is dug, and an unbaked clay pot brought from the potter is put in the pit.

A winnowing fan is put on the pot and a clay lid on the fan; some oil is poured into it, and then a wick is put in and lit. The Kolpula woman sits facing this light inside the enclosure, and she stares steadily at the light. All the goddesses are thought to appear to her through that light. Outside the enclosure, the Baindla priests stand and invoke the goddess, beating their special drums. The Kolpula woman goes into trance, closes her eyes, and is taken possession of by one of the goddesses. The people outside break a coconut, kill a chicken and pour a libation of toddy on the ground where the sacrifice takes place. The woman's face is washed with toddy. Before she becomes unconscious, she utters the name of the goddess who is troubling the village, and states what should be offered to this goddess, and when, in order to appease her. If that goddess wants a new shrine built, she tells the people this and her instructions are later faithfully followed.

In the following rite, the Kolpula woman gets up into the platform near the shrine to the goddess Uradamma. A sheep is let loose as an offering to Uradamma, and the priestess pierces its stomach with her sword. The entrails, liver, and lungs are removed. The lungs and liver will be put in the Kolpula woman's mouth and the intestines round her neck. A new sari and blouse are dipped in the blood of this sheep and then the Kolpula woman puts them on. Lime, vermilion and black ash *bottlu* are put on her whole body, and a broken pot on her head. She holds a broomstick in her left hand, a winnowing fan in her right hand, and goes through all the streets of the village, starting from the shrine of Uradamma. Her brother and the Baindla priests follow her, and the Madigas beat drums in front of her. She grasps an old wall, thinking that the cholera goddess may be hiding in the wall. Then the priests, the priestess, and the accompanying Madigas go to a tank and bathe. There they cook rice and mutton curry, prepared with the rest of the sheep, have a feast and drink toddy.

The main ceremony three or five days later is intended to send the cholera goddess away from the village. Money is collected from each house (between eight annas and two rupees from each family) and used to buy male buffaloes. They sacrifice one to Durgamma, one to Uradamma, one to Maisamma, and one to the foreign goddess in the centre of the village. Near the Potalingamiah shrine a goat is sacrificed. The Potarazu kills the goat by biting its jugular vein with his teeth. The head toddy-tapper puts *naivedyam* before the Potalingamiah, and his mouth is tied so that he may not speak to anyone. In the centre of the village, a wooden image of the cholera goddess and another three or five images to represent the soldiers or bodyguards of this foreign goddess are put up. The Baindla priest draws a diagram and places three images inside the diagram. The toddy-tapper brings the toddy and pours it on the ground over the diagram. A big heap of cooked rice is put on the diagram. On that heap the meat and blood of the buffalo are sprinkled, as well as saffron and vermilion. All the buffalo heads are put round this diagram. The fat surrounding the intestines is spread over the heads of the buffaloes, and saucer lamps are put on each of these heads. The tongue of each buffalo is pulled out and one of its forelegs is placed between the jaws. The Baindla priest sings songs, in order to satisfy the foreign goddess. This whole heap is then collected in some big basket, and the skins are taken out of the village; piles of this rice are put on the borderline of the village. This is called the 'second meal' for the goddess.

Then all the village people go out with their cooking utensils and foodstuffs and have a picnic.

Three or five days after driving away the foreign goddess, the villagers try to placate the local goddesses. The Madiga headman sacrifices a buffalo at the Uradamma shrine. The meat is cut into small pieces, which is buried nearby along with the skin. The dung of the buffalo is mixed with the rice and all the village menials collect the rice into baskets and go round the village sprinkling it on the way. Meanwhile, the Neerudu drags along a live pig. After this circuit of the village, they come back to Uradamma and bury the pig alive with the remaining rice in another pit. The Potarazu, wearing his special anklet, bites the back of the sheep and then goes round the village with the Baindlas, keeping all the entrails in his mouth.

If cholera should break out in the village soon after a violent death has taken place there, the villagers may attribute this to the ghost of the dead person seeking vengeance, rather than to a 'foreign goddess'. They send off such a ghost with the same animal sacrifice and other ceremonies as in the case of the 'foreign goddess'.

2. The Festival of Maisamma

A buffalo and a pig are sacrificed to Maisamma. Heaps of cooked rice mixed with the dung of buffalo are given to the Potarazu and the Baindlas, who go round the village, sprinkling rice on the way and then come back to Maisamma and bury the remaining rice along with the buffalo and the pig. In all these rites the sacrifice is done by the Neerudu (a Mala).

3. Cattle Disease Ceremonies

As in the case of cholera, a cloth is tied up to the beam of the veranda containing saffron rice, copper coins and cactus, and two coconuts and a cactus are also tied up in the cattle shed. The rest of the ceremonies are like the 'cholera worship', but with the following differences. In addition to fixing posts at the four main entrances of the village, another 'gate' of two posts is set up at the Uradamma shrine. The cattle are driven through this Uradamma 'gate', then down the lanes of the village, and finally out through the entrance gate. At one of the entrances two men stand one on either side with a brass pot containing buttermilk and porridge. The men dip margosa branches in the brass pots and sprinkle each one of the cattle as it passes through the gates. When the cattle disease has somewhat subsided, the 'sending off' ceremony of the foreign goddess and two body-guards is performed. To meet the expenses of these ceremonies, the village headman collects one rupee for each head of cattle from the cattle owners.

4. Ceremony against Smallpox

The place where the patient lies is cleaned with red earth and the patient is kept in clean clothes. The relatives go daily to the shrine of Poshamma to worship, offering toddy and onions. They make vows while the patient is seriously ill, and if the patient gets better, they fulfil the vows, generally the sacrifice of a sheep, goat or chicken. Nobody should approach the patient with sandals on; women during their menstrual period should not go near the patient. Anyone visiting the patient should go in only after washing his feet outside, and drum beating should not be heard. Nothing should be fried in the house. The patient is given rice and porridge. If the patient gets a little better, they dip the margosa branches in water and sprinkle the water on the patient. Three days after that they smear his body with a mixture of margosa leaves, saffron and sweet oil, and give him a bath. They repeat this at three-day intervals. Each family with a sick person should do this. The whole village sends the image of Poshamma out of the village with the same sheep, buffalo and pig sacrifices as in the case of cholera. On the following day all go out for a picnic and have a grand feast.

E. *Miscellaneous Ceremonies*

1. *'Trampling'*

If a dead person appears in one's dream, it is believed that he has appeared in the form of a ghost. If any illness comes after this dream, toddy is poured on the ground in the direction of the grave of the dead person who appeared in the dream. Some cooked rice with dry fish curry is placed on the spot where this toddy was poured.

2. *'Taking a leaf cup'*

This leaf cup should be made with seven different kinds of leaves. Red rice is mixed with lime water, saffron rice is prepared, and black rice is mixed with soot. Three balls are made out of these three kinds of cooked rice and put in the leaf cup. The patient is made to stand, while an elder or magician holding his leaf cup in his hands brings the cup around in a large circular motion, starting from above with his hands above his head, twice in front of the patient and three times behind him. The 'cup' is taken at night and left at the place where three roads meet. It is believed that whoever first sees this 'cup' or crosses over it will be possessed of the demon concerned.

If anyone falls into a well, but is pulled out and survives, the same circular motion is made with a live chicken over the person, and then the chicken's head is pulled off (not cut off). The head is thrown away but the rest of the chicken is eaten. This is done so that the ghost inside the well may not later kill the person who fell in.

3. *'Lowering'*

This ceremony is performed for many people who feel ill. A Baindla priest, or black magician, is called, who takes the patient to a place well away from the village, draws a diagram on the ground, puts coconuts and five copper coins at each corner of the diagram, and in the centre one rupee. The patient is made to sit within the diagram; coconuts are broken and coconut milk poured on his head. Limes are cut and dripped on to his head. A circular motion is made around the patient with a chicken. Then the chicken's head is pulled off and the blood allowed to drip on the patient's head. The magician pours toddy in the palm of his hand, recites some mantras, and sprinkles the toddy on the patient's face. All the things which were put within the diagram are taken by the magician as his fee. Then the patient and the magician must return to the patient's house without looking back, lest the ghost follow them. Patients who go to the government or mission hospital have this ceremony performed before they go to the hospital.

4. *Action against Black Magic*

In cases of longstanding illness, nervous breakdown, or fits, people invariably suspect those who are not on good terms with them. They suspect that their enemies have got some black magician to cast a spell. They therefore hire another black magician who they think to be more powerful, and have him perform the 'Lowering' ceremony, to make the other magician's black magic ineffective. People do in fact go to black magicians and pay them to cast spells on their enemies. If there is a strong suspicion of either the instigator or the magician whom he employed, they may be summoned before a village panchayat and severely punished.

Recently in Wadiaram, five men were suspected of black magic but only three could be caught. In the presence of the whole village, the village headman and other influential leaders of the village pulled out their front teeth, poured into their mouths dirty water from the Madiga pots in which hides are cleaned, and made them drink it. There is a police station in Wadiaram, but the police did not interfere. They generally let such 'justice' take its course. In Jangarai village, one Mala caste headman's wife was suspected of having employed a black magician, because the headman's brother's son had become ill. After she was scolded and threatened, she ran away to Hyderabad, never to return. Had she remained, she might have been severely beaten or even killed, just on the ground of suspicion.

To determine who is instigating or performing black magic, an Erukala woman is consulted. She indicates rather vaguely the direction in which the guilty person lives, and the relatives of the sick person are quick to draw their own conclusions. There is no recognized method, such as an 'ordeal', for proving or disproving the suspicion.

APPENDIX B: MUSLIM VILLAGE FESTIVALS

1. *Muharram*, commemorating the martyrdom of Hassan and Hussain, sons of Ali and Fatima, and grandsons of Muhammed, is often called *Pirila Panduga*, the 'Festival of the *Pirs* (Saints)', and is also celebrated by many Hindus and most of the Christians. In front of the village mosque, or the *kacheri* (shrine), where the standards and flags of the pirs are kept, the village menials dig a large pit and build a low wall around it. Every night during the festival a bonfire is lit in the pit, and many people run around it shouting, 'Hassan, Hussain, Dhoola'. On the seventh day the spear on which Hussain was slain is paraded. The thirteenth and last day of the festival is most important. The representations of the pirs are taken out and worshipped, and vows are made to them. A fast is observed on that day and sugar is distributed, over which the *Fatihah* (first chapter of the Quran) is repeated. Elegies are sung when the standards of Fatima and Hussain, the sword of Ali, and the sacred horseshoe are paraded. Hindus also carry the standards of the pirs, fall into trances and describe their visions. Some Hindus construct cenotaphs and carry them through the streets. During the processions some men and women, in fulfilment of vows, throw themselves on the road and roll in front of the cenotaphs and standards of the pirs.

2. During the month of *Rāmzān*, Muslims are supposed to abstain from both food and drink throughout the daylight hours, during which time one should engage as much as possible in meditation and prayer. The twenty-sixth day is marked with special prayers to commemorate Mohammed's receiving the Quran from Allah. There is considerable feasting during the nights, but the high feast comes on the day after the new moon has been seen, called *Īd-ul-fitr*. The day is marked by wearing new clothes, attending

special community prayers, visiting friends and distributing a special sweet pudding to them, and by a great feast.

3. Another widely celebrated festival is *Baqr-Īd*, the 'festival of the sacrifice of the cow'. Muslims go to the mosque for prayers, and when they return they sacrifice goats in the name of Allah, if possible one for each member of the family. The meat is then cooked and meat dishes and other delicacies are distributed to relatives and friends.

4. The *Urs* are religious fairs held on the death anniversaries of the *pirs*. The word is an Arabic term for 'wedding', and has the connotation of the mystic union of the saint with Allah at death. They are attended by Hindus and Christians, too; sometimes there are more Hindus than Muslims present. Many Hindus from the villages surveyed go to an urs held in the nearby village of Kolicheleme in commemoration of a certain Sheikh Sahib. A Mala priest (a *potarazu*) from Jangarai goes every year to attend this urs, because a son was born to him after he attended it some years ago. Both Hindus and Muslims make vows of various types, which they will carry out if the pir grants their request. They have great confidence in the saint's goodwill and the efficacy of his blessing.

5. *Kanduri* is usually a vow fulfilled every year according to the promises made by the devotees. It is one of the chief observances at the time of an urs. Sheep and goats are slaughtered by the mullahs at the tomb of the pir. The family takes the sacrificed animal home, and cooks mutton curry and saffron rice. A portion of this food is offered as *naivedyam* at the *dargah* (tomb), and then food is given to five fakirs who are waiting there to be fed. The members of the family, along with their relatives and friends, share the remaining food. A definite share of the sacrificed animal, along with some money, is given to the mullah or fakir who officiated at the sacrifice. In Jangarai some Hindus who have made vows to a pir named Madar Sahib celebrate Kanduri instead of the Hindu Poli before they thresh the paddy after the harvest.

CHAPTER 4

The Congregations in the Jangarai Section

A. *The Wadiaram Pastorate*

The congregations in the Medak Diocese are grouped in 'Pastorates' which are subdivided into 'sections'. There were thirty village congregations in the Wadiaram Pastorate, and nine of them were included in the Jangarai section. All villages which have at least twenty-five Christians are considered to have 'congregations', though some have no regular gatherings for worship or other corporate expressions of their existence. These villages with larger or smaller congregations in their 'outcaste' precincts are scattered among about thirty villages without congregations, in most of which there are no Christians at all. There are completely non-Christian villages within a few miles of the nine villages with Christian congregations.

The congregations in the Wadiaram Pastorate were for many years a part of the much larger Ramayampet Pastorate. Two Methodist missionaries had established a dispensary in Ramayampet in 1904, following the successful growth into a small hospital of the dispensary they had started in Medak in 1896. These missionaries and their successors not only cared for the dispensary in the market town, but toured the surrounding villages and supervised the work of the evangelists.

Particularly important was the period after 1921, when Miss Green was appointed to Ramayampet. For many years she not only cared for the sick but also fostered the village schools and directed the work of the evangelists. She was assisted by Pastor A. Timothy, during whose years of service most of the village churches in this area were founded. The older Christians in the Wadiaram Pastorate look back to 'the good old days' when the Christian community in the area was rapidly expanding, and still remember with gratitude and appreciation the work of those two pioneers. Pastor Timothy was over eighty when he recounted to us some of the incidents at the very beginning of Christian work in this area. He said that one of the earliest converts in Medak, in 1889, was Bodanapu Venkiah, the police patel (chief) of a village near Ramayampet. Venkiah later became an evangelist, working in Medchal, a village which is now in the Wadiaram Pastorate.

In 1931 the Wadiaram Pastorate was detached from the enormous Ramayampet Pastorate and given a resident pastor. For several years the pastor was under the supervision of a senior minister who lived either in Medak or in Hyderabad. There had been eight pastors or ordained presbyters in charge of the Pastorate between 1931 and 1959. In May 1954, the boundaries of all the pastorates in the Diocese were revised according to the recommendations of the Resources

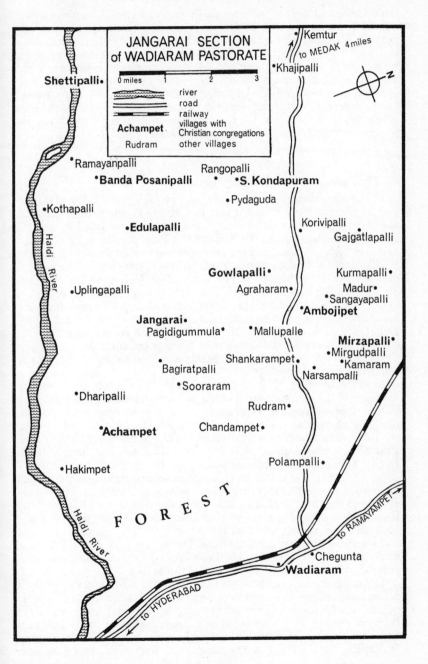

JANGARAI SECTION
of WADIARAM PASTORATE

0 miles   1   2   3

river
road
railway
Achampet · villages with
Christian congregations
Rudram   other villages

· Kemtur
to MEDAK 4 miles
· Khajipalli

Shettipalli ·

Haldi River

· Ramayanpalli
Rangopalli
· · **S. Kondapuram**
Banda Posanipalli
· Pydaguda
· Kothapalli
· Korivipalli
Gajgatlapalli ·
· **Edulapalli**
Kurmapalli ·
Gowlapalli · Madur ·
Agraharam · · Sangayapalli
· Uplingapalli
· **Ambojipet**
Jangarai ·
Pagidigummula · · Mallupalle
Mirzapalli ·
· Mirgudpalli
Shankarampet · · Kamaram
· Bagiratpalli Narsampalli
· Sooraram
· Dharipalli
Rudram ·
· **Achampet**
Chandampet ·
· Hakimpet
Polampalli ·

F O R E S T

Haldi River

to RAMAYAMPET

· Chegunta
· **Wadiaram**
to HYDERABAD

Commission. At that time seven village congregations from three other adjoining pastorates were added to the existing pastorate to form the present Wadiaram Pastorate. In 1958 the total Christian community in the thirty congregations, in addition to a few Christians in other villages, was 4,095. Of these 929 were communicant members, 2,380 were non-communicant adults, and 786 were baptized children. Pastoral care was provided by the presbyter, living at the pastoral headquarters of Wadiaram, and eleven evangelists living with the congregations in the villages. Four evangelists were living in the Jangarai section, responsible for its nine congregations.

B. *The Founding of the Congregations*

The first baptisms in the Jangarai section took place in the village of Bandaposanipalli on June 9, 1912; this village is closer to Medak than the rest of the section, and along with the Chettipalli and Edulapalli congregations was part of the Kolicheleme Pastorate until the reorganization in 1954. At present there are twenty-nine Mala families and eight Madiga families in the congregation. The caste structure of the congregation reflects the history of the Hyderabad Methodist District: the Malas were the first to respond in relatively large numbers, often the entire Mala caste in a village. Later Madigas began to seek baptism, and through deliberate church policy were included in the same congregations with the Malas. Many of the more recent congregations show a third stage: the decision of Madiga communities to become Christian in villages in which the Malas were and have continued to be unresponsive to evangelism.

An older member of the Ambojipet congregation told us about the founding of the church there. There was a devoted Christian of a nearby village, named Velpala Yesuratnam, who was arranging to give his daughter in marriage to a boy in Ambojipet, but insisted that the boy should become a Christian if he wanted to marry his daughter. The boy, Prakasham, finally agreed to be baptized, not alone, but along with his family, and later this family persuaded all the other Mala families to be baptized. Two of the elders were also given some gifts at that time by an evangelist, in order to influence them to become Christians. This was in 1914, and in 1920 the Madiga families in the village were baptized and joined the congregation. At present there are still four non-Christian Mala families, mainly of the subcaste of Baindlas (magician-priests), but all of the Madigas are Christians. During the period of the survey, in August 1959, two Sudra families were baptized, the first non-'outcaste' families to become Christians in the section.

The congregation in Chettipalli began in 1917 and consists of both Malas and Madigas. It is one of the 'second village' congregations—those which have been without a resident evangelist for many years, and have been assigned to an evangelist as an extra or 'second' village. There are two other similar congregations in the Jangarai section, Edulapalli and Mirzapalli, both started in the same year, 1927. The special features of these neglected congregations will be discussed later in this chapter.

The Madiga community in Jangarai was also first baptized in 1927, but this congregation has had a resident evangelist much of the time. The older Christians there told us how the congregation began. For several years the only strong congregation nearby was in Ambojipet; the evangelist there used to visit Jangarai occasionally, but for a long time there was no response to his preaching. At that time the Madigas in the village were forced to work part of the time for the landlords and the police corps without pay (the widespread system of *yetti* or forced labour). One day one of the Madigas was severely beaten and threatened with arrest on false charges by the police patel. To escape this injustice, the Madigas sought the help of the evangelist who had visited them, and he in turn led them to the Rev. C. W. Posnett, long time Chairman of the Hyderabad Methodist District, in Medak. Through his personal influence and his letters to higher officials, Posnett had the police chief brought to trial and punished, the first time any such action had been taken against the village official. When the Madigas saw that the terror of the village, who feared no one under heaven, had been punished, they looked upon Mr. Posnett as their champion. Later they invited the evangelist back to Jangarai to give them instruction for baptism, and eventually they were baptized, on May 1, 1927. None of the nine Mala families in Jangarai has ever become Christian, though two Christian families of Mala background are members of the congregation. One is a family which emigrated from a village in Sarjana pastorate some years ago, while the other is the family of the widow of an evangelist. The main body of Madigas in the village are Christians, but there have been nine non-Christian families in the Madiga subcaste of Bandelas, who are traditionally devotees of Vishnu. During the period of the survey in 1959, nine of the Bandela people were baptized, the first converts from new families since the original baptisms thirty-two years before.

In Kondapuram villages the beginning of interest in Christianity came when the caste headman of both Malas and Madigas learned that the children in a nearby village were being taught to read and to sing by Christian evangelists. They invited the evangelists to come to Kondapuram to teach them how to read and instruct them in the Christian faith. The present Christians in the village say that the original decision to become Christian was made in order to have their children educated and in order to escape from the tyranny of the patels (village officials). Both the Mala and Madiga communities were baptized at the same time, and have worked together much more harmoniously in this congregation than is the case in some other villages.

The first Sudra to join the congregation was baptized during the period of our survey (May 1959). He is a toddy-tapper who came back from Sadhu Joseph's services healed of his leprosy, and immediately started taking an active part in the life of the congregation, (see p. 148 below).

Achampet is a village farther away from the main road (five miles) than the previous village mentioned and three miles beyond Jangarai. When the Madigas of Jangarai became Christians, the Madigas of Achampet heard much about the new religion from their relatives and other members of the same caste, and they cordially received the evangelist from Jangarai whenever he came to visit them. The five older Christians who remember when the congregation began said that the visiting evangelist gave money for a feast to some of the leaders of the Madiga community. Soon thereafter these leaders decided that the entire caste in the village should become Christians. The first baptisms took place on June 26, 1932. All the Madigas are Christians (about twenty families), but none of the similar number of Malas ever became such, even though they live very close to the Madigas in Achampet, and even though most of the evangelists working in the Madiga congregation have been Mala. Indeed, a rather bitter rivalry between Malas and Madigas has continued in this village.

Eighteen years elapsed between the founding of the Achampet congregation and the establishment of a Christian community in Gowlapalli. Even before Independence and the end of the Nizam's rule in Hyderabad State, the expansion of the Church had slowed down. Now with a Congress party government supported by the Hindu majority, Christians feared they could no longer count on the benevolent neutrality of the Muslim ruler, or the influence of the British missionaries in their midst. Moreover, with the establishment of government schools and the awarding of scholarships to Harijans (outcastes), the church was losing its monopoly on education. There was also the effort of the Arya Samaj to reconvert outcaste Christians to the Hindu community, aided by the inclination of some government officials not to regard Christians as 'Harijans' in awarding scholarships, land or housing grants. It was in this new situation that the beginning of the Gowlapalli congregation took place.

In 1947 there was an enterprising Madiga in this village who had become a leper. He refused to accept his fate and learned that there was a Christian mission leprosy hospital some miles away at Dichpalli. He very much wanted to go there, but he was under the impression that as a non-Christian it would be difficult for him to be admitted. He decided first to go to the nearby mission hospital in Medak and get a letter of introduction from the mission doctor in Medak to take along to Dichpalli. When the doctor asked him, 'Which is your village and what is your name?', the leper was taken aback with the sudden realization that the answers to these simple questions would reveal that he was not a Christian. He decided to tell a lie and answered with some fear and trembling, 'Madam, my name is Yesudas ['Servant of Jesus'] and I come from Jangarai' (the nearest village to his own where he knew there were Christians). The doctor gave him a note and sent him to Dichpalli, where he was admitted to the leprosy hospital and treated for a year. While he was in the hospital, he regularly attended Christian prayers, and he later reported that while he was in the hospital, he had experienced the love of Christ. When he was pronounced cured and sent home, he decided he should become a Christian. At the time of his baptism two years later he emphasized that his decision was based on his gratitude for having been cured by Jesus, but in recounting the experience to us more than ten years later, he revealed for the first time his initial lie and how that had preyed upon him, and he indicated that his decision was strongly influenced by his fear of the curse of Jesus for, quite literally, the taking of His name in vain. Whatever his motives may have been, it is quite clear that he did not consider becoming a Christian as an individual decision. He was not baptized before leaving Dichpalli but returned home to Gowlapalli to try to convince the entire Madiga community there that they should become Christians.

In the meantime Gowlapalli had been affected by the tremendous political upheavals which occurred in Hyderabad State during the year that Yesudas was in the hospital. After Indian Independence came the period of uncertainty as to whether Hyderabad would join India, during which the Hindu majority were increasingly terrorized by the Razakars, a kind of private army of Muslim extremists intent on perpetuating Muslim rule. When the Indian Government finally intervened and ended the Nizam's autocratic rule (the Police Action), most of the weapons of the Razakars fell into the hands of the Communists, who waged an armed insurrection against the Government for several months. The Hindu landowners had suffered from the attacks of both the Razakars and the Communists, and many of them were determined to keep political power henceforth in their own hands. Some of the landlords in Gowlapalli had severely beaten and imprisoned nine of the Madigas, claiming that they were Communists. The Congress Party leader in Medak came to the village and got the men released, and effected a superficial reconciliation between the Madiga community and the Hindu landowning castes (Kapus and Reddis). However, their fear and resentment remained. It was into this situation that Yesudas walked when he returned from Dichpalli, healed of his leprosy. His fellow Madigas listened attentively when Yesudas urged them to become Christians. Many of them hoped to gain some protection under this new religion against the continuing and renewed persecution of the high-caste Hindus in the village. They came to a group decision, and the men signed a document declaring that they wanted to become Christians and sent it to the presbyter in Wadiaram. The presbyter arranged for an evangelist to come to live in their village and instruct them in the Christian faith, and eventually, on November 12, 1950, all the Madigas in Gowlapalli including Yesudas were baptized. As was the case a generation before in Jangarai and Achampet, the other major outcaste community, the Malas, did not share in this decision to become Christians, and have shown no interest in joining it in the years since its founding.

Because of the remarkable character of Yesudas's conversion and missionary efforts, this story of the founding of the Gowlapalli congregation became well known in the Diocese and was publicized in Methodist missionary circles in England, but the group baptism was not the end of the story. The higher caste Hindus of the village were opposed to Christianity, and the landlords bitterly resented the conversion of these outcaste Madiga labourers to an alien religion. The Christians in Gowlapalli feel that the Hindu landlords have resisted any change which would better the lot of the outcastes: they do not like to see these Christians come up in the world, and do everything they can to hold them back. The persecution and oppression which the Madigas hoped to escape after they became Christians have only intensified. Some of the caste Hindus have tried to persuade the Madigas to renounce Christianity and return to their traditional role in the village Hindu community. Their most effective instrument of persuasion has been the withholding of land grants and other concessions available for 'Harijans', on the grounds that by becoming Christians they cease to be 'Harijans' (Gandhi's new name for the outcastes, meaning 'children of God').

In 1954 the Tehsildar (administrative officer) from Medak came one day to the large roadside village of Shankarampet, a few miles away. Twelve of the Christian men of Gowlapalli, led by the same Konka Yesudas who was instrumental in founding their congregation, went to the Tehsildar with a petition, asking for their share of the government lands available for Harijans. The Tehsildar told them that they would not be given lands unless they gave up their Christian religion and submitted the petition with their old Hindu names. Again it was Konka Yesudas who persuaded the others, but this time it was to declare before the Tehsildar that they were not Christians and to submit their Hindu names. It was not their intention completely to renounce Christianity, but for the sake of some badly-needed farm lands they were willing to deny their Christian religion for the time being, and to give their Hindu names, instead of the Christian names they had been given at baptism. When he learned what had happened, the evangelist scolded these men, but no further disciplinary action was taken. In the circumstances, all this is not too surprising; what is remarkable is that a number of the younger men in the congregation, who had taken only a very minor part in the community decision for baptism four years before, refused to follow their elders' examples in giving their Hindu names. Like most other Christians in this area, these young men regularly used their old Hindu names in common speech, but they refused to use their Hindu names officially if this implied a renunciation of their Christian faith. Instead, they reprimanded the older men and declared their intention of remaining loyal to Christ, whatever their elders might decide and however much it might cost them. This congregation, founded in a period of conflict, continues to reflect that conflict, not only in the competition for leadership between the evangelist and the original lay leader, Yesudas, and in the divergent decisions of the elders and young men, but also within the same Christian mind and conscience, as is made evident in the following statement of one Christian in Gowlapalli, nine years after the congregation began (1959):

> One cannot get on well in the world if he tries to live a truthful and honest life. We have been undergoing great hardships from the time we became Christians, and have been suffering great loss. Last year we nearly resigned our church membership in order to avail ourselves of the privileges and concessions offered to the Harijans by the Government— wells for drinking water, house sites and housing materials, lands for

cultivation, scholarships for Harijan children attending government schools, a reserved seat for a Harijan in the local village panchayats, and a supply of bullocks. All these are being given to the Harijans and scheduled tribes in the village. A Mala is given the reserved seat for Harijans; two of the Malas receive housing aid; and a Lambadi (gypsy) is given a pair of bullocks. But when the grant came from the Government for the construction of some of our Madiga houses, the village officials returned that money solely on the ground that we are Christians. How can we afford to lose all these benefits from the Government? We are still wondering if we have made a mistake in accepting Christianity.

A few miles from Gowlapalli is the hamlet of Mallupalle, and during the period of our survey in 1959 the first decisive events occurred there in a long and perhaps even more remarkable process, leading to the founding of another small Christian congregation in the Jangarai section. In 1959, however, there was only one Christian family in Mallupalle; this story, will be told, therefore, in Chapter 7 on 'New Converts and Inquirers'.

C. *The Membership of the Congregations*

The official membership of the Church consists of all baptized Christians. Except in the 'second village' congregations, this includes almost all the members of Christian families, since most of the children are baptized. The Church of South India accepts infant baptism and urges all Christian parents to have their children baptized as soon as possible. Adults may be baptized by immersion, pouring, or sprinkling. All baptized children and adults are 'members of the Church and share in the privileges and obligations of membership' (*Constitution of the Church of South India*, III, 1).

When baptized children are fourteen or older, they are expected to be confirmed by the Bishop or presbyter, after careful preparation by the evangelist. Those baptized as adults are occasionally confirmed at the same time, but usually they are expected to have a period of Christian living and further instruction after baptism before being admitted to communicant membership. Only communicant members are supposed to participate in the Lord's Supper, and they are supposed to share in the government of the church, if they are twenty-one or older, only provided they meet the further qualifications of accepting the rules of the Diocese, contributing regularly to the church, and evincing their active participation by regular attendance at congregational worship and by Christian witness and service. Then they may vote in the election of members of the local 'Leaders' Meeting', the Pastorate Committee, and the Diocesan Council, and on much the same conditions are eligible for election to these offices. Admission to the 'Women's Fellowship', and the award of a 'Bishop's licence' to laymen trained as 'Voluntary Church Workers', also presuppose communicant membership. One form of church discipline, though it is very rarely practised in the village congregations, is to refuse communion to a person under discipline. Baptized adults who have not been confirmed are not communicant members; they are sometimes referred to with the designation 'on trial'.

Each village congregation is provided with a church roll, in which the names of all Christians, family by family, are recorded, with all the particulars of each member: date of birth, parents' names, date of baptism, whether confirmed or 'on trial', married or single, and, if he died during that year, the date and cause of death. There is also one large church roll and a baptismal register for all the congregations in the Pastorate. Once a year the presbyter scrutinizes the village membership rolls with the aid of the evangelists, and prepares the annual statistics for the Pastorate, which he then sends to the Diocesan statistician. The following were the statistics recorded for the Jangarai section as of August 31, 1959.

Name of the village	Communicants	Non-communicant adults	Baptized children (under 14)	Total Christian community	Percentage of adults who are communicants	Trained leadership in 1959
					%	
Jangarai	40	59	17	116	40	Evangelist
Gowlapalli	39	67	48	154	37	Acting superintending evangelist since June
S. Kondapuram	46	63	41	150	42	Evangelist
Achampet	52	31	25	108	62·6	Superintending evangelist until May, when he left for deacon's training
Ambojipet	31	40	31	102	43·7	Retired evangelist in mission house
Bandaposani-palli	36	90	41	167	28·6	Evangelist
Edulapalli	5	39	12	56	11·4	No evangelist
Chettipalli	—	68	14	82	0	No evangelist
Mirzapalli	3	64	—	67	4·5	No evangelist
Totals	252	521	229	1,002	32·6	

Even in the villages with resident evangelists, some children of Christian parents have not been baptized, and there are many parents who do not seem to attach much importance to baptism, since they need repeated urgings from the evangelist before they finally bring their children for this. Some parents even refuse to have their children baptized; this is especially true when they are planning to marry their daughter to a non-Christian in a non-Christian ceremony. 'She will soon be married; why do you want our daughter to be baptized?' The roughly equal number of non-Christian girls (and a few boys) who are married *into* Christian families are brought for baptism sometime when the presbyter is visiting the village, usually without much instruction but often after a period of several months or even years of living in those Christian families.

The Church's official distinctions between non-communicant adults and communicant members are not much in evidence in the actual life of these village congregations. There are many baptized adults who have been 'on trial' for many years, and many spend their whole lives 'on trial'. Some of those who are confirmed do not know that they are communicant members, and those who do know do not understand much about the significance and privileges of being a communicant, nor about the meaning of the sacrament of the Lord's Supper. There are a few, however, for whom this sacrament means a great deal. Church elections are held at meetings of the congregation in which communicant and non-communicant adults are present without distinction, and all of those present vote. This wide discrepancy between the official conception of Church membership and the actual practice of Church members is an indication of serious problems affecting many Christians in South India. These problems will be discussed below in Chapter 10 on 'Baptism and Communicant Membership'.

D. *Worship*

The congregation gathers at the nightly prayer services, which are more elaborate on Sunday night or on the night of the presbyter's visit. On Sunday the evangelist normally follows the first order of service from the Telugu *Book of Services*, while on other nights he abbreviates the service as he thinks best. The order is generally as follows:

1. one or more lyrics,
2. a brief passage of Scripture, often a miracle story or a parable,
3. a short explanation of the Scripture lesson,
4. another lyric (or lyrics), and
5. a prayer by the evangelist, concluded by the corporate praying of the Lord's prayer.

The regular meeting place is usually a broad veranda on one side of the evangelist's house. (In Gowlapalli there is a separate prayer shed.) There is considerable disorder during these evening prayers, with people coming and going during the service. People sit on the ground or floor, usually not in neat rows but higgledy-piggledy, sometimes talking and laughing, or even sleeping, while the service is going on. There are some Christians, however, who take part in the service reverently and listen to the Bible lesson and sermon quite attentively. They often correct the others who disturb the service.

The survey was conducted during the hot season (March–June), when attendance is usually at its best. The average attendance in the five villages in which we (the Lukes) lived ranged from 14% to 19% of the congregation on weekdays and 14% to 31% on Sundays. Attendance is considerably higher on the few occasions when the presbyter visits and conducts the service. During seed-time, harvest, and the rainy season, on the other hand, attendance at congregational prayers is often very low. The most regular attendants are the young men and the children; the older people are very rarely there except when the presbyter is visiting.

The presbyter leads a service of Holy Communion whenever he visits, generally following the Methodist order of service. When the presbyter reads the liturgy, many regard it as a *mantram* (set ritual formula) comparable to that which the Brahmin priest recites at wedding ceremonies. Most of the young men join in some of the responses. Some consider the communion elements they receive from the presbyter as a kind of *prasādam* (the food blessed by consecration to a Hindu deity, and distributed to the worshippers as an embodiment of divine grace and blessing). Many confirmed members take communion as a matter of course, without attaching much meaning to it. Some of the communicant members do not know they are such and thus entitled to partake; the evangelist sometimes walks over to them and sends them forward to the Lord's Table. Some do not seem to know what the elements stand for, or sometimes even what they should do with them. Many of the adults are not allowed to take communion because they have never been confirmed, but there is no general difference observable between the communicants and non-communicants, either as to their general conduct or as to their understanding of Christian faith. There are a few communicants who take communion after getting drunk on their evening visit to the toddy shop. On the other hand, some communicants in each congregation take Holy Communion very seriously and prepare for it beforehand. They attend the communion service in clean clothes and join in the service with reverence and with penitence. They come to the Lord's Table longing for fellowship with the Lord.

There are not many literates in these congregations and not many people own Bibles, as the following statistics of the five congregations specially studied makes clear:

	No. of Literates	No. of Bibles
Jangarai	2	0
Achampet	9	8
Kondapuram	5 ·	4
Ambojipet	4	1
Gowlapalli	8	8

At the evening prayers it is the reading of the Bible which is the central item. Usually the evangelist or his wife reads the Scripture lesson; when the presbyter is visiting, the evangelist asks one of the literates in the congregation to read. It is usually the young men who own Bibles and can read from them—but they do not know how to use Bibles in their homes for private and family prayers, or how to look up references in the Bible. They say that they find the Bible puzzling and that they often do not understand what they read. The congregations' knowledge of the Bible and their understanding of the Christian faith will be discussed in Chapter 8 below.

Because most of the Christians are illiterate, the words which they can sing or recite together are very important in their corporate worship. Most can recite the Lord's Prayer, and some know the Confession and the Creed by heart, even if they can give no account of what they mean. In two congregations the Lord's Prayer and the Creed are sung in the worship service. The congregation does not sing many lyrics from the hymn-book; much of what they sing comes from other sources: revival songs, songs from Sadhu Joseph's book of lyrics, and parable action songs. The parables and miracles of Christ are expressed in simple poetic metres and fitted with popular village tunes which can be easily learned and remembered. The older people find it difficult to learn anything new, the more so as they so rarely come to evening prayers, but some of them still remember some of the lyrics which they learned before their baptism.

In addition to the nightly congregational prayers, there are occasional 'family prayers', but by this term village Christians usually mean the prayer service held by the evangelist or presbyter when he visits a home. If they know the evangelist is coming, they clean the house and spread a mat on the floor to sit on. They also put out a brass plate containing uncooked rice and a few copper coins as a 'family prayers collection' or 'thank-offering'. If it is the presbyter who is visiting, the wife sometimes washes his feet, the same mark of respect a Hindu family would offer to a guru. The order of service is like that of congregational prayers and is led by the evangelist or presbyter. If the family can sing, they are invited to join in a lyric. The prayers are largely intercessory prayers for members of the family. The presbyter is often taken to homes where someone is ill, and he prays especially for that sick person.

There are a few Christian families (an average of one or two per congregation) who have their own prayers before, or more commonly after, the evening meal. The members of the family, and sometimes their neighbours, sing a lyric, and if there is a literate, he reads a passage from the Bible, chosen somewhat at random, one day from one book, the next from another. Sometimes the lesson is picked by allowing the Bible to fall open. One person prays, usually a young man, especially if there is one in the family who has had training as a Voluntary Church Worker. He prays for the members of the family by name, for the welfare of its cattle and lands, and for the healing of any member of the family who is ill. Occasionally the young men in the congregation who have had training as Voluntary Church Workers will go as a group to the various Christian homes and conduct evening prayers.

E. *Financial Support of the Church*

The salaries of presbyters and evangelists are paid by the Diocese, and the contributions of the families in these village congregations are expected to be channelled from the congregation through the Pastorate into the funds of the Diocese. When these congregations were established, the pastors and evangelists were paid by the Hyderabad Methodist District, almost all the funds of which came from the Methodist Missionary Society in Great Britain. It was recognized that the new converts came from the poorest social groups, and it was felt that the stationing of an evangelist in a village should not be made dependent on the ability of the Christians in that village to support him. It was expected that the Christians would contribute according to their very limited means and that with increasing size and improving economic status, the village congregation would move steadily in the direction of fully supporting its own evangelist, as well as contributing to the support of its presbyter and other church expenses. However, this aim of gradual progress towards 'self-support' was not realized. The village Christians grew to regard their evangelist (and even more so, the Indian minister in charge of the circuit) as a relatively rich man whose salary was guaranteed by the Methodist Mission, even if they did not give him any collections. The evangelist was expected to collect a certain share of his salary, but he usually did not take any great pains to imbue the congregation with the principles of Christian stewardship, and if he could not gather the required amount from his congregation, he would make up the difference out of his own pocket.

Thus though self-support was in theory accepted as an aim, there was little religious motivation or practical necessity to strive for it. With the inflation of the war and post-war years, however, the mission grants from Britain could not provide salaries for so many evangelists. Moreover, both the Medak Diocese and the Methodist Missionary Society took steps to increase the giving of the congregations, the former, as part of the 'New Pattern of Church Life', calling for a progressive increase in local giving, and the latter, through a phased reduction of mission grants to established work, in order to provide funds for newer mission fields (such as Kenya) and new work within the Medak Diocese itself. The rates of reduction in the years immediately prior to our survey were: 2·5 % in 1955–56, 7·5% in 1956–57, and 17·5% in 1957–58. In 1958–59 the progressive cut was suspended, and no further reduction made. In order to maintain the same size of staff, the Diocese worked out a system whereby each Pastorate was expected to raise 29% of its payroll (3·5 months' salaries) plus all local expenses. It was left to each pastorate to determine how they raised this amount, though it was assumed in principle that local giving would be raised to at least this level. However, in the Wadiaram Pastorate, as in many of the other rural pastorates in the Diocese, the presbyter simply assessed each evangelist a certain amount monthly, regardless of the contribution he reported. From June 1958 to January 1959 this monthly rate was Rs. 27·38. After January 1959 it was reduced to Rs. 22, but this was still three or four times the average of what evangelists were collecting; the rest was deducted from their salaries, a deduction which in the case of the junior evangelists sometimes came to as much as one-third of their salary.

In February 1960 the 'contract system' was abolished and evangelists asked to pay simply what they received. Further cuts in the Methodist Missionary Society grant were deferred for a few years in order to give time for a more genuine and equitable meeting of the problem than that achieved through the 'contract system'.

In 1954 the Medak Diocese introduced the 'Pledge Card' system into the village congregations. At the beginning of the year the congregation was called together, and promises of the total amount to be given during the year were secured from each family. The Diocesan aim was a yearly offering of Rs. 15 from each family. The promise which each family made was entered on its pledge card. Each family was expected to put its card up on some wall or door-post of the house, and to keep it throughout the year. In a few congregations, however, the cards were not distributed; and in the congregations where they were, many families simply used them as wall pictures. In many cases where promises were made, they were not redeemed, and only a few families actually fulfilled their pledges. Some families have promised one rupee during the year, some two or three, while others promise five or more. In Gowlapalli there were two families in 1958 which met the Diocesan aim of Rs. 15; they were the only families in the section to do this.

An older norm for family contributions was two measures of paddy (Rs. 2) at the winter harvest, and one measure of paddy at the summer harvest. It is clear from the statistics, however, that only a few families contribute even this much in 'harvest collections'. Christians also make contributions under several other headings:

1. 'Thank-offerings' at weddings, baptisms, and such special occasions as recovery from illness or a safe delivery.
2. 'Thank-offerings' during family prayers (see above).
3. Sunday service collections. A total of a few naya paise are put on the collection tray when it is passed during the Sunday night service; most of those present do not give anything.
4. Jathra collections. The Jathra is intended primarily to bring Christians of the Pastorate together in fellowship. It is also hoped that it will be one means of increasing giving. Very few people brought gifts to the Jathra held in Wadiaram during the period of study, in May 1959.
5. A handful of grain at every meal cooked. Only in Gowlapalli has this method been adopted by a few Christian families. A handful of grain is put into a small earthen vessel before the meal is cooked, morning and evening throughout the week. The grain thus collected is then brought and offered at the worship service Sunday night.
6. The 'first-fruits'. A few families offer the first-fruits of the different vegetables they grow around their houses.

The following is the information gathered from the village collection books kept by the evangelists on the total giving in four of the congregations studied. It is of course possible that the giving was in fact somewhat more than this, and that the evangelist did not record every gift he received. It was our impression, however, that while this may sometimes happen, the records are substantially accurate—this means that the average giving per family, including all categories, is far below the old norm for harvest collections alone. Nevertheless, we were told that the total giving was now far more than it was ten years ago.

Ambojipet (71 adults)	No record maintained by the retired evangelist living there, and no collections forwarded to the presbyter.		
Kondapuram (109 adults)	January – December 1958		Rs. 64·81
Achampet (83 adults)	January – December 1958		Rs. 81·81
Gowlapalli (106 adults)	January – December 1959 Family 'Thank-offerings' Weekly Sunday offerings Harvest collections	Rs. 15·78 20.35 12·68	Rs. 48·81
Jangarai (99 adults)	January – December 1959 Family 'Thank-offerings' Weekly Sunday offerings Harvest collections	Rs. 119.82 16·71 20·25	Rs. 156·78
	The total contributed by the wealthy widow of a retired evangelist	Rs. 89·81	
	The total contributed by the rest of the Jangarai congregation	Rs. 66·97	

In the villages where there are no resident evangelists, Christians rarely give anything to the church, partly because they but rarely see the evangelist who is responsible for them, and partly because they see no reason to contribute to the support of an evangelist who is not stationed among them. In villages where there are evangelists, many Christians expect a 'return' from their contribution to the evangelist: free medicines, free education for their children, and assistance in their family difficulties or court cases. These they expect, as their 'right', and if such aid is not forthcoming, they may refuse to give any offering to the evangelist at all. When one evangelist asked a Christian to pay the cost of pills, she said, 'Why should I pay? Have I not paid you the collections? It is all included in it'. When another evangelist reminded a Christian of her promise, she replied, 'Our professional beggars and traditional priests have stopped coming to us, and now you have come in their place to pester us to give collections'.

When Christians were asked why they give to God, some answered, 'Because there are some poor people in the world and the collection we give is given to them in God's name'; others said, 'Because God cared for us and blessed our crops, our cattle and children'; while a few others answered, 'Because God saved us from sin'. One elder of the congregation in Gowlapalli had this to say: 'The non-Christians offer fowls, goats, sheep, etc., to their goddesses and they just sprinkle some blood or keep a little food before them, and then they bring everything back to their homes and eat. But in the Christian religion we cannot hope to get the sacrifices back when we offer them to Christ'.

The information gathered on the economic condition of these Christians, which will be summarized in the next chapter, indicates that poor as these Christians are, their giving to the church usually represents only a very tiny share of their total expenditures, and that it is far less than what is spent on various items which we would not consider economic necessities, such as tobacco and toddy, extra expenses of the Hindu festivals, and even contributions to the traditional Hindu mendicants. It should be remembered, however, that for the village Christians these other expenses are not 'luxuries' but part of the normal pattern of life; it may be giving to the church which seems a 'luxury', since it is not regarded as essential to the maintenance of the evangelist, and in any case it is an 'extra' on top of the 'necessary expenses' which always amount to more than a family's income.

The remark of the Gowlapalli elder quoted above has a number of implications. He did not compare the offering to the church with the gifts expected by Hindu gurus or religious beggars, but rather with the offerings made to the Hindu deities. There may be a tone of complaint in the comparison, for the Hindu gets back, and expects to get back, most of the sacrificial offering with a divine blessing, whereas the rice given to the evangelist is not returned but consumed. Nevertheless, the comparison shows the influences of Christian teaching, that the offering to the evangelist is a sacrifice to Christ. If the entire congregation should come to feel that they worship a God who demands costly sacrifices as well as providing great blessings, a profound change may come in the attitude towards Christian giving. It is perhaps not a coincidence that this remark should have come from an elder in the newest congregation, the one where Christian giving has been taken very seriously by at least a few families, and where a new religion which some may have entered with the hope of gaining increased security and material welfare has so far turned out for many to involve costly sacrifices: loss of the free land and other benefits designated for Harijans.

F. *Fellowship in the Christian Community*

At the time our study began, the congregations in the Jangarai section consisted of the Madiga community in a village, or of both the Madigas and Malas. The most obvious problem of Christian fellowship, therefore, involves the relation between Malas and Madigas. The first Madiga converts did not enter the church until about a generation after the first Mala converts, and there was considerable resistance on the part of the Malas, who considered themselves superior to the Madigas and resented the Madigas' 'boasting' of their equality with Malas as their fellow-Christians. Often trouble was caused by the non-Christian relatives of the Mala Christians, who felt indirectly threatened in their claims to separateness and superiority. Later on fresh difficulties arose in the mission boarding schools when children from both these castes were admitted. The Malas had a generation's 'headstart' in the church and this fact, coupled with continuing caste consciousness, has meant that the number of Madiga children entering the boarding schools has been very low, and that therefore only very few Madigas have become evangelists. (Only one of the eleven in the Wadiaram Pastorate in 1959 was a Madiga, and he was not one of the four in the Jangarai section.) It was also difficult for these Madiga evangelists to find educated wives within the (British) Methodist Church, and some had to arrange to marry Madiga girls in other denominations.

Gradually the tension between the two castes has lessened; Christians belonging to both castes sit and worship together, and they partake of Holy Communion together. When they are at meetings at the Pastorate headquarters in Wadiaram, they eat together and drink water from the same well. But in their own villages they still neither eat together nor drink from the same well. In Kondapuram and Ambojipet, where there are both Malas and Madigas in the congregation, only the Malas draw water from the 'mission well' in front of the evangelist's house. The caste barrier is thus rigidly maintained within the village on matters of food and drink and marriages.

The Christians of Madiga background have had no objection to having an evangelist of Mala background living among them, and in general they are much more willing, in this area, to mingle with Malas, whether Christian or non-Christians, than are the Malas with them. In Achampet there have been a succession of Mala evangelists serving an entirely Madiga congregation, and these Mala evangelists have always engaged a Mala woman of the village as a servant in their home and have reserved the 'mission well' for their own use and that of all the Malas in the village—all of them non-Christian. It is uncertain whether this policy was due to the lingering caste feeling of the evangelists themselves, or their reluctance to change a custom which seemed to leave a door open to Malas to come into the Church. However that may be, the Christians have not been happy about this, and when the congregation was left without a resident evangelist during the period of our survey, the Christians seized the opportunity to start using the well at the evangelist's house, even though they had another well within their Madiga *basti* (precinct), whereupon the Malas at some expense sank a well in their basti. In Jangarai, the all-Madiga congregation has for many years used the mission well at the evangelist's house. The present evangelist, who is a Mala, gets his water from a well in the house of the wealthy widow of a retired evangelist in the Mala basti. One reason why the Malas in Achampet, Jangarai, and Gowlapalli have not become Christians is that they fear they would be forced to mix with Madigas in the church, and thus give substance to the Madiga claim to be equal to them.

Another major obstacle to Christian fellowship is the quarrels between families and individuals. Such quarrels are frequent and bitter, and settling them is a major task of the congregation. Land disputes between Christians are usually taken to the civil courts instead of being settled within the congregation, 'before the saints' (1 Cor. 6:2). A few years ago in Jangarai, the retired evangelist quarrelled with some of the Christians over a piece of land and filed a case against them in the court at Medak. Two or three years before our study, a long-standing quarrel between two brothers in the Kondapuram congregation culminated in one brother killing the other. Many petty quarrels are settled within the congregation, either by the evangelist, or by an unofficial Christian panchayat. Sometimes no panchayat is held, because it is feared it would lead to further misunderstandings and complication of the quarrel; the losing party might gather supporters and become a continuing clique working against the leadership of the congregation. Moreover, the influential men in the congregation find it difficult to render objective judgments; they feel they must act to safeguard their own interests, or keep silent on matters in which the decision might later affect them and their families. Sometimes parties are formed because of the influence of people outside the congregation, in particular, when a Christian receives support or incurs disfavour from one of the rich landowners or from a leader of one of the political parties. In two villages especially, such outside influences were contributing to the breaking of fellowship within the local congregation.

In recent years young people have been less and less inclined to accept unquestioningly the authority of their elders, and they now come to independent decisions; this sometimes causes real tension within the congregation. On particular occasions there is also tension because of different conceptions of Christian discipleship. Especially when one or two Christians refuse to participate in some traditional practice or festival, many of the others ridicule or berate them. When two women refused to take part in the Holi festival, many of the other Christians poured scorn on them. Sometimes Christians are persuaded by such social pressure to conform to the majority practice. Even when they insist on being different, however, the tension subsides after the particular incident. There does not seem to be any ostracism, on the part of the majority, or any sense of decisive difference and self-conscious superiority to the 'spiritually indifferent' on the part of the minority.

At times the divisions and tensions between Christians are so conspicuous that they cannot escape the notice of their non-Christian neighbours. These are not looked upon as anything unusual by the rest, for the same kinds of rivalries and jealousies exist within the Hindu caste communities, and there, too, the community solidarity in belief and practice is being increasingly broken by the independent opinions and decisions of a minority, very often of the younger men. Solidarity within the local community is still strongly felt within these villages, however, and Christians feel this solidarity within their local congregation. If they are all of one caste, this sense of belonging is a reinforcement of their caste solidarity; but the sense of unity and of common belonging, transcending in importance immediate quarrels and tensions is also felt in those congregations composed of more than one caste. Christians further have a sense of belonging to a much larger community of which the local congregation is only a part, but this larger community is rather vaguely apprehended; it becomes real in its leaders (the presbyter and the bishop) and in its impressive institutions, of which village Christians are very proud: the school, the hospital, and especially the great cathedral in Medak.

People from one village meet people from other villages at the weekly market held in a large village on the road between Wadiaram and Medak, and also at the various Hindu religious fairs held at shrines in nearby villages. The Christians in one village in the Jangarai section have little contact with the Christians in the other villages a few miles away. They rarely come together for sectional meetings. Some go to meetings at the Pastorate headquarters in Wadiaram, but even then they apparently gain little sense of a fellowship including all the Christians in the thirty scattered congregations in the Pastorate. Occasionally there is intercession for someone outside the congregation. In Gowlapalli and Kondapuram, Christians prayed for the Christian healer Sadhu Joseph when his tent was burned by Hindu extremists near Medak. They also prayed for the solitary Christian family suffering persecution in the nearby village of Mallupalle and a few went along with the investigator (Mr. Luke) to 'intercede' with the family's non-Christian relatives (see Chapter 7). The young men in Achampet remembered in their prayers the mission hospitals in Medak and Dichpalli, both the patients and the medical staff.

G. The 'Second Village' Congregations

The three congregations which have had no resident evangelist for many years are quite evidently different from the rest. The sense of being a Christian community has not vanished, but there are no regular meetings of the congregation for worship, and few other outward signs of a Christian community. Officially, there are no longer any 'second village' congregations; the evangelist is expected to give equal attention to each of the two or three congregations under his charge, but these congregations had had very few visits from an evangelist or the presbyter in recent years. Moreover, these congregations have lacked a physical centre. In addition to the importance attached to the physical presence of the evangelist and his family, there is the importance, both practical and symbolic, of the evangelist's house, the veranda of which serves as the normal meeting place of the congregation.

In the Chettipalli congregation, founded in 1917, there are no communicant members. According to the church roll, there was one baptism in 1941, three in 1945, twenty-five in 1950, and nine in 1957. At the time we went there in 1959 with the evangelist appointed to visit them regularly and the superintending evangelist of the section, the Christians were embarrassed; they could not make out who we were. All but six had forgotten the Christian names given to them at baptism, and they showed no outward signs of distinction from village Hindus. They remembered two evangelists many years ago who visited them regularly, but they complained that since then 'no evangelist has ever shown his face here'. They also claimed that the presbyter had visited them only once in the past ten years:

> Our non-Christian neighbours are scornfully reminding us that our guru has stopped coming. What else can we do when our guru does not come? We are going to our previous non-Christian gurus, and since we and our children are ignorant of the Christian religion and Christian festivals, we are resorting to the worship of idols. If this evangelist had been coming, we would have collected some grain and given it to him as an offering.

For the last twelve years the Edulapalli congregation has not been cared for by any evangelist. After the initial baptisms when the congregation began in 1927, there were ten baptisms in 1939, ten in 1948, six in 1950, and seven in 1954. Only three remembered their Christian names, though five are listed on the church roll as communicants. They participate fully in the village religious practices: solemnizing their own marriages with traditional rites, celebrating all the non-Christian festivals, and worshipping the idols of the Hindu deities. All but two had forgotten what they had been taught many years ago about Jesus Christ and about the Christian festivals. There are two men, however, one of whom is literate, who have faint memories of what they were taught. When asked where Jesus was born, they replied, 'You come to visit us once in ten or twenty years—how can we remember the name of the place where Jesus was born?' When we visited Edulapalli, we were invited into the home of the police patel (a Hindu of one of the landowning castes) and served tea. The patel urged us to station an evangelist in this village who would conduct a school for all the children of the village, since this is a small village without a government school. He promised to donate a two-acre piece of wet land, the crops of which could be used for the support of the evangelist; and the Christians of the village promised to help with the construction of a house for an evangelist, if only we would send him.

The most neglected congregation is that in Mirzapalli. This is ironic, for the Christians there still remember that the evangelist from a village four miles away visited them regularly for two years before they were baptized in 1927, and he promised that if they would become Christians, they would be given free education, free hospital treatment, as well as deliverance from the burden of *yetti*, compulsory labour for the village patels. They say that it was for the sake of these advantages that they agreed to become Christians. The church roll shows sixty-seven adult Christians, of whom three are communicants, and no baptized children under fourteen. However, these figures are quite inaccurate, because for some years the evangelist officially in charge of the congregation has simply made the same notation by each name as in the previous year, without visiting the village at all to see whether

D

these church members were even still alive. After the first baptisms in 1927, there were thirty more the following year, 1928. In 1932, ten baptisms were recorded, but in the twenty-seven years from that date until our study in 1959, there were no further baptisms! The Christians there said that at the beginning an evangelist had lived in the village, in the home of one of the Christian families, but after two years he was forced to leave the village because of a clash with the village officials, who demanded that Christian prayers should not be held in the Madiga *basti.* Since that time no evangelist has been stationed there, and they claimed that in all the intervening years they had had only three or four visits from evangelists, and that never once had the presbyter in Wadiaram, only four miles away, come to visit them:

> You come to us once in twenty years. Our traditional Madiga guru writes down our names and visits us at least once in five years, but you are worse than he. The Mashti and Dakkali (itinerant religious dramatists) visit us at least once a year, but you have completely forgotten us. We also have forgotten everything you taught us in the beginning.

It is possible that these Christians may have exaggerated the extent of their neglect; there were still five who remembered the Christian names they had been given so many years before, but there is no doubt that their resentment had a strong basis in fact. That resentment itself, however, was one of several indications that they still considered themselves Christians, however much they might have returned to their traditional practices and their traditional religious leaders. Moreover, like the Christians of Edulapalli, they pleaded for the stationing of an evangelist who would teach their children to read, and they made the concrete offer of a vacant house belonging to a Christian in which he could live.

H. *Distinctive Features of the Individual Congregations*

In spite of having so much of their Christian tradition and their village environment in common, the six congregations which have now or recently had resident evangelists show a number of variations. The three older congregations consist of both Mala and Madiga families, and two of the three (Bandaposanipalli and Kondapuram) are both larger than average (over 150) and more prosperous: a number of families, both Mala and Madiga, own their own lands. The third older congregation, Ambojipet, is smaller and poorer, and in recent years has suffered from being in the care of a retired evangelist who was allowed to live in the evangelist's house but was no longer paid any salary by the Diocese, and for that reason felt little obligation for the pastoral care of the congregation. At the beginning of our period of study, Ambojipet appeared to be one of the least active or self-conscious congregations about its specifically Christian activities; but during the period of study itself, some of the most interesting new developments in the section, both in lay leadership, and in a new interest in Christianity on the part of some Sudras, occurred in Ambojipet. One distinctive influence on the congregation there is its accessibility. It is on the road between Wadiaram and Medak, and this makes it easier to travel to the larger towns like Medak, or even to Hyderabad, fifty miles away. Some Christian families have moved away from the village, some to Hyderabad and two to the sugar factory farther away in Bodhan. Those who went to Hyderabad occasionally come back to visit their relatives.

Of the three all-Madiga congregations studied, Jangarai is the oldest but also the most immersed in traditional village culture. Its group of young men are far behind those who in the other congregations lead in specifically Christian activities and sometimes make the most distinction between their Christian life and their participation in the life of the village. In Jangarai it is the women in the congregation who are more active. This is understandable, because two widows of evangelists('Bible women') were in charge of the congregation for some of the years in the previous decade, when an evangelist was resident only intermittently. In 1959 both the evangelist's wife and the wealthy widow of a retired evangelist who had settled down in that village were active in gathering the Christian women for worship. None of these women could read but they sang many lyrics, most of which they had learned from the present evangelist's wife, who is full of energy and enthusiasm. Some of the younger women started to learn to read, but were sent back to their homes by the chiding and discouragement of the older women. This group of Christian women have also struggled with the problem of their participation in the traditional village and caste rites, though only a few of them have had the courage to refrain from the religious practices in which others joined.

The Christians in Jangarai are much poorer than those in Konda-puram; here, only a few own any land. Whereas in Kondapuram most of the Christians have houses with tiled roofs, the Jangarai Christians are crowded into eighteen small thatched huts, with as many as three families to a hut, and hardly space to walk between them. All attempts to get fresh house sites have so far been blocked, on the grounds that these outcastes are not Harijans, but Christians.

It seems incongruous that this desperately poor congregation should have within its membership by far the wealthiest Christian family in the section. At the edge of the village is an enclosed plot containing a grave covered by a cement slab and marked by a large upright granite cross. This is the grave of a Christian who died in 1958, a year before our survey; he was a retired evangelist who had settled down in Jan-garai and lived there for eighteen years. He had some funds when he retired, and he multiplied his capital many times over by lending it at the high village rates of interest. He bought lands, built a large house in the Mala basti, and left about eighteen thousand rupees when he died. The man himself had the reputation of being a miser and a grasping money-lender. Though he had been an evangelist, he rarely attended Christian worship and contributed only a pittance. His widow, on the other hand, had become an active member of the congregation, assisting the present evangelist's wife and contributing financially far more than her husband ever did, indeed, more than the rest of the congregation together. Yet she seems quite humble in her unusual state of wealth; she does not seek to dominate, but is willing to participate as an equal in this poor, largely illiterate, and almost entirely Madiga congregation.

The congregation with the most decidedly Christian stamp is that in Achampet. One outward sign of this is the cross painted on many of the houses. For many years the superintending evangelists of the Jangarai section had worked in this congregation. Just before we (the Lukes) came in June 1959, the evangelist had left for a year's course of ministerial training, and for the first time in its history, the congregation was left without a resident evangelist. This produced something of a crisis, but one which the congregation was able to resolve. (See the section on 'Lay Leadership' in Chapter 6 below.) The Christians in Achampet gratefully remember the services of some of the past evangelists, especially Atigari Samuel, who is now a presbyter working elsewhere in the Diocese. They said that he worked day and night for their spiritual growth, even to the neglect of his health. It was he who taught most of the young men to read the Bible and to conduct worship services. 'It was as if an angel were moving in our midst, so intimately did he know us when he lived among us and visited our homes. Oh, he was such a great tower of strength to us!' There were also words of special appreciation for the wife of the most recent evangelist, who conducted a regular day school for the children and an active Sunday school.

The young men clearly have a much more extensive knowledge of the Bible and of Christian beliefs than do most of the Christians in the section. They are enthusiastic about calling people for worship, and can conduct the worship themselves. They like to sing revival songs, though they are unable to articulate any personal experience of 'revival' or explain what it means. The young men have bought instruments and formed a band. In addition to playing at special Christian services, they hire themselves out to play at both Christian and non-Christian weddings.

Many of the women and older men know little about the Bible, yet it is clear that the more effective Christian teaching of a succession of able evangelists and their wives has affected not only the young men but the whole congregation. Almost two-thirds of the adults are communicant members, which is nearly double the proportion in the section as a whole. Fewer Christians participate in non-Christian rites; and those that do, participate less fully that the Christians in many of the other congregations. However, many marriages have been performed by the Madiga caste headman (a member of the congregation) with traditional rites instead of by the presbyter with a Christian marriage service. There is a very large proportion of intermarriage between the Christians of Achampet and non-Christian Madigas in other villages. (This general problem will be discussed in the section on 'Marriage' in Chapter 9 below.)

The congregation consists of the entire Madiga community in Achampet. Five of the twenty families are engaged in the traditional Madiga occupation of tanning leather. Four of the young men went to the mission school at Ramayampet for special training in the tannery. Two young men who were educated in mission schools up to matriculation are now in government service. They return from time to time to visit their relatives, and exert some influence on them as educated Christians. Only a few families possess any land of their own. No one has as much as two acres. Those without land cultivate other people's land as tenants, returning half the produce to the landowners and keeping the other half. The congregation is thus not so well off as some others in the section, but it has a much neater and more prosperous appearance than the Jangarai Christian basti; all but five of the twenty houses have tiled roofs.

As was noted above, there is a sharp rivalry in Achampet between the Christians, who are Madigas, and the non-Christian Malas. On two occasions during the congregation's history, the Malas were preparing to become Christians, but both times the Malas in other villages dissuaded them. The Christians are proud that their young men can read, unlike the Mala young men, and point with pride to the greater neatness and cleanliness of their basti. It is precisely this pride in their Christian achievements, however, which reinforces the ancient caste barriers between the two groups, and makes it more difficult for the Malas to 'swallow *their* pride' and join the Christian congregation.

The beginning of the Gowlapalli congregation and something of its subsequent difficulties have already been recounted. More will be said about Gowlapalli when we discuss lay leadership, for it presents a classic example of a clash between the original lay leader of a congregation and the official leader appointed by the Church, the evangelist, who is sent in from outside. Attention has already been drawn to the conflict between the young men and their elders, which is sharper in this congregation than in any of the others. On the whole, the Christians here are very poor; only three of the thirty-one houses have tiled roofs. There are twelve families who own as much as or more than one acre of land; the rest are day labourers in the fields of the landowners of the higher Sudra castes, and they are therefore subject to whatever economic pressures the landowners exert. The Gowlapalli congregation is largely Madiga, but it is less homogeneous than the congregations in Jangarai and Achampet. Five families belong to the Madiga sub-caste of Bandelas, and there are two Mala Christian families who migrated to the village. The Christians constitute the majority of the outcaste section of the village, but there are ten non-Christian families, seven Mala and three Dandem. During the summer of our study, a lame boy from one of these Mala families was baptized and joined the congregation.

Perhaps it is noteworthy in how many respects the Gowlapalli congregation is *not* different from all the other congregations in the section, which have been in existence for at least a generation longer. Its small proportion of communicant members, weak penetration of Christian teaching, and extensive participation in non-Christian rites is very similar to that of congregations in which there have been one or two generations for Christian nurture. In some respects, indeed, this congregation is 'ahead' of many of the others. In 1959 there were eight literates, all owning Bibles. In the nine years of the congregation's existence, there had already been two boys from this congregation who had gone out to the mission boarding school in Medak and after further training become evangelists. One Voluntary Church Worker has completed his training and received his 'Bishop's licence'. He devotes much of his free time to helping the evangelist.

The 'newness' of the Gowlapalli congregation shows up most clearly in the resistance, both outside and inside the congregation, to the kind of Christianity which has come to be accepted in the other villages. The Hindu landowners have not reconciled themselves to any form of Christianity, no matter how 'syncretistic' it may be or how insignificant a minority it affects, for they fear it will become a force disrupting the socio-economic and religious structure on which their political power is based. We shall see in the next chapter that the Kondapuram Christians could openly take the Communist side in the village election without being subject to the sort of harassment Gowlapalli Christians receive for mere suspicion of Communist sympathies. There are a number of reasons for this, one of which is the greater economic independence of the Christians in Kondapuram; many more of them own land, and therefore do not have to work as tenants or day labourers for Hindu landowners. Yet one additional important reason appears to be that Kondapuram has become accustomed to non-Hindu minorities; the small Muslim group has been there for a long time, and the Christians have apparently also become a recognized minority, though much lower in the social scale. Their distinctive cults are not merely tolerated, but to some extent admired; yet it is tacitly agreed that the minorities will co-operate in religious matters of overriding importance to the whole village. In Gowlapalli, on the other hand, the Christian Church is still new and 'questionable'. There are Christians who are doubtful whether it is worth the trouble it brings; there are also Christians for whom it is bringing a different kind of trouble: the disturbance of their consciences. They find that they cannot accept the widespread compromise involved in the simultaneous participation in Christian and Hindu forms of worship, a compromise which has become almost a matter of course in most of the older congregations. For many Christians in Gowlapalli, Christianity is still a religion which demands a choice, but they are uncertain what that choice should be.

CHAPTER 5

The Life of Christians in Village Society

A. *Forms of Livelihood and Standard of Living*

The majority of villagers depend on agriculture for their livelihood. Rice is grown on the highly prized 'wetlands' which can be irrigated from the tanks (village reservoirs), and ragi or ambali (eaten as porridge or gruel) is grown on other lands which depend on the monsoon rains and very occasional showers during other parts of the year. Ownership of land is of great economic importance to the villager, even if he has some other occupation in addition to farming, or chooses to leave his land to a tenant instead of working it himself. Land has more than economic significance, however. It has even more symbolic value than the other principal forms of property, cattle and jewellery.

The Christians in these villages are almost all members of the 'outcaste' groups, and only a few of them have more than a very small plot of land; many of them have no land at all. (There are significant differences between the Christian congregations in the Jangarai section in this respect, as we noted in the last chapter.) They are therefore very much attracted by the prospects of receiving free land from the Government, and correspondingly frustrated if they see this land denied them because they are Christians. Those who are not farming for themselves (as owners or tenants) work for landowners on long-term contract or as day labourers; a few have traditional positions as village messengers and servants. While those who own their own farm land have somewhat more economic security, they do not have enough capital for such major expenditure as the purchase of seed for sowing or of new cattle; they therefore have to borrow money at high interest from money-lenders or village officials (patels).

Among the Christians of Mala extraction, the Neerudus who watch over village tanks and flood gates possess rent-free gift land (*inam*) granted to them by the Government for their regular services all the year round. For other services rendered in connexion with religious festivals and village ceremonies, they get one measure (3 seers) of paddy and one bundle of paddy sheaves per acre from the agriculturists at each harvest, in addition to what they get during ceremonies. The Begaris do not hold any rent-free gift lands like the Neerudus, but get the other concessions from the agriculturists in return for their service. Begaris also take part in the religious ceremonies. In these villages there are no Majkuris (village peons) among the Christians.

Among the Christians of Madiga background, there are some who render semi-official service, *yetti* (menial service), to the village and to the Government, for which they are granted some rent-free land. For their other religious duties and drum-beating they are paid one measure (worth 8 annas) of paddy and one bundle of paddy sheaves per acre by each agriculturist. Some Madigas pursue their traditional occupation of leather work, while others labour as servants for higher caste families. Some work in the fields of the landowners and get a share of the produce at each harvest.

Women and girls of 7 to 14 work in the fields during the agricultural seasons, for three to four seers of paddy a day. Some women (especially Madigas) have permanent menial jobs working for higher caste families. Instead of daily wages, they are paid twenty rupees worth of paddy at each of the two harvests.

There are two main agricultural seasons during the year: one for crops planted in June–July and harvested in October–November, and the other, which is shorter, for crops planted in December–January and harvested in April–May. For four months of the year agricultural labourers have no work in the fields. During these periods without work, both adults and children often go out into the surrounding scrub jungle to collect fuel, beedi leaves, broomsticks and glue material. They also pick wild berries and wild figs when they are in season. A person can sometimes earn as much as twelve annas or even a rupee from a day of such gathering.

Village Christians are so poor that even the children must contribute to the family income. As soon as a boy has courage enough to twist a bullock's tail, off he must go with the landowner's cattle to pasture. Boys between the ages of six and fourteen are paid from three to seven rupees a month.

Very few Christians in this area own milk cows or buffaloes, which would supply them with milk and butter. Only two Christian families (one in Kondapuram and one in Gowlapalli) possess a buffalo. Most families cannot afford to keep these animals; but even if they could, they would not be able to sell milk or butter in the village, because high-caste people would not use food which the outcastes have touched. The very few who do keep cattle usually sell their dairy products to the Muslims. All the Christians keep poultry, and occasionally earn a little money by selling eggs and poultry to wandering traders who go about from village to village collecting them.

Statistics were gathered from ten Christian families (two from each of the five congregations most closely studied) about their sources of income and types of expenditure. The figures were manifestly inaccurate in certain respects; families do not keep financial records, and hence indicate what they *expect* to earn or to spend in a given category. However, even their guesses were of considerable interest, since they give some clue as to their living *standards*: what they consider the normal yield or wage or expense on a specific item in the course of a day, month or year. It is quite probable that in many cases a family's income does not come up to expectations, or that there are extra unforeseen types of expenses, in which case the family simply has to spend on various items less than they regard as normal. To some extent families can meet the disparity between income and expenses by borrowing money, and this is done to pay for a wedding or to meet other major expenses. However, the interest rates are so high or the conditions of repayment so onerous that such loans do not cover the disparity between expected and actual income, or between 'normal' expenses and actual income. The family has to restrict its expenditure still further.

It was noteworthy that a relatively large proportion of their meagre income is spent (or at least expected to be spent) on a number of items which look like luxuries rather than bare subsistence. These include tobacco (for the men), toddy (for everyone at festivals, and for some men every night after work), and lavish gifts and hospitality on special occasions, notably at weddings, and to a lesser extent at other ceremonies connected with the life cycle. Another category of 'luxuries' include gifts to religious professionals. Most of these Christian families contribute far more to the itinerant Hindu beggars than they do to the resident evangelist or the presbyter.

It seems quite clear that many of these 'luxuries' are not regarded as luxuries at all, but as a normal part of village life, and as necessary as daily food. Perhaps to these village Christians it is their offerings to the church which seem the least necessary, since they believe that the 'Mission House' or the Bishop in Medak will see to it that their evangelist does not starve, and it is only the 'thank-offerings' they make on special occasions which come into one of the familiar village categories of 'normal', and therefore 'necessary', expenditures.

It should also be noted that there is a good deal of variation from family to family, not only in the *per capita* budget, but in the proportion spent on different items. A more extensive survey might have revealed even more variation. Two of the ten families had spent money in the previous year on litigation. Only one of these families had spent nothing on toddy; and that was the family of Narayana Paul, the convert baptized during the period of our survey, who is from the caste of toddy-tappers! His father is supplied free toddy by other members of the caste, but the rest of the family does not drink at all.

B. *The Course of Life*

Villagers get up early in the morning, and the women busy themselves with their household work while the men go to their work in the fields. The left-overs from the previous night's meal are given to their small children, and then the women cook the major midday meal by ten in the morning. The men may return from work to eat, or have their wives take the meal to them in the fields. Then the women either join the men in their work or go to do other work during the busy season, leaving their babies at home in the care of the children who are still too small to work. After returning in the evening from work, they cook the evening meal. When the members of the family have finished supper (between 8 and 9 p.m.), they go to sleep immediately or attend night prayers at the evangelist's house. Some women come to night prayers bringing their babies with them. Others who leave them with the old people (usually the mother-in-law) are anxious to get back home. In the middle of the service one can sometimes hear a mother-in-law calling loudly for her daughter to come home. Some of the men feel uneasy, for at any time they may be called away by their masters. In Gowlapalli during one night service, a patel sent the village messenger to call a young Christian lad from the service, but the boy refused to go until the service was over. After a day's hard labour the men cannot be attentive for more than half an hour. Yet during most of the year this is the only time when the evangelist can teach them.

Besides the daily round and the cycle of the seasons (hot season, monsoon, and cold season), the life of village Christians incorporates the accepted pattern of the life cycle of every individual in the village, but makes modifications of the traditional pattern at certain points.

For the first three months of a child's life, the mother nurses it and cares for it constantly. If it is the mother's first baby, the older women in the family teach her how to take care of the child. After the naming ceremony (*Purudu*) on the twenty-first day, the mother is allowed to resume her domestic duties, and when the baby is three months old the mother may go out to work in the fields. The mother usually nurses the child until her next pregnancy, but gradually introduces it to some soft food. From early infancy children are very much attached to their parents, but between the ages of 2 and 5 they begin to make friends with other children. Only in a few homes do the children receive any Christian teaching from their parents. Except in the Christian homes in Achampet, no grace is said before meals, nor do the parents hold any family prayers. But children learn bad habits and abusive language by observing their friends and relatives and other older people in the community.

The Telugu word *pantulu*, translated as 'evangelist' or 'catechist', means 'teacher', and the evangelist and his wife are expected to provide a number of forms of education for both the children and the adults of the congregation.

(1) The evangelist's wife (*pantalamma*) is supposed to gather together the five- and six-year-olds every day to teach them songs and nursery rhymes and, gradually, how to read and write.

(2) In the early days of the Methodist Mission, the establishment of a primary school (up to the fourth standard) was considered an essential part of the nurture of new converts. These schools taught by the evangelist and his wife had a basic curriculum of reading, writing and arithmetic, in addition to Bible study. It was maintained that if these children were in grace, they had to be able to read the Bible for themselves. However, it proved difficult in many villages to achieve a day school in which the attendance of children remained regular long enough for them to achieve permanent literacy. Children must soon become 'breadwinners' like their parents, watching the crops and taking the cattle to pasture, and even the younger children are wanted at home, to mind the baby while their parents are at work. It is therefore difficult to persuade illiterate parents to send the children to school. Even

so, children will come for a time; at harvest time or during special seasons, however, they play truant with their parents' consent (or at their instigation). For a time the Methodist District had a system of subsidies designed to compensate the children and their families for their loss of earnings while attending day school. The evangelist also received an increment to his salary, based on the number of children he taught and their standard of attainment. This system of financial aid was discontinued a generation ago.

Other forms of education included in the evangelist's responsibility are (3) the night schools, for older children and young adults, and (4) adult literacy classes. These will be discussed below.

In the congregations surveyed, the nursery school is the only part of the 'day school' which is functioning. In order to help the evangelists improve the day schools, the Diocese has appointed a full-time supervisor of village schools, but the strength of these village schools has continued to fall. Moreover, very few children from the villages are sent to the boarding schools of the Diocese. Most of those in the boarding schools are the children of 'paid church workers' (evangelists and presbyters) and the children of other educated Christian parents living in mission compounds or in the cities. The Principal of Boarding School in Medak informed us that only twenty-four village children (thirteen girls and eleven boys) were enrolled out of a total of 545 pupils.

A very recent development is the establishment of one-teacher Government elementary schools in all the villages surveyed. These schools are open to Christian children, but many of them are attending neither the Government school nor the evangelist's 'day school'. Thus a great many Christian children are getting neither a secular nor a Christian education, which means that there will be very few educated, or even literate, leaders in these village congregations in the next generation.

On Sunday morning the evangelist holds a worship service that is attended mostly by children and is in the nature of a Sunday school. Sunday schools in the area surveyed are poorly attended and little care is expended in teaching them. In order to encourage and improve Sunday school work, in 1958 a Sunday school rally was organized for the Jangarai section, in Jangarai, to which about a dozen Christian children from each of the other Christian congregations in the section came, after learning the set syllabus for the rally in their villages. They were examined and three prizes were given to the evangelists for their work. By this treat and prize-giving method, the enthusiasm and the interest of the evangelists and the children were aroused.

Adolescence is another significant stage in the life of village Christian children. The adolescent group consists of boys between the ages of 12 and 18, and of girls of the puberty stage between 10 and 15. The boys seek children of their own age-group for play and gossip. They become romantic and self-conscious. They are supposed to be under the control of the parents and elder brothers, but in these days of increasing freedom and individualism, the youth are becoming independent and are trying to defy the traditional authority of the family. Young boys in this stage develop romantic feelings for adolescent girls, and make secret efforts to attract girls to have sexual relations. Sex is one of the common subjects of talk and gossip of youth, and they share with each other in private talks the experience of their love affairs. They are fond of vigorous country games, folk dances and folk plays, particularly Chirutala Ramayanam and Bhagavatam. They try to exhibit their skill, art and strength through these and other such displays.

During the period of adolescence, girls are expected to learn all the domestic duties. Marriage arrangements are made for them at this age. They have to be careful about their dress and should not wander about recklessly in the village. At this age they get into love affairs with boys and young men, but they also fear that their waywardness may fall under the critical eye of the community. They become self-conscious and feel shy when older people raise the subject of marriage, sex, etc., in order to tease them. They spend their leisure time in playing games, in folk songs and folk dances with girls of their age-group.

Recognizing the important position that youth occupy in the congregation, the Diocese has sponsored young men's and young women's 'guilds' (Yavana Samaj and Yuvati Samaj). After the evangelist has taught them the special songs and motto (Romans 12: 1) of the youth organizations, the young people are supposed to be formally initiated into their respective guilds during a ceremony at the annual Jathra at the Pastorate headquarters, conducted by the diocesan youth secretary. A number of distinctive insignia have been devised to indicate their membership in the guild: a green shirt or blouse (symbolizing life and growth) and a red badge on the shirt pocket showing an open Bible and a torch. The guild is also expected to have a green flag with a white cross on it, which can be carried at the front of processions. In addition to bringing people to the night prayers and sometimes conducting the worship themselves, the youth guilds are supposed to have weekly meetings and to engage in social service. Youth rallies are also expected to be held for the entire Pastorate.

In the congregations surveyed, there are only two organized guilds. In Achampet there is an excellent young men's society at work, which is a great help to the congregation. In Jangarai there is a fairly strong young women's guild, guided by the evangelist's wife. In the other congregations studied, the youth are not formally organized, although they constitute most of the attendance at night prayers and often take the lead in activities of the congregation.

Christian youth are much attracted by the dramatic dances enacting stories from the Hindu Epics and Puranas. There are Christian versions of Hindu folk dances and dramas which are popular in some congregations elsewhere in the Diocese, but they do not seem to have been taken up by the Christian young people in the Jangarai Section. In Ambojipet there was one remarkable instance of local adaptation of the *Chirutala Ramayanam* to tell a Christian story. That will be recounted in Chapter 7 below. When the young people are involved in predominantly Hindu groups dramatizing episodes from the Hindu scriptures, they become a problem for the congregation instead of its principal dynamic. This problem already exists in several of the congregations.

During the period of survey, we learned of a number of instances in which youth were led into the habit of drinking or became involved in extra-marital sexual relations. For these congregations, drinking and adultery are serious problems, and they are temptations into which young people are easily led.

Night schools were introduced in the villages, to provide both religious and secular education for young people who had to work in the fields all day. Written examinations in Bible, composition, and arithmetic are held twice a year, and those who pass these examinations still receive a small prize or financial reward. At times older people in the congregation, who are illiterate, join them and learn to read, following the adult literacy method first introduced in Medak by Dr. Laubach in 1937. The night schools are frequently the place where young people come into living touch with the Scriptures, and it is therefore regrettable to have to report that the night schools are not functioning in most of the Jangarai congregations. Jangarai is the only congregation that has a regular night school, which is attended by five non-Christian boys as well as by two Christians. In Gowlapalli a night school is conducted but meets irregularly.

After the adolescents are married, which is frequently below the legal age of 18 for boys and 15 for girls, they live with the boy's family. During the early years of marriage the girls return to their parents' home (in another village) for frequent visits, especially at the time of festivals. In this period the boy and girl are still very much under the influence of their respective families, so that the quarrels which sometimes develop between the girl's and boy's parents can occasionally even lead to their divorce. A girl's traditional training for her role in life is exclusively domestic and begins in the home of her own parents. A girl also receives intensive domestic training from her mother-in-law. This 'apprenticeship' is likely to be particularly onerous during the early years, and this is especially true if there is a period after marriage before the young wife becomes sexually mature, able to consummate the marriage and bear children. After a girl's first child is born, especially if it is a boy, her status in the family improves, but she does not have much independence until she has two or three children. She is not supposed to speak to her husband in public, and the crowded living conditions and long working hours make it impossible for the young couple to have much privacy, even for casual conversation.

In these circumstances, since the young husband and wife have much to draw them apart and little opportunity to get to know one another, it is not surprising that suspicion often flourishes. Many a husband has to listen to the complaints of his mother about his wife and his wife's complaints about her mother-in-law. Husband and wife tend to be jealous of any interest in another member of the opposite sex, and they may express their suspicions in taunts and threats. Wives frequently suspect their husbands of excessive drinking or extra-marital intrigues, while husbands or their families often watch the wife to make sure she is not secretly sending anything to her parental home, or committing adultery. If a couple has quarrelled, the husband's family watches to see that the wife does not mix poison in his food! When the couple becomes older and has children, it becomes more independent and sometimes is the centre of a new joint-family unit. However, the legacy of early mistrust remains and even older couples have secret liaisons, sometimes in other castes. A very few men maintain a house for another woman in a different village.

Old people have their own age-group. As long as physical strength permits, they continue to work at home. When they can no longer do so, they return to their own room (if there is a separate room) and often feel that they can only mark time until their death. Grandparents are very fond of their grandchildren; they are often found carrying or fondling them. They are as lenient towards their grandchildren, whom they tend to spoil, as they are critical of their children's behaviour. They depend on the loving care and generosity of their sons and, even more, of their daughters-in-law. Some old people find it very difficult to adjust to this life of complete dependence.

The middle-aged and the old people play an important role in the affairs of the congregation. All important decisions in the church are supposed to be referred to them for comment. If they are not consulted on an issue, some try to create divisions in the church fellowship and put obstacles in the way of carrying out the congregation's decisions. The older people find it difficult to reconcile themselves to new ways of life and hence usually advocate the old and familiar in thought and practice. A tension thus frequently develops between the older and younger members of the congregation. Many of the older people do not take an active part in worship. but if elected to the Pastorate Committee, they will attend the meetings, and if paid the usual fees, they will take part in the informal courts (panchayat) of the congregation. They consider themselves too old to learn Christian songs or Bible stories: 'We have become old and are nearing the grave. We cannot learn anything. It is enough if our young men and children learn.'

C. *Political Changes in the Village*

India's adoption of a secular democratic form of government with adult franchise gave village people opportunity to take part in the general elections conducted in the country in 1951–52 and 1956–57. The new constitution makes offences arising out of untouchability illegal, and gives equal rights to women with men in matters of marriage, divorce, inheritance and succession. Child marriage is abolished by law. In 1959, however, all this legislation had scarcely affected any of the villagers in the area under survey.

There is a growing feeling of independence among the village Christians, who interpret political freedom in terms of relaxation of the rules of caste authority and the social prohibitions. When the Congress Government first came, the villagers assumed that they were all free citizens and that there would be no difference or distinction on the basis of caste, wealth or creed. In this mood the villagers in Jangarai (including the Christians) beat the Mali patel, who was a cruel and callous village official. A woman described the changing attitude of the present youth in the following words: 'Just as the currency has changed from Halli Sicca (Nizam's currency) to Indian Government currency, and from annas and pies to naye Paise, so also the attitude of these young men is changing.'[1]

The Congress Party has been in power since democratic government was established after Independence and the Police Action. The Communist Party has been the major opposition party, and at times has been especially strong in some parts of Telengana. It has had some influence in industrial areas, and among high school and college students, as well as among the lower caste and poorer people in the villages. We found that many village officials and landowners were discontented with the current leaders of the Congress Party, since they felt that both the major parties were equally corrupt and disinclined to bring them real benefits. However, they see no third option, since neither the socialist nor the conservative parties are active in this area. Some village leaders believed that the Congress leaders had enjoyed special privileges and amassed great wealth, and were willing to give the Communists a chance to see whether they could prove themselves less corrupt than the ruling party.

The Christians of the villages do not know much about the merits or demerits of the policies of either of these parties; they judge, or side with, a party simply according to the practical help they receive from it. In Jangarai village, the Christians voted for the Congress Party in the first general election, in gratitude for their help in getting some land. Before the 1956 election, however, the Communist Party leader in Medak helped the Christians in a court case. As a result, in this second election the Jangarai Christians voted for the Communist candidate. Both Christians and other groups vote for the party which helps them in their immediate difficulties, and tend to shift suddenly from one party to another according to the material benefits they receive.

In 1956 village councils (*gram panchayats*) were established in the revenue villages with a population of from one to five thousand. During 1959, the year of our survey, the provision for local democracy was extended to smaller villages, grouping a revenue village with another contiguous village or villages, so that the total population would be between one and five thousand. The councils consist of from six to twelve members and a few seats are reserved for members of scheduled castes and tribes in proportion to their percentage of the local population. Members of the panchayat serve for three years.[2]

Elections to the gram panchayat for Kondapuram took place on May 5, 1959. Kondapuram, with two adjacent hamlets, was yoked with Khajipalli to constitute one panchayat, and the voting booths were set up in Khajipalli. There were two Christian candidates in Kondapuram, one on the Congress ticket and the other on the Communist. Most of the Christians in Kondapuram, along with the majority of their fellow villagers, voted for the Communist candidates, who won the three seats assigned to the village on the gram panchayat.

The Christians were influenced partly by the desire to side with the majority of the village, whom they knew beforehand were in favour of the Communists, but there were other reasons as well. In the first place, they were angry at the Congress Party because they believed that on Palm Sunday, Congress followers in Medak (eight miles away) had burned the tent of Sadhu Joseph, who had been conducting healing services in the Medak area. Secondly, the Christians (and others) were impressed by the propaganda technique of the Communists, who presented their ideas through *burra katha* (ballad singing), a means which the Congress leaders did not use. Furthermore, the Congress leaders from Medak visited the villages only once in a car and were unable to answer the fire of questions from the antagonistic villagers, whereas the Communist Party members visited the village four times, staying two days each time, mingling freely with the lower caste people and accepting water to drink from them (something no one normally does from a member of a lower caste).

When the Communist Party leader from Medak visited Kondapuram just before the election, he had a private conversation with the evangelist. The Communist leader told the investigator that many evangelists were complaining to him about their financial difficulties. We do not know whether this conversation with the evangelist influenced the Christians to vote Communist, but it is a fact that when Communist Party workers go to a village, one of the first men they call on is the evangelist. One of the Communists elected to the panchayat committee is a Christian, Nathaniel (from the Madiga community), who was later elected as the vice-chairman of the committee.

The Congress Party won all three seats for Khajipalli, thus producing a tie with the Communist Party, which won the Kondapuram seats. It was decided that the only way to choose the chairman and the vice-chairman was by lot. Both times the lots were cast, a Communist member won. A Muslim from Kondapuram became chairman and the Christian Nathaniel was chosen as vice-chairman. Those who had voted for the Communist candidate in Kondapuram were jubilant. Most of them were Hindus, but they told the investigator that they had been aided in securing the winning lots by Jesus Christ! Moreover, they requested the investigator (as a Christian presbyter) to go to their homes and pray for them. When the elections were over, members of the Communist Party in Kondapuram attended Christian worship to give thanks to 'Lord Jesus' for bringing them success in the panchayat elections.

In Rayelli, another village in the southern section of the pastorate, Christians were informed that the Congress Party would not include one of them among its candidates. They then appealed to the Communists, who selected a Christian named Daniel as one of their candidates, and promised all the help possible to secure his election. Not only was he elected to the panchayat, but his fellow members chose him to be chairman. Both Daniel of Rayelli and Nathaniel of

Kondapuram are among the relatively few literate men in their congregations.

In the Gowlapalli election only one party was represented, the Congress, but it was split into two factions supporting rival candidates: Brahmins and Reddies on one side, and Munoor Kapus on the other. The faction led by the Reddi-landowners won, whereupon the Kapu landowners became very angry with the Christians, many of whom work on their lands, suspecting them of voting for the victorious Reddi candidate.

Elections bring long-standing jealousies and antagonisms between different castes and religious communities out into the open, and sometimes further accentuate them. Feeling sometimes runs so high that one group will take extreme measures to embarrass or harm their opponents: involving them in court cases, hiring a black magician to work them ill, or hiring men to beat or even kill them. On the other hand, for the groups in the village, like the outcastes, who have previously had no power, universal suffrage has brought a new feeling of worth; their support has to be solicited even by candidates of higher castes. Sometimes their votes have no real effect on the power structure; at other times, as in Kondapuram, the lower castes and minority groups attain real influence, especially if they can learn to work together across caste lines. Thus the new political situation has brought new inter-caste co-operation as well as the intensification of rivalry between castes.

Almost all the Christians in these villages have both a Hindu name and a Christian name, the former given them at the traditional naming ceremony, the latter at baptism. As far as the church is concerned, it is their Christian baptismal name which is their official name, but these names are not found on the voting lists prepared by the village officials for the Government in the villages surveyed. Only the Hindu names of the Christian voters are entered on the official list. Most of the Christians are illiterate and thus unaware of this, and some would not be greatly disturbed if they did know. The Christian evangelist is aware of this fact, but he frequently does not care or dare to challenge the village official. Similarly, it is often the Hindu names of Christians which are entered when the census is taken in these villages, with the result that there is sometimes no indication in the government records that there are Christians in those villages.

Before Independence, when Telengana was under Muslim rule, village people used to greet one another with the word *Salaam* (an Arabic word which means 'peace'). Now they greet with the word *Namaste* ('reverence to you', a Hindi word which is used for greeting respectfully) or *Namaskāram* ('I make reverence', its Telugu equivalent). One village elder greeted the author saying 'Salaam', and immediately a woman standing by checked him and said, 'You should not use the word *Salaam* any longer; in this new India you should say *Namaste*'.

This change from a greeting with Muslim connotations to a word with a Hindu background is symbolic of the change in political and cultural atmosphere in Telengana since the end of the Muslim ruler's absolute reign. Up to 1948, every Muslim in the village, however humble his occupation and circumstances, felt himself superior to Hindus and Christians, for he belonged to the religion of the Nizam! In these particular villages there was no persecution of Muslims at the time of Police Action, and there has been no real discrimination against them since. There is a feeling that there is some discrimination in appointments and retirements in the State Government services, but there are still many Muslims in the police and in other government services. In spite of their relatively favourable economic and social position (they live in the caste section of the village), there is a feeling of depression and dissatisfaction among some of the Muslims. They have been removed from their previous privileged position, and they feel that the Hindu majority, especially the landowners and local leaders of the Congress Party, can discriminate against them at any time. Some Muslim officials are afraid of doing their duty lest they offend the powerful Hindus, especially the Congress members of the State Legislature, who have influence with the cabinet ministers of the State Government.

The Muslims do not recognize caste rules, either among themselves or in their relations with caste and outcaste people in the village. They will accept water from anyone, employ outcaste servants within the house, and will eat together with Christians outside the village (when travelling or in the city). In order not to displease the caste Hindus among whom they live, they will not do this in the village. In the two of the five villages where there are Muslims, their relations with Christians have been friendly. The recent election in Kondapuram has brought them closer together—under the Communist banner!

The village Christians in Achampet greet the pastor or evangelist with the word *Jai Christu* (Victory of Christ) which is an adaptation of the nationalist greeting before Independence, *Jai Hind* (Victory to India). They do not use this greeting among themselves or to non-Christians, but only when they meet a pastor or an evangelist. The Christians in the other four villages use the word *Namaskāram* as a respectful greeting to the presbyter or evangelist. To caste Hindus and Muslims they use the Hindi form, *Namaste*. Muslims greet one another (as equals) with the expression *Salaam alekum* and greet respected Muslims with the deferential word *Adaab*.

D. *Economic and Social Changes in the Village*

One major project of the Central and State Governments since Independence has been the introduction and gradual extension of the Community Development Programme. It was started in Telengana in 1952 with what were called 'Community Projects'. Later 'National Extension Service Blocks' were introduced. There are also 'Multi-purpose projects' for tribal areas.

A three-year programme of intensive social and economic development was planned for the villages included in a particular 'block'. It was first intended that after three years, these blocks would enter a 'post-intensive' phase. In April 1958 the system was changed to that of two stages: a first five-year stage and a second stage of indefinite length. The Community Development Projects provide for agriculture, animal husbandry, irrigation, health and rural arts, crafts and industries, and rural housing activities. The Multi-purpose Projects make provision specifically for the work of co-operatives.

The underlying principle in these various projects is that the people should feel that it is their programme, and value it as a practical contribution to their own welfare. The State has therefore directed its efforts to securing the active participation of the people at all levels. Villages are to contribute in cash, kind and labour, and at State, District, and block levels there are to be advisory boards with non-official groups of citizenry represented. The official responsibility for formulating and executing the programme of Community Development is being transferred from the planning agency to the new institutions of democratic local government: the village panchayat, and the bodies representing the panchayats at the Taluq and District level (*Panchayat Samiti* and *Zilla Parishad*, respectively).[3]

At the District headquarters of Ramayampet is a Block Development office, which during this first stage concentrates on the improvement of agriculture. In Stage II it will turn its attention to the development of cottage industries in the villages and small industries in the market towns. This block includes eighty-three villages in three revenue circles. In addition to the Block Development Officer, there are Extension Officers for each of the various departments in the block area—agriculture, co-operation, irrigation, panchayats and animal husbandry; there are Social Education Officers (one man and one woman), Medical Officers (a doctor, Health Visitor, Health Inspector), and twelve village level workers (ten men and two women).

While the loan co-operatives have not generally functioned well since 1952, the co-operatives within the Development Blocks have on the whole made good progress. The objective of these co-operatives is to undertake all the necessary financing of agriculturists for short, medium, and long-term purposes—these would therefore be marketing co-operatives, co-operative credit societies, village industry co-operatives, co-operative farming societies, etc.

In order to become a member of the co-operative society, one has to pay at least Rs. 11, i.e., half a Rs. 20 share and an administration fee of Rs. 1. He may then borrow on the security of his lands up to a maximum of twenty-four times his land revenue if the land is in the block area, or twelve times the land revenue if it is in a non-block area. To belong to a grain bank, each member has to pay into the pool 25 seers of grain as his share, plus 5 seers of grain as membership fee; then he is entitled to borrow up to ten times his land revenue from the grain bank. There are now two Deputy Registrars for Medak District, who sanction loans.[4]

Most Christian families in the villages studied have not yet gained very much from the various programmes of Community Development. They are too poor to pay the membership fee in the co-operative credit societies, and even if they were members, their illiteracy would make it very difficult for them to check on the management or help

to decide policies. Four of the five villages are within a block development area in which it is possible to get loans at a much lower rate of
interest than that which prevails in the village. These *takkāvi* loans
have a 6% interest rate per annum and can be repaid in instalments
over a period of five years. Unfortunately, however, a great many
Christians do not own any land which they could use as security.

Two Christians in Gowlapalli applied for loans to buy new bulls,
and one asked for a loan in order to sink a new well for irrigation. (All
three of these men own some land.) These applications were made to
the village level worker, responsible for nine villages, who passed them
on to the Block Development Officer in Ramayampet. At the time of
our study the applications had not been acted upon. The Block Development Officer did sanction an outright grant to build a parapet wall
around the well of the Christians in Jangarai. Prior to the investigator's
living in these villages and helping Christians with their applications,
no one had realized that they could apply for such benefits, and the
evangelists and presbyter had not considered it part of their responsibility, either to be informed themselves about the new social welfare
legislation, or to help Christians in their applications for grants and
loans.

The State Government has set up a Social Service Department,
particularly for the social and economic uplift of Harijans and other
scheduled castes and tribes. This Department offers financial aid for
purchasing farm land and house sites, buying bullocks, constructing
houses and digging wells. We found that Christians of Harijan origin
were being denied these benefits. When an application for housing aid
was sent to the Social Service Officer, Medak District, by the Christians
in Gowlapalli village, the officer concerned replied, 'With reference
to your application cited above, I have to inform you that there is
no housing-aid provision for Christians, even for the first generation
also'.[5]

Educated Christians consider this policy of the Social Service
Department a discrimination against Christians, which is contrary to
the Indian Constitution. The Constitution in Article XXV (1) grants
religious freedom to all citizens of India, and it declares India to be a
secular state which will give freedom to every religion but favour none.
Article XV expressly forbids the State's discriminating against any
citizen on grounds of caste or religion. On the other hand, some Government leaders justify the exclusion of Christians from the Harijan
Community, and therefore from the benefits accorded to this backward
community, on two grounds. First, by becoming Christians, converts
leave the social structure of Hinduism and are therefore no longer
'outcastes' or 'untouchables'. Second, since Christian converts have
been given education and various aids to improving their material
status by Christian missions, they are not properly in the same category
as non-Christian outcastes. Some government departments follow out
the logic of this second argument by granting Harijan benefits to
converts (sometimes also their children), but not to Christians of the
third generation. Many Hindus do not believe in either of these argu-

ments and see this policy as one of discrimination, but they are divided between those who favour such discrimination and those who oppose it. The continuing poverty and illiteracy of most of the Christians in this area and the continued 'outcaste' stigma attached to them in the eyes of higher caste Hindus undercut both the arguments advanced for excluding them from the category of Harijans.

Some educated Christians, both Indian and foreign, have at times advanced the view that by becoming Christians, converts ceased to be part of the Hindu caste system; they ceased to belong to any particular *kulam*. This theory is at such variance with the continuing sense of caste membership which even educated Christians have, that it has never been taken very seriously, but it has been stated so often by Christian leaders that it is rather embarrassing when Hindus take this theory as a reason to exclude Christians from benefits to Harijans. Even as a theological principle, however, this theory seems very doubtful. It assumes that membership in a caste is like membership in a religious sect, which is dissolved in principle when one joins the Christian community. The caste, however, is far more comparable to an extended family, tribe or nation. It is a 'natural' community into which one is born and from which one can never entirely escape. The theological question should not be whether caste is a reality, but whether this reality can be subordinated and transformed to make possible the greater reality of Christian fellowship.

Christian churches have made repeated efforts to persuade the Government to end economic discrimination against Christians belonging to the outcaste communities. Shortly after the period of our survey, the Andhra Pradesh Government agreed to classify Christian converts from scheduled castes as 'backward classes', entitled to receive grants for education and other purposes. The Education Department has implemented the decision by making 'Harijan scholarships' available to Christians. At that time (1960) the Social Service Department had still not been willing to extend other Harijan benefits to outcaste Christians.

On their own initiative, without application from the Christians, the Social Service Department in 1958 provided two wells for drinking water for the Harijans in Gowlapalli, one for the Malas and the other for the Madigas (Christians). Here the Government did not know that the Madigas were Christians, since their Hindu names are listed in the census. Some Government waste lands have been given free of cost to the Christians in Jangarai, Gowlapalli and Kondapuram, but this was because they wrote their Hindu names in their applications for land.

Three of the big villages in this area (Chandampet, Shankarampet and Wadiaram) have been electrified, and the villagers there were very much excited at this development. When the first 'switch on' ceremony took place, the villagers broke coconuts at the main switch and did puja, so that nothing untoward might happen.

The Government is gradually introducing into all the villages primary education which is both free and compulsory. In all these five villages there are Government one-teacher primary schools which were opened three years before our survey. Christian children are admitted to these schools, which are situated in the caste section of the village, but they are made to sit at a distance from the caste children. The number of Christian children enrolled in these new Government schools was as follows:

Gowlapalli	5
Achampet	4
Jangarai	2
Ambojipet	1
Kondapuram	0

Even the attendance of these few children is sporadic, because the teacher is so often absent. Before June 1959, four of the five teachers lived in other villages where they could obtain better accommodation. The Gowlapalli teacher was the only one to live in the same village. In June 1959, however, a new teacher came to Jangarai and took up residence in the village, with the result that the school now meets regularly. For some time after the panchayat elections in Konda-puram the Government school was closed. Some of the villagers believed the Congress leaders in Medak kept a teacher from being sent in order to 'punish' the village for voting Communist. The village teachers have no headmasters over them and the inspector visits very infrequently (once or twice a year). Only when the village officials take an interest in the schools do the teachers come regularly. Such is the case in Achampet, Gowlapalli, and now in Jangarai, where the officials have provided a house for the teacher as well as for the school. These teachers receive about Rs. 70 a month, a relatively good salary for the village. Some teachers in nearby villages (not included in the survey) augment their income by such occasional pursuits as giving injections and doing electric wiring.

There is no tuition for these Government schools (though some teachers give extra tuition to the same children out of school hours, illegally collecting a fee). Pupils may attend these one-teacher schools for three years and then go to a full-fledged primary school in one of the larger villages for another two years. These villages are from one and a half to four miles away. Here, too, the education is free and Christian children can get aid for buying books and school supplies. The Education Department has for some time considered first and second generation Christians of outcaste background to be eligible for scholarships and other concessions. Since January 1959, it has decided to give this aid to all Christians of Harijan origin who are studying in the middle schools and high schools and colleges. In March 1961 the Government decided to give residential and non-residential scholar-ships to all outcaste Christian children, even those in primary school.

There are no children from these five village congregations in primary schools, nor in any of the three middle schools within ten miles. These middle schools are also free, and Christians of Harijan origin can get help to pay boarding fees, as well as money for books and school supplies. There are also government high schools in the towns of

Medak and Ramayampet (between eight and fifteen miles away from these villages). Here there are fees, but Harijan Christians can gain exemption ('freeship') as well as the other financial aid available from middle schools.

There are Christian teachers in two of the larger villages near the area surveyed (Shankarampet and Chandampet) in which there are no congregations. It has been difficult for them to secure housing in these villages, though they could have done so easily if they had given their Hindu names, as some Christian teachers and other Christian government employees have done elsewhere. Now they have moved their residence from Shankarampet to Ambojipet, where there is a Christian congregation.

One feature of the new political and social situation is the introduction of the national holidays: Independence Day and Republic Day. These holidays are not regarded in the same light as the traditional religious festivals in the smaller villages, and they are therefore not really 'celebrated' by anyone in the village. In the larger villages, however, Hindus observe the new national festivals, but many village Christians think that because they are baptized, they should not do so. They associate Independence with 'sending away the English missionaries'. This is the boast of many Hindu landowners, and Christians feel belittled by that boast. Christians admit that they belong to a 'foreign religion': the religion of the English missionaries. Moreover, the flag-raising ceremony is made into a Hindu act of worship, and while few Christians really object to receiving *bottu* (the mark of blessing on the forehead) they have an uneasy feeling that perhaps they ought to object, and this may lead them to stay away from the flag-raising altogether.

It is interesting to contrast the Christian minority's attitude with that of the Muslims. The latter do not feel themselves foreigners. Many still regard the former Hyderabad State as 'our kingdom which the Hindus have snatched away from us. The backboneless Nizam has surrendered it'. For them the national festivals are festivals of the Hindu rulers, but they join in on these occasions because they believe it politic to please these new rulers.

There is a further fact of importance. Villagers tend to regard the national festivals not as national, but as Congress Party festivals. They call the national flag the 'Congress flag' (the two flags are quite similar and were the same in the period when the Congress Party was leading the fight for independence). Christians know that Congress leaders (village landowners) are not well disposed towards Christians, and this leaves them rather indifferent about the 'Congress flag' and the 'Congress festivals'. The evangelists have generally not been concerned to enlighten members of their congregations about the meaning of the national flag and the national festivals, or to teach them about the positive significance of Indian nationhood.

There are a number of indications in these villages of their increased contact with urban life. Most of the men now buy and wear ready-made shirts. Only a few of the villagers used to wear them, and up to twenty years ago no outcaste man wore a shirt. Now they almost all do. We find women wearing jackets (blouses) instead of *ravikes*, and adopting modern fashions such as using hair clips, face powder, soaps, coconut oil, wearing skirts and bodices under their saris, etc. Most of the villagers use mill yarn cloth. For the first time, people in the villages have taken to drinking coffee and tea, in addition to toddy. A few of the young people go to the cinema in Medak once a week, smoke expensive cigarettes on special occasions, and go to restaurants when they visit cities.

Two Christian young men from Achampet who were educated in mission boarding schools and passed matriculation (end of secondary school) are now employed in government service in Secunderabad. They come back once a year to this village to spend their vacation. They bring with them their new attitudes and new ways of life and share them with their relatives. They send offerings quite regularly year by year to the congregation at Achampet and help the evangelist in his work while they are in the village. Their relatives also visit them now and then. The other Christians in the village try to emulate them and wish that their children might be educated like them. There is more desire on the part of the parents in this congregation than in the other four surveyed to give secular education to their children, and the young men in the congregation are trying to imitate the two educated men who have grown to be clean in their habits and dress.

There is one young man from Ambojipet who is employed in the Railway Workshop in Secunderabad and earns Rs. 90 a month. He comes home to his village every weekend and then goes back to his work in the city. He regularly gives all his salary to his brother at home, who gives him back part of it as pocket money and supplies him with all the necessary rations to take into the city each week. He attends worship services in his village, helps the congregation in its activities and gives his offerings. He does not miss any of the Pastorate Jatras and other special meetings held in Wadiaram. Quite recently he got his son admitted into the Railway Boys' School in the city. Two other families from the same village went to Bodhan twelve years back, and since being employed in the sugar factory, they have settled down there permanently. They seldom come back to their village.

A few families from Kondapuram and Jangarai are employed at the sugar factory in Bodhan as seasonal labourers. They spend part of their time there (between October and May every year) and the rest of the time in their villages. They return to their villages with a considerable amount of money (about Rs. 200) and pay off their debts. Their Christian giving has not increased in proportion to their income. They do not come for prayers, and they encourage others to stay away, speaking lightly of religious matters and persuading the young people to go with them to the cinema in Medak. They show no respect towards the evangelist or the elders and often oppose them. Along with the other Christians they frequently join in the ceremonies during Hindu festivals, but they seem to do so more for the fun of it than because of any fear of the village Hindu deities.

The young men from Achampet and Ambojipet, on the other hand, do not take any part in the Hindu festivals while they are at home. Their education and experience in the city seem to have strengthened their Christian faith and weakened the hold of village Hinduism upon them.

APPENDIX A:

TYPICAL VILLAGE INCOME AND EXPENDITURE

(I)   TYPES OF INCOME

1. *Patta* lands or/and *inam* lands.
2. Daily wages   (*a*)   Men
                   (*b*)   Women
3. *Madiga tanam* (*a*)   Leather work
                   (*b*)   *Dappu* (drumming)
                   (*c*)   Religious festivals: bullock cart Rs. 0.4.0.
                                                   bonam   Rs. 0.1.0.
4. *Vathan: Neerudu* or *Begari.*
5. *Jitam:* monthly salaries.
6. Other economic pursuits.
7. Sale of cattle or lands.

(II)   TYPES OF EXPENDITURE

1. Food: (*a*) Rice ¾ seer for a man per day
                    ½ seer for a woman per day
         (*b*) Curry stuff—Market expenses.
2. Clothing: for men: (*a*) Dhoties   for women: (*a*) Saris
                      (*b*) Shirts   (*b*) Ravike
                      (*c*) Turban
                      (*d*) Blanket
3. Ornaments for women: (*a*) Bangles
                          (*b*) Rings for toes
4. Toilet: soaps and coconut oil.
5. Tobacco: for men and women.
6. Toddy.
7. Betel for women.
8. Life cycle: (*a*)   Delivery
               (*b*)   Purudu
               (*c*)   Coming of age
               (*d*)   Marriage
               (*e*)   Funeral rites and *dinalu*

9. Agricultural operations: (a) *Lagodi*
                                   (b) Seeds
                                   (c) Manure
                                   (d) Land tax
                                   (e) Buying bullocks or he-buffaloes
                                   (f) Forest watchman per plough
                                   (g) *Pullera* —grazing tax per cattle
                                   (h) Workers—carpenter, potter, blacksmith, cowboy, washerman, barber, *neerudu*, *begari, majkuri, thalari, erukali*, etc.

10. Religious festivals.
11. Medicines.
12. Entertaining relatives.
13. Religious priests or professional beggars: (a) *Gurram Malliah*
                                                          (b) *Sindhollu*
                                                       (c) *Dakkali*
                                                     (d) *Mashti*

14. Litigation.
15. Debt.
16. Support of the church: (a) Sunday collection—very few pay—normally 1 cent per family.
                              (b) Family thank-offerings.
                              (c) Harvest: (i) Summer
                                              (ii) Winter

(III) DETAILS

LEATHER WORK (see I, 3 (a))

1. If the Madigas receive skins of dead cattle from others, half of the skin goes to the owner of the cattle, and the other half to the Madiga who receives it. One skin costs between Rs. 8 to Rs. 9 (for a small one) and Rs. 12 to Rs. 15 for a big one.

It costs Rs. 7 to Rs. 8 to cure one hide of a cattle.

2. Some Madigas buy raw skins at Rs. 8 to Rs. 9 a small skin and Rs. 12 to Rs. 15 a big skin.

If the Madiga sells after curing the skin, he will get Rs. 30 per skin.

If he makes articles out of one skin and sells them he will get Rs. 35 per skin.

3. Usually one Madiga can work on 40 skins of cattle a year out of which 10 skins will go as wastage during work. So he will profit on 30 skins a year,

4. One pair of sandals he makes, he sells at Rs. 4 or Rs. 5 per pair.

He sells one *Thondam* (leather used for buckets in irrigation) at Rs. 8 to Rs. 12 according to the size and quality.

He sells one *Baradi* pair (leather straps used for tying bullocks to the yoke) for Rs. 3 to Rs. 6.

5. On the whole one man will earn (profit) Rs. 180 to Rs. 200 a year on leather work apart from other expenses.

Dappu (*Drum beating*) (see I, 3 (b))

1. For each wedding he gets about Rs. 3 to Rs. 4.

2. For each funeral he earns about Rs. 00.25 to Rs. 00.38.

3. For each religious festival where drum beating is needed he gets about Rs. 00.31.

4. For his *Dappu Bicham* he gets about Rs. 50 a year from the agriculturists in the village.

Neerudu Vathan (See I, 4)

One gets as *Neerudu Bicham* from the agriculturists in the village at Rs. 75 per agricultural season at each harvest. That is to say, he earns about Rs. 150 per annum.

Begari Vathan (see I, 4)

1. *Begari* gets his *Bicham* from agriculturists: about half of what the *neerudu* gets, i.e. Rs. 75 per year.
2. At each funeral, he takes the cloth covering the dead person.

AVERAGE EXPENDITURE ON DIFFERENT ITEMS (see II above)

Food

> 1 child between 2–3 years: 1 quarter seer rice a day.
> 1 child between 4–7 years: 2 quarters seer rice a day.
> 1 man needs ¾ seer rice a day.
> 1 woman needs ½ seer rice a day.
> Two persons need for curry stuff, etc.: Rs. 7 per mensem.

Clothing

> *1 man* needs per annum 1 pair of dhoties (Rs. 9) ⎫ 1 blanket, for
> 4 shirts (each shirt costs Rs. 3.8.0), and 2 tur- ⎬ 3 years (costs
> bans (each turban costs Rs. 3). ⎭ Rs. 12 to 18).
> *Children* between 2 – 3 years: 4 shirts and 4 shorts (each shirt
> 6 annas, each pr. shorts 6 annas).
> *Children* between 4 – 7 years: (4 shirts and 4 shorts (each shirt
> 12 annas, each pr. shorts 8 annas).
> 4 frocks for girls at 12 annas each.
> *1 woman* needs 2 saris (1 sari Rs. 9)
> 4 ravikes (each costs 10 or 12 annas) a year.

Ornaments

> Bangles—each woman puts on bangles three times a year, and each time she spends about 6 annas–12 annas. On the whole, one woman needs Rs. 2.8.0 worth of bangles.
> Rings—*Kanchu* rings cost Rs. 1. Each woman needs Rs. 1 worth of rings for toes per year.

Tobacco

> 1 anna per day per man – i.e. Rs. 1.14.0 a month or about Rs. 22.7.0 a year.

Betel

> Each woman needs Rs. 8 to Rs. 12 worth of betel and zarda at 8 annas per month at least.

Coconut oil

> 12 annas a month or Rs. 9 a year (at 3 annas a week).

Soaps

Washing and bathing – 6 soaps a month.
Each soap costs 2 annas or 1 anna.

Toddy

If addicted to daily drinking – each person takes at 4 annas a day
or Rs. 7.8.0 p. m.
When relatives come – Re. 1 worth of toddy for 3 persons.
When heavy work – each man takes 6 annas or 8 annas worth of
toddy.
Festivals – Re. 1 or Rs. 2 worth of toddy for each festival.
Average – Rs. 2 to Rs. 4 per month per family which is not habituated
to drink daily.

Life cycle

Delivery—for washerman: Rs. 1.4.0 gift plus Rs. 1 toddy plus Re.1
worth of rice if a girl is born and Rs. 2 worth of rice
if a boy is born.
for midwife: 1 ravike plus feeding her for a week plus
6 annas toddy on third day and 6 annas toddy on
twenty-first day.
for sweet oil for the baby – at 2 annas a week.
Purudu —Naming ceremony Rs. 20.
Sāre expenses incurred by the parents of the girl for the
first delivery:
Sari and ravike to the girl,
Shirt and turban to the son-in-law,
Shirt and cap to the baby.
For the subsequent confinements, the parents of the girl
give only ravike to the girl and shirt to the baby.
Coming of age—to washerman: 1 pair of sandals.
barsala: food and drink Rs. 35 rice ⎫
Rs. 10 toddy ⎬ Rs. 60.
Rs. 15 goat ⎭
Gifts (sarelu) by the parents—*Sāre* expenses incurred by the parents
of the girl: 1 Sari, 5 ravikes, 5 coco-
nuts, 5 seers of rice, 5 garlic,
5 turmerics, 2 shirts, 1 chella and
1 dhoti to son-in-law, *odi biyyam*
to the daughter and son-in-law.
Marriage—Rs. 300 each marriage for the boy and Rs. 150 for the
girls' parents.
Funeral rites—Rs. 30 to Rs. 50 including *dinalu* (memorial feasts).

Medicines

Serious illness	Rs. 100
Ordinary illness	Rs. 50
Small illness	Rs. 10 or Rs. 20
	Rs. 20–Rs. 50 a year per family.

Barber

He does not touch or shave the outcastes, so the barber gives razor –
for each 'head' Rs. 2 a year.
Each crop – 4 annas (two months a crop, i.e. 6 crops a year).

Washerman

    Whitewashes the house for weddings or festivals.

    Washes clothes at 2 addas per man and 5 addas per woman in the family.

    Each family should pay Rs. 4 to Rs. 6 a year to the washerman (8 to 12 addas of paddy a year).

Potter

    Supplies pots. Each family to pay 8 to 10 addas of paddy a year, i.e. Rs. 5 a year.

Festivals

    For each festival Rs. 2 to 5 per family.

Priests

    Gurram Malliah Rs. 1.8.0 per family for 3 years because he visits Malas once in three years.

    For Madigas
        Dakkali comes once a year as .3 per family.
        Sindhollu comes once in three years Rs. 1.8.0 per family.
        Mashti comes once in three years – Re. 1 per family.

    Average about Rs. 2 per year per family.

Agriculture

    Lagodi: quarter of the produce goes for *lagodi*.

    If they borrow grain 10 *thumulu* at Rs. 15 per *thumu*, they have to pay back at the harvest Rs. 10 per *thumu*, or pay back 15 *thumulu* Land Tax.

    Artificial manure—at Rs. 45 per bag per acre.

    Pullera—Pasture at 4 annas 'per tail'.

    Forest watchman—Rs. 2 per annum.

    Cowboy—at Re. 1 per pair of cattle per month.

Village artisans

    Carpenter   4 addas per acre and 4 bundles of paddy sheaves.
    Blacksmith   4 addas per acre and 4 bundles of paddy sheaves.

Village menials

    Potter 4 addas plus 1 bundle.
    Barber 4 addas.
    Washerman 4 addas.
    Neerudu 4 addas plus 1 bundle of paddy sheaves.

Thalari	2 addas	,,	,,	,,	,,
Begari	2 addas	,,	,,	,,	,,
Majkuri	4 addas	,,	,,	,,	,,
Madiga	2 addas	,,	,,	,,	,,

Others

    Fakir   2 addas (it is called 'molla bicham').
    Erukali   4 addas (supplies baskets, thadakas).
    Medari   1 addas (supplies winnowing fans, grain storing baskets).
    Kolpula   1 addas.
    Potharaju 1 addas.

    The above payments are made by the farmers at each harvest and they are their perquisites.

Professional beggars

  For Malas *Gurram Malliah*
       Mala Mashti
  For Madigas Nulka Sandayya
       Sindhollu
       Dakkali
       Mashti

(IV) SUMMARY OF FAMILY BUDGETS

Achampet

 1. Zuloori Shantamma (widow)—family of 3 (2)
  Income   322.0.0
  Expenditure 715.5.0 (250 covered by loan)
 2. Boda Benjamin—family of 8
  Income   1,086.0.0
  Expenditure 2,070.6.0

S. Kondapuram

 1. Legala Reuben—family of 6
  Income   1,014.0.0
  Expenditure 1,184.14.0 (170.14.0 covered by loan)
 2. Thudumu Elia—family of 5
  Income   393.0.0
  Expenditure 859.2.0

Gowlapalli

 1. Bhupala Swamidass—family of 2
  Income   465.0.0
  Expenditure 501.15.0
 2. Konka Yesudass—family of 2
  Income   327.8.0
  Expenditure 564.12.0

Ambojipet

 1. Malga Yesudass—family of 5
  Income   828.8.0
  Expenditure 1,281.11.0
 2. Narayana Paul—family of 5
  Income   870.0.0
  Expenditure 1,310.7.0 (including debt of 150—is this interest?)
       Wedding Expenses in a previous year Rs. 550.

Jangarai

 1. Chinnangolla Jacob—family of 5
  Income   375.0.0
  Expenditure 555.2.0
 1. Chinnangolla Devadass—family of 5
  Income   535.0.0
  Expenditure 1,469.0.0

APPENDIX B: DIVORCE

Village people accept the permanence of the marriage tie as a general principle, and do not approve of divorces taking place just because of quarrels. When adultery is suspected by a few and gives rise to gossip, the friends and relatives of the people involved (especially of the woman) do their utmost to hush the scandal, in order to avoid the necessity of divorce. This village disapproval of divorce is shared by Christians.

In actual practice, however, there are difficulties which sometimes lead to a divorce. Many times quarrels arise between husband and wife over the children or over the wife's treatment by her mother-in-law. Behind these quarrels is often a lack of understanding, love and trust between husband and wife. The husband or his family sometimes suspects the wife of mixing poison in the food or medicine she gives him. Sometimes a wife leaves her husband temporarily because of his harsh treatment; after her grievances are redressed in a local panchayat she returns. Sometimes a wife leaves her husband because she has become involved in sexual relations with another man, in that same village or in her parents' village. She may leave her husband for brief periods and then return, or she may leave permanently. In some cases a divorce is arranged by the wife's parents, who want her to return home and contribute to the family income.

Serious marital difficulties, domestic quarrels, and all divorces are dealt with in the caste councils. If it is the wife who wishes the divorce, or if she is judged the guilty party, she (or the man who marries her after the divorce) must pay her husband a fixed amount. (In the villages studied, this was Rs. 150, but it varies somewhat from place to place.) If, on the other hand, it is the husband who wishes the divorce (or is adjudged guilty), he must pay his wife a slightly larger compensation than she would pay him (Rs. 200 in these villages). Both husband and wife are free to marry again. The fine or compensation is often used for the expense of remarriage.

According to the rules of the Church of South India and the Indian Christian Marriage Act of the Indian Government, these divorces are illegal, since divorces should be obtained in a civil court. However, because village Christians are poor and ignorant of these rules, they do not go to law courts to procure legal divorce certificates. The Church is then faced with the problem of people who regard themselves as divorced by the caste court, but whom the presbyter may not remarry because their divorce is not legally valid. There are now a number of such divorced persons in the congregations surveyed. In the Methodist Church in Hyderabad State before the establishing of the Church of South India, the Church was authorized by the Nizam's Government to have divorce cases heard by a minister in a church panchayat, and divorces might finally be granted by the District Chairman. This is no longer possible in the present situation, with the result that, in divorce as well as in marriage, the village Christians follow village mores which are considered illegal by both Church and State.

CHAPTER 6

The Ministry and Lay Leadership

A. *Types of Leadership in the Church*

The official view of the Church's leadership would divide it into the two categories of clerical and lay, or the ordained ministry of bishop, presbyters and deacons, on the one hand, and the lay ministry of paid and voluntary church workers, on the other. The evangelist or catechist (*pantulu*) is considered a layman, not only in the negative sense that he is not allowed to celebrate Holy Communion or perform marriages, but also in the positive sense that he is eligible for election as one of the lay representatives to the Diocesan Council.

From the standpoint of the village congregation, however, the evangelist is not one of the people (*laos*) but the paid representative of the 'Mission' or the Diocese. He is stationed in the congregation by the decision of the presbyter, who after a few years may and frequently does transfer him to another village. The evangelist and his wife are outsiders, and they sometimes belong to a different caste from that of all the members of the congregation. Within the local membership there are different kinds of leaders: some traditional caste officials; some distinguished by special training to which they have been sent by the evangelist; and some informal leaders of opinion respected for their shrewd judgment, their influential connexions with powerful families of the village, or possibly heeded because of their youthful vigour and enthusiasm. In terms of the official functioning of the congregation, the 'paid lay leadership' of the evangelist and his wife has overshadowed the voluntary leadership of other members of the congregation. The Diocese has been concerned with the relative weakness of 'lay leadership' and has taken certain steps to remedy this weakness. Both the situation existing at the time of our survey in 1959, and the recent efforts to change that situation, will be dealt with in this chapter.

B. *Evangelists*

During the famine years from 1897 to 1900, hundreds of orphaned and homeless children were saved from death by being taken into the various boarding schools of the Hyderabad Methodist District. It was from this group of school-children that the first evangelists were selected. After a short period of training in Medak, they were sent to the many new congregations in the villages. The process of taking the brightest children from the village congregations into the boarding schools continued after the famine. While this policy ensured a supply of evangelists, it took many of the most intelligent children away from their congregations.

The District aimed to station one evangelist and his wife in each village where a Christian congregation was established. When there was an urgent need for more evangelists because of the rapid rise in the number of congregations, the District adopted the scheme of 'combing out' the village congregations in search of village Christian youths who had attended the evangelist's school in the village and learned enough to read and to understand the Bible. Some of the most promising of these young men were sent immediately into the villages as 'emergency evangelists', while the others were sent to Medak for further training before going to the villages.

The importance of the evangelist's wife has long been recognized, since women in the village have been considered to be most deeply attached to the traditional domestic and family observances, and hence the most difficult group in the congregation to persuade to follow Christian practices. To enable them to exercise a Christian influence on the village women, the wives of evangelists were given some training, either before or after marriage. Experienced women missionaries and senior Indian women taught them how to preach, teach, nurse the sick, do the housekeeping, and set an example of Christian living to other Christians and the rest of the village. The evangelist's family is in some respects the centre of the Christian community, and the evangelist and/or his wife may be called on for help when there is any trouble in the larger 'family'. Whether there be domestic quarrels, marital infidelities, sickness, or other trouble, the evangelist and his wife are called in and expected to know what to do.

Until 1940 there were three grades of evangelists:

'A' grade—those who studied in mission boarding schools up to the third form;

'B' grade—those who studied in mission boarding schools up to the fourth standard; and

'C' grade or 'Emergency'—those taken straight from village schools.

All the evangelists had a three-year course at the Medak Training School, the syllabus varying according to their previous education (see Appendix A). At the end of the course, the students would relate their call and Christian experience, and would be presented with a Bible and a hymn-book, as well as with their certificates, at a special valedictory service. They were then stationed in the villages, first for three years on probation and thereafter as regular evangelists.

From 1910 to 1916, when there were many in the villages asking to become Christians, the District followed the policy of refusing to baptize a village group until it could provide an evangelist who would continue to live in that village after the congregation was founded. In the years up to 1940 a few evangelists were put in charge of two or three congregations, but almost every congregation had its own resident evangelist. After 1940, however, the number of evangelists

E

and new candidates for training decreased. In the two years prior to our survey in 1959 there were no new candidates.

In addition to pastoral care and preaching, the evangelist and his wife are expected to teach a day school and a night school, with the primary purpose of teaching Christians and any others interested how to read the Bible. The evangelist is to instruct the congregation in the fundamentals of Christian faith, conduct Christian worship, maintain church discipline and encourage giving.

In 1914 an order of 'Superintending Evangelists' was established to assist the presbyter by taking charge of a 'section'; viz., five to ten congregations. They are selected from among the evangelists who have proved themselves through many years of experience. The superintending evangelist, like the other evangelists, is directly responsible for two or three villages, but in addition is supposed to visit all the other congregations in the section regularly and to assist the presbyter in his visits to the section. Many of the 'S.E.s' actually tour very little, but the S.E. of one of the other sections in the Wadiaram Pastorate manages to visit each of his eight congregations twice a month. To do this he has to be away from his own village half of each week, during which time he leaves his own congregation in the charge of his wife.

Because of the marked decrease in the number of evangelists since 1940, each evangelist is assigned two or three congregations. In principle, he is just as responsible for the Christians in the other villages as for those in the village where he lives, but in practice most evangelists pay very few visits to their 'second village' congregations. The result of this neglect in the Jangarai section was indicated in Chapter 4. There are a few evangelists who do take seriously their responsibilities to their other congregations. One man in the southern section had for a time been in charge of five congregations, four in other villages. He told us that he spent one day a week in each of the other four villages, returning home every night. (Two of the villages were one mile away; the other two were three miles away.) The remaining three days he spent in his own village. The evangelist said that he left much of the work with his own congregation to his wife. Such regular visitation of 'second village' congregations is quite exceptional.

In order to remedy the neglect of the congregations without a resident evangelist, the 'New Pattern' of work in the Diocese included the provision that all the evangelists in a section should consider *all* the congregations in the section as their joint responsibility. A report to the Medak Diocesan Council in 1957 confirms our own findings in the Jangarai Section that no change in the evangelist's methods or attitudes has yet occurred:

> When the new pattern was inaugurated, we envisaged a system according to which paid workers in each section of a pastorate would work together as a team taking the whole section as its sphere of work. Though in a few pastorates this may be in operation, on the whole in most of the pastorates each worker is still under the impression that he is responsible for his own and perhaps another additional village, and each S.E. still

thinks that he is responsible for the few villages in his section in which there are paid workers.[1]

Even within their own villages the evangelists are not doing all that the presbyters and the Diocese expect of them. Reference has already been made to the irregular meeting of the primary schools. The teaching, preaching and pastoral care of the evangelists suffer from a number of handicaps that will be discussed more in detail later in the chapter: spending time in other work to supplement a meagre income, inability to teach and preach effectively in the time that is available, inability or unwillingness to develop and utilize lay leadership, and failure to develop effective teamwork with other evangelists and the presbyter, for mutual encouragement and better tackling of common problems. The evangelists of a section do meet occasionally and sometimes they go together to visit villages where there are no Christians. They also sometimes gather when the presbyter visits the section. Once a month all the evangelists go to the Pastorate headquarters for a monthly meeting, sometimes called the 'Agents' Meeting'. They turn in the offerings they have received, receive their salaries, and report on the work they have done during the previous month. In the Wadiaram Pastorate the evangelists normally arrive in the evening and stay overnight. The next morning they begin with a communion service and then hold a business meeting. They are finished by noon and able to return to their village that afternoon.

Even an ineffective evangelist can be of great significance for a village congregation, simply by the fact of his living there. This quickly comes to light when the question arises of transferring the evangelist to another village. The evangelist's family is expected to set an example to other families in the congregation and very often does so, but there have been cases where evangelists' families have shown the same failings that so often are evidenced in their congregations: abusive language, quarrels between husband and wife, or marital infidelity.

Evangelists' families seem to be frequently neglecting their private devotions, and little literature is available to encourage and stimulate them. For some time they have used the Telugu edition of *The Upper Room*, a manual of daily devotions issued once a quarter. Every year they gather in a summer school for the renewal of the spiritual life, and they take a yearly examination on an assigned book of the Bible. This examination is intended to encourage them to undertake regular Bible study throughout the year, but in practice many evangelists prepare for the examination at the last moment.

C. *The Present Plight of the Evangelist*

At the time of our survey in 1959, the evangelists in the Jangarai section seemed to be in the midst of a severe crisis of morale. The immediate manifestations of the evangelists' plight were economic, but behind these were other indications of the evangelists' inability to cope with a rapidly changing situation in the Church and in society at large.

Until about 1940 the evangelist's salary made him relatively better off than most of the members of his congregation, and this salary was guaranteed from the 'Indian Agency' of the Methodist Missionary Society. While 'self-support' was held up as an ideal, both the evangelist and his congregation were convinced that the evangelist's salary would continue to be paid even if the congregation contributed practically nothing to his support. Although goals of local giving were set, they were so low that the evangelists could easily make up the difference themselves between the expected figure and what they actually received.

However, the years of the Second World War brought more inflation than salary adjustments could keep pace with, so that the evangelist was no longer richer than most of his congregation. Moreover, after the inauguration of the Church of South India in 1947, two related developments took place which greatly aggravated the evangelist's financial state. The New Pattern of church life envisaged a progressive increase in local giving, the training and utilizing of a nucleus of lay leaders in each village congregation, and the eventual transfer of many of the evangelists into previously unevangelized areas to work in new congregations or among new inquirers. At the same time that the Diocese decided it should reduce its dependence on foreign funds, the Methodist Missionary Society in Britain decided it should divert part of its funds from well-established mission fields to newer work in such places as Kenya. To accomplish these ends, it was agreed that there should be a phased reduction in the amount of funds made available to the Diocese for continuing existing work.

By 1959 the local contribution expected from each pastorate amounted to three and a half months of the annual payroll for that pastorate (i.e. salaries of the presbyter and evangelists, and items for repairs of church property and other expenses). In most pastorates the required amount was deducted from the monthly pay of the evangelists in lieu of their turning in the offerings they had received. This practice of assessing contributions from the congregations for which the evangelist is responsible goes back many years, but the amount assessed was now much larger, and the evangelists had been told it would continue to increase. In theory the emphasis on stewardship in the New Pattern would result in at least a comparable increase in the offerings of each congregation, but in practice the increase fell far short of meeting the assessment. In the Wadiaram Pastorate, the amount assessed was almost twice the average amount the evangelist received in 'collections', so that on the average the evangelist had to pay half the amount himself. Since the amount assessed from each evangelist was usually the same, an even greater strain was placed on the junior evangelists receiving a lower salary. Moreover, there is considerable difference in both the ability and willingness to give of different congregations; the unfortunate evangelist with a congregation accustomed to giving very little had to meet most of the assessment out of his own meagre salary. Far from stimulating the less competent or less experienced evangelist to persuade his congregation to increase their offerings, it seemed to reduce him to a state of acute anxiety and despair, in which he did no effective work and developed a strong sense of resentment against the presbyter and all the evangelists with higher salaries and more generous congregations.

Many evangelists have tried to meet their financial crisis by supplementing their income in various ways, all of which are irregular as far as the Diocese is concerned, since both the evangelist and his wife are supposed to devote all their time to the care of their congregations, and they are not allowed to earn additional income through any other work. (Evangelists who retire at 60 rather than 65, called 'active supernumeraries', are paid a small pension plus half the regular salary, and they are allowed to earn money through part-time work.) Some of the types of work by which the evangelist and his wife earn additional funds are the following: farming their own plots of land or working as day labourers for a landowner; giving injections and dispensing medicine; midwifery (the evangelist's wife) and delivering calves and other veterinary duties (the evangelist), making beedi leaves (country cigarettes), selling broomsticks, and writing applications to the Government for illiterates (charging Rs. 1.25 for each application). Some evangelists fall back on help from relatives, and many borrow money, so that they become as deeply in debt as many of the members of their congregations.

A few months after our survey, in February 1960, the 'contract system' of fixed assessments was abolished, following a visit to the Medak Diocese by the Rev. Donald B. Childe, Secretary of the Methodist Missionary Society. Evangelists were asked to turn over to the presbyter only as much as they received, and the M.M.S. provided a special 'cushion' fund to absorb the difference between the percentage of self-support attempted and the actual amount received in offerings. Moreover, in January 1961 both presbyters and evangelists began to receive a dearness allowance of Rs. 12 per month, made possible by another special M.M.S. grant. The financial situation of the evangelists was further improved by the increasing availability of Government scholarships for their children, as 'Christians of Harijan origin'; if no Government scholarship were obtained, the Diocese agreed to pay half the school fees.

These improvements in the evangelists' economic situation have improved their morale, but they have not touched the more fundamental aspects of the evangelists' plight. One way to express that plight is to point to the evangelist's ambiguous position: he is neither a recognized 'clergyman' nor a real 'layman'. The Telugu term *pantulu* suggests that he is primarily a teacher; in many areas he is quite ineffective as a teacher, and the coming of Government schools makes this role more questionable. In most cases he is definitely not an 'evangelist', since he is concerned with the nurture of the congregation rather than the proclamation of the Gospel outside the congregation. He functions as a pastor, but the Church has been unwilling to ordain him, because of his low educational attainments; sometimes he is sent for further training and eventually ordained, but then he is no longer the pastor of one or more congregations, but the supervisor of a number of evangelists shepherding a still larger number of village congregations. We might say that the pastors of the congregations are not ordained ministers, and the ordained ministers are only to a very limited extent pastors.

At a time when educational standards are generally being raised, the desirability of maintaining a corps of evangelists with less than a secondary education has been seriously questioned in the Diocese. Indeed, it was decided in 1958 not to admit for training any more men who had not matriculated; but the result of raising the admission standards was that no qualified men applied. For the school year 1961–62 the requirements were temporarily lowered to those who had passed at least the eighth standard, and a few men enrolled. There are apparently very few young men with sufficient education to go into some other occupation who feel attracted to or challenged by the vocation of evangelist. Many church leaders would be happy to see the place of the evangelists gradually taken by the VCWs (Voluntary Church Workers). At the time of our survey in 1959 too few VCW's had been trained to make any significant number of replacements. More important, however, the actual functioning of the few laymen who have been trained and the vast size of the pastorates gives little hope that a combination of the VCW's and the presbyter will solve the problem of pastoral care. We shall return to this problem in later sections of this chapter.

Part of the present uncertainty and lack of enthusiasm on the part of many evangelists stems from the extent to which material considerations have influenced the vocational decisions of evangelists in the past. It is true that all candidates were interviewed during their final year of training and asked to relate their call to Christian service, and many were motivated by an experience of Christ's contrasting love, yet many were undoubtedly motivated by the fact that until 1940 the position of evangelist was the most attractive and secure job they could obtain with the education available to them at mission expense. An evangelist was qualified to attempt the examination that would give him a Government normal training certificate, and after a few years' service as an evangelist, he could seek employment at a higher salary in the Government schools. After the order of 'pastors' was initiated, there was a chance for a junior evangelist to be promoted to the post of superintending evangelist (from 'little' *pantulu* to 'big' *pantulu*), and after that, if he were one of the fortunate few, to the position of 'pastor'. Each promotion brought with it a significant increase in salary and social status. Being an evangelist also made it possible to educate one's children at very low cost in mission schools, often with the hope that the children would later be able to secure better paying jobs in the cities. In more recent years the financial attractions of becoming an evangelist have markedly decreased, but this has not lessened the motive of securing the best possible employment. In the recent past, however, some of those who have tried to find a better paying job have turned to the evangelists' training as a last resort. In this respect, the

Church is affected by the general Indian problem of the 'educated unemployed': a rapidly increasing number are going to school in the expectation of securing much better jobs than their fathers have, but they actually go into a society with a very limited number and type of such 'better jobs'.

The fact that the position of evangelist is no longer considered a desirable avenue to personal and family advancement is one reason why so few Christian young men seek to prepare themselves for this work and why the present evangelists lack satisfaction in their work, but there is also another important reason: the increasing sense that the position of evangelist lacks dignity. To some extent this is the result of the lack of any ecclesiastical status beyond that of 'paid lay worker', and the fear that even this status is not assured for the rest of their lives. Apart from the talk of discontinuing the post of evangelist altogether, there is the policy of increasing self-support (which remains in effect even though the progressive reductions of the M.M.S. grant have been temporarily suspended). It is simply inconceivable to many of the evangelists that their congregations would contribute enough to support them. One evangelist quoted approvingly the opinion of the New Pattern he had heard from a presbyter: 'This *guri* (aim) of raising collections is our *uri* (hanging).' There is an obvious insecurity about their future; if they are not paid to be evangelists, what other kind of work could they find above the labour of the uneducated villager? The insecurity is made worse, however, by the lack of dignity evangelists feel in their present status. This often means, in particular, the *indignity* which they feel in the way they are treated by their superiors, the superintending evangelist and the presbyter.

The S.E. is the presbyters' representative in the section; he is expected to report to the presbyter on the work and conduct of the junior evangelists, and all their requests to the presbyter should go through him. While there are instances in which the S.E. has served as a helpful counsellor to the other evangelists, he often seems more eager to exercise his authority over them than to help them through regular visits. The evangelists suspect that the S.E.'s reports to the presbyter may be coloured by his desire to please the presbyter and be recommended for the training leading to ordination as deacon. Moreover, they are jealous of the S.E.'s role in arranging for repairs to their houses, often suspecting the S.E. of collusion with the presbyter in the misappropriation of some of the funds budgeted for these repairs.

The evangelists consider the presbyter to have almost absolute control over them, for he can recommend that they be promoted, transferred, disciplined or even dismissed, and his recommendations are usually accepted by the District Church Council or the Diocese. They consider it prudent, therefore, to try to please the presbyter and do his bidding. This attitude on their part adds to the presbyter's temptation to order them around like servants, rather than work with them as colleagues. Such servile obedience, however, is not genuine loyalty or affection; indeed the evangelists often regard the presbyter with much bitterness and suspicion. The presbyter generally does not show the evangelists the full accounts of the pastorate, either how much he is receiving from the village congregations through the evangelists, or how he is spending the funds for building repairs and other local expenses. Presbyters are supposed to show their accounts to the pastorate finance committee, but in most rural pastorates this committee actually does not exist.

The master–servant relationship is a familiar pattern in traditional society, and it is not surprising that it should characterize the relations between the evangelists and their ecclesiastical superiors, but there are several factors in the present situation which make the evangelists increasingly unhappy and restive.

The evangelists share the sentiment of their congregations that in the new independent India, with its democratic Government, the traditional master–servant relationship should no longer be tolerated. The Christians who work for a landowner may not be able to do very much about his imperious attitude, but they certainly resent it, and if some practical form of protest is available, they seize upon it, as they did in the panchayat board elections. Likewise, the evangelists resent being ordered about by the presbyters, even though they may obey the orders given; some evangelists complain that the presbyters behave as though they were living twenty years ago, before Independence, in the way they try to keep the evangelists under their thumb. The evangelists certainly acknowledge that there are some presbyters who are very kind and considerate; they treat them as a loving father treats his children; but there is none, they say, who treats them like a brother.

The other reasons for tension have already been alluded to; they arise from the contemporary situation of the Church. The decreasing proportion of mission subsidy has increased the presbyter's pressure on the evangelists to gather more in 'collections', while at the same time the efforts of the Diocese to encourage voluntary church workers to assist and possibly replace the evangelists lead the presbyter to recognize and honour the voluntary laymen, and to ignore or denigrate the one who has been regarded as the head of the congregation for the last two or three generations: the evangelist.

These various factors tend to reinforce one another in producing a situation of tension and mutual misunderstanding. That situation is further aggravated by the relatively infrequent contacts between the presbyter and the evangelists, especially the infrequent visits of the presbyter to many of the village congregations. We shall look at this problem more directly in the next section.

D. *The Ordained Ministry*: *Presbyters and Deacons*

From the beginning of its work in Hyderabad, the Methodist Missionary Society aimed at the cultivation and training of Indian ministers with the same advanced level of theological training and the same status in the Church as the missionaries from England. Therefore likely candidates capable of higher education and ministerial training were carefully selected from the mission boarding schools, especially the Normal Training School at Medak and Wesley Boys' High School at Secunderabad. The students usually were not sent to do a B.A., but after a period of theological training went as evangelists to the village for a year or more in order to gain practical experience. Those selected for B.D. training were sent to the United Theological College in Bangalore. At the end of the first year they took the qualifying examination which they had to pass in lieu of a B.A.; after that came the three-year course leading to the B.D. At the United Theological College many of them met for the first time students and faculty from other denominations and language areas, especially of South India.

After receiving the B.D., they worked as assistant ministers under the guidance of a senior minister, remaining on probation for four years. During this period they had to preach a trial sermon and write examinations on prescribed books each year, and in general prove that they were worthy of ordination to such a high calling. After this period of probation they were made 'superintendents' in full charge of a circuit or pastorate.

As the Church grew in numbers and extent, many new circuits had to be formed. There were not enough ministers to serve as superintendents of all the circuits, so it was impossible to provide an ordained man to administer Holy Communion in the village congregations of each circuit. To meet the situation produced by such rapid expansion, the District introduced a new category below the minister called 'pastors'. Men of the highest integrity, long experience and outstanding abilities among the superintending evangelists were given a licence to administer the sacraments.

The Church Order of the Church of South India had no provision for such a category of 'pastors', so the pastors were given a year's additional theological training at the Andhra Union Theological College in Dornakal and were subsequently ordained as presbyters. However, the C.S.I. makes provision for ordained deacons, and the Medak Diocese has been ordaining some superintending evangelists each year as deacons, after a year's course at the A.U.T.C. in Dornakal. (In 1959, this course was shifted to Medak.) Deacons may be ordained as presbyters two years after their ordination. Deacons are put in charge of one section in a Pastorate, and are also expected to help the presbyter with his work in the other sections. They are allowed to baptize, to solemnize marriages, and to assist the presbyter in the celebration of the Lord's Supper.

An ordained presbyter who is not yet given full responsibility for his pastorate, but works under the supervision of a more senior presbyter, is known in the Diocese as an 'Assistant Presbyter'. Presbyters in charge of or supervising one or more pastorates are designated as 'Presbyters-in-Charge'. There are three grades of salary among the ordained Indian ministers. 'Presbyters-in-Charge' who have had a full theological training in a theological college, as well as presbyters with university secular degrees, are put on the first scale, 'Assistant Presbyters' on the second, and 'Deacons' on the third. In 1959 the starting salaries per month were as follows:

	Starting basic salary	Travel grant	Helper's allowance
First	Rs. 95	Rs. 22	Rs. 30
Second	Rs. 80	Rs. 18	Rs. 30
Third	Rs. 60	Rs. 18	—

In addition, they receive children's allowances like the evangelists. All the presbyters' and deacons' wives are supposed to give honorary service to the Church. Some of them are highly educated, for the Hyderabad Methodist District emphasized the importance of ministers having educated wives. Whatever their educational qualifications, they are not supposed to take up other work. They are expected to help their husbands and to take the lead in developing the women's work in the pastorate. They are given travel grants from the Women's Fellowship Fund for their touring in the villages, whether with or without their husbands.

The special function of presbyters and deacons in the Church of South India is to preach the word of God and to administer the Sacraments. They are responsible for both the pastoral and the evangelistic work of the pastorate or pastorates entrusted to their charge. In most of the rural pastorates the presbyter is responsible for about thirty village congregations, and has the assistance of eight to twelve evangelists. The presbyter is expected to visit these congregations as often as possible. Usually he goes to a village one afternoon, visits some of the families in the congregation, and after dinner conducts a worship service that includes a sermon and the celebration of Holy Communion. This is a long service, usually lasting from two to three hours. If there are any baptisms to be performed, they are also included in this same service. The next morning the presbyter leaves for another village or goes back home.

The presbyter is unable to get well acquainted with the congregation on such brief visits, but he rarely finds it possible to stay longer. In earlier years missionaries and ministers would sometimes camp in a village for several days, and the Diocese still owns tents that can be used for this purpose. The presbyter does not feel he can spend longer in any one congregation when he has so many others to visit, as well as much paper work awaiting him at home in the pastorate headquarters. It is probably also true, however, that presbyters are discouraged from staying longer than the minimum time in the villages by the lack of the kind of accommodation to which they have grown accustomed from years of urban living. One important consideration is the lack of any toilet facilities in the evangelists' houses. The various inconveniences of village living seem to affect not only the length but also the frequency of the presbyter's visits. At the time of our survey in the Jangarai section, the presbyter managed only three or four visits a year to the congregations with a resident evangelist, and virtually none to the congregations without. If this were typical, it would mean that the presbyter spent less than 50 days a year visiting the village congregations. Undoubtedly there were more accessible congregations in other sections that were visited more frequently, and there are certainly many pastorates where the presbyter spends much more of his time touring in the villages, but the picture of brief and relatively infrequent visits by the presbyter is not peculiar to the Wadiaram Pastorate, and it has much to do with the inadequacies of Christian teaching and pastoral care that characterize the congregations studied.

The presbyter is also with the evangelists during the monthly meeting at the pastorate headquarters, and he has some other contacts with the evangelists and some members of the village congregations through the various special meetings and training courses at the pastorate head-quarters. Sometimes village Christians make the trip into the pastorate headquarters to see the presbyter about some problem.

The presbyter is directly responsible for the congregation in the village or town where he is living. In Wadiaram village there is no local group of converts to Christianity, and there are only a few Christians who have moved into the village because it is the headquarters of the pastorate. In other pastorates located in larger towns, the care of the town congregation absorbs much of the presbyter's time.

In rural pastorates like Wadiaram the presbyter is in sole charge of the finances of the pastorate. Keeping account books, looking after church property, and keeping detailed church records require him to spend much of his time in his office. In a town pastorate, educated laymen can perform some of these duties and can share the responsibility for management of the pastorate finances, but the presbyters shoulder this task alone. Some of the presbyters who were ordained after Church Union from the ranks of the evangelists have not had training in bookkeeping. They find it difficult to keep the books without making mistakes, and sometimes hire the aid of the accountants in mission institutions.

The Medak Diocese has many committees, each with a large member-ship. Travel to the place where the committee is to meet and attendance at the meetings take much of the time of many of the presbyters, especially the more senior ones, and this further reduces the time they have available for visiting village congregations. The presbyters who are serving as chairmen of the District Church Councils spend a very large proportion of their time in committee work. While they hold this office, therefore, they are usually given the help of an extra assistant presbyter or deacon. Such assistance makes possible more visitation of the villages by an ordained minister, but they are in some respects an inadequate substitute for the frequent presence and guidance of the senior presbyter in the village congregations.

Special problems arise for pastorates under the care of an 'assistant presbyter' subordinate to an 'absentee superintendent' who lives in another pastorate or at the diocesan headquarters. The superintending presbyter is in charge of the finances, and sometimes is unwilling to share much of this responsibility with the assistant presbyter resident in the pastorate. The superintendent decides how many congregations he will visit himself and how often. The superintendents regularly come for the monthly 'Agents' Meeting' of the evangelists. The experience of the superintendent can be of great help to the assistant presbyter, but if the senior presbyter is very critical, the junior man is likely to become resentful and discouraged. Moreover, the assistant presbyter does not have much authority in the eyes of the evangelists, as long as they know that there is a man above him. The evangelists sometimes go to the 'absentee superintendent' with complaints against the assistant presbyter. Control of finances is frequently a sore point between the two men. If the superintendent insists on keeping complete control himself, the assistant presbyter may be suspicious of his motives. On the other hand, the senior man often feels that the assistant presbyter is not ready to assume such a large financial responsibility. The resident presbyter sometimes feels at the mercy of his supervisor, for the superintendent has to submit a report on his work at the end of the year, and that might affect his next stationing.

A somewhat different problem of teamwork and personal relationship occurs when an evangelist who has been ordained as a deacon resumes his work in a rural pastorate. Such a deacon often feels that he is now above the level of the evangelists, yet he may not be altogether accepted as an equal by the presbyter. Many senior presbyters feel that the deacons are actually doing less than they did as superintending evangelists; they think they are equal to the senior presbyters, and should spend their time ordering evangelists around. Some deacons have a tendency to side with the evangelists against the presbyter, or vice versa, according to the way in which they are treated by the presbyter. On the other hand, some of the deacons remain quite humble after ordination, take up their work with even greater enthusiasm than before, and remain friendly with both the evangelists and the presbyters.

In some respects the presbyter of a rural pastorate has more authority than the bishop of a C.S.I. diocese, for the presbyter, in practice, has the final word on most matters pertaining to his pastorate. Most important in the eyes of the evangelists, he has full control over the finances of the pastorate, with no one to question his accounts or challenge his decisions, This unchecked authority is resented by the evangelists, and their resentment hinders the discharge of their joint responsibility with the presbyter for providing pastoral care to all the village congregations. The lack of effective lay participation in the government of the pastorate through a completely functioning pastorate committee means that the constitutional check to the presbyter's arbitrariness is not present in the rural pastorates, while the lack of effective lay leadership in the village congregations makes much more difficult the provision of pastoral care for all the Christians in the pastorate. Hence the problems of ministerial leadership are closely connected with the problems of lay leadership, and to these we shall turn later in the chapter.

There has been much discussion in the Diocese in recent years about the reduction of the size of the dioceses and the pastorates, and about reorganizing the present system of diocesan administration and the present pattern of church life in the light of the resources of the Indian Church. Though more presbyters and deacons have been ordained and the size of the pastorates has been somewhat reduced, they are still too large for the presbyter to have frequent contact with and close supervision of the village congregations. Our study suggests that the problem of pastoral care is further aggravated by the reluctance of a number of presbyters to spend very much time in the villages, and by the lack of friendship and wholehearted co-operation in many pastorates between evangelists (both junior and superintending), the deacon (if there is one), and the presbyter (or presbyters, if there is both a resident assistant presbyter and a superintendent living elsewhere).

In spite of the fact that the presbyter has a position with much more financial security and dignity than that of the evangelist, there have been very few young men in the Diocese in recent years who have offered themselves for ministerial training. One general reason for this is that the relatively few who have the educational qualifications are enabled by that education to take pre-professional and professional training in a number of fields which seem more attractive than the vocation of presbyter. More specifically, there are three kinds of people in the Medak Diocese from whom volunteers for the ministry might be expected to appear. The first category is that of village Christians, but only very few of them have received enough education to qualify for theological training, and still fewer are able to undertake higher theological education at the B.D. level. If the family is able to sacrifice enough to make possible higher education for one or more children, it wants the newly educated member of the family to get the most remunerative employment possible, in medicine, government service, or various technical jobs. All of these professions pay more than the Church. This same consideration affects the decisions of young men in the other two categories: children of church workers and children of urban Christian laymen. In addition, the children of evangelists and presbyters have often been affected by their fathers' unhappy experiences in church work. Children of men who have served in urban pastorates have encountered the problem of the presbyter's dealings with organized groups of laymen on greater lay control of the machinery of church government at all levels. Children have also experienced their parents' apprehension that foreign financial support would soon be stopped and the Diocese would be unable to pay ministers' salaries. Neither church workers nor laymen seem to feel any obligation to present a son for ministerial training as an act of sacrifice, and very few young men feel called to what they regard as an uncertain and often unhappy task.

At the time of our survey in 1959, the situation with respect to ministerial candidates looked very bleak; there was no one from the Medak Diocese either at the United Theological College in Bangalore (B.D., in English) or at the Andhra Union Theological College in Dornakal (Licentiate in Theology, in Telugu). The one encouraging report was the offer of the headmaster of a Government middle school to enter the ministry, a decision which entailed leaving a secure position with a considerably higher salary than he would receive as a presbyter. By 1962 there were three students from the Medak Diocese taking the

L.Th. course at Dornakal, and one student was getting practical experience in the villages in preparation for starting the B.D. course at Bangalore in June 1963. (The most recent graduate of U.T.C. in Bangalore was there from 1955 to 1958.)

This slight increase is due in part to the Diocese's increasing awareness of the seriousness of the problem and the efforts it has taken to encourage men to apply for ministerial training. To some extent this is a revival of past emphases. When the Wesley Boys' High School was established in Secunderabad in 1912, its specific purpose was to provide the Hyderabad Methodist District with Indian leadership. Many of the more highly educated ministers in the Diocese were drawn from this school and from the Normal Training College, which was established in Medak in 1922 with the late Bishop Whittaker as its first principal. The principals and hostel superintendents of the High School and the Normal Training College watched the students in their care, and made a special point of encouraging the final year students to offer themselves for the ministry. Many of the present presbyters trained in Bangalore chose to study for the ministry through the personal influence of the Rev. L. Simpson, for many years the superintendent of the Wesley High School Hostel, or of Bishop Whittaker. Both these men kept looking for young men whom they thought should receive higher theological education and challenged them to undertake this training. For the past several years the Diocese had an evangelist stationed at the Wesley Hostel so that he might have an influence on the students and persuade some to take ministerial training. In 1959 the Diocese decided to appoint a presbyter as hostel superintendent in view of the urgent need of candidates for the ministry. In 1962 a presbyter was also appointed as warden of the Senior Boys' Hostel in Medak. A new experiment is a one-year pre-vocational course in Medak following high school. Students are encouraged to explore the possibilities of some variety of church work and are helped to prepare for the qualifying examinations for an arts course in the university or for professional training. Within the first three years (1960–63) an average of about three of these P.V.C. students each year decided to study for the ministry. The relative success of these recent efforts appears to indicate that despite the decline in the presbyter's financial position and social status, some young men do respond if presbyters and other church leaders watch for those who would be capable of theological study and encourage them to reflect on their vocation. Effective vocational guidance requires a combination of personal concern and persuasive Christian teaching. The latter is the subject of the next section of the chapter.

E. *The Teaching and Preaching of Evangelists and Presbyters*

It is expected that Christian teaching and preaching will be one of the chief responsibilities of both evangelists and presbyters. Evangelists have some opportunity to 'preach' at the nightly prayers, the Sunday night service, and on their occasional evangelistic visits to other villages. 'Teaching' of the Christian faith is expected to be an important part of the day school for children and the night school for young people, especially in connexion with learning to read the Bible. Teaching of Christian beliefs and duties is also assumed to be a large part of the evangelists' preparation of candidates for baptism or confirmation. Presbyters usually preach at the evening service every time they visit a congregation; they preach at the communion service during their monthly meeting with the evangelists, and they give more systematic instruction in the Christian faith during special meetings and special courses at the pastorate headquarters. Because of the nature of the presbyter's visits to the village congregations, he does not often have the opportunity to 'teach' in the village congregations.

In view of these relatively numerous opportunities for preaching and teaching, it may seem surprising that so many Christians in the villages have such an inadequate grasp of Christian teaching and seemingly so little understanding of Christian faith. Part of the reason for this is the small and irregular attendance at night prayers after a long exhausting day; there is also the problem of illiteracy; most of the Christians cannot read the Bible or any other religious book or pamphlet for themselves, and they are therefore dependent on what they hear from the evangelist and presbyter, and from the few literates in the congregation. Yet the character of the teaching and preaching done by presbyters and evangelists is also an important aspect of the problem. Both evangelist and presbyter tend to confine their teaching and preaching to a rather narrow range of subject matter (different in the two cases), often presented in such a way that the congregation does not understand what the evangelist or presbyter is intending to say.

The Diocese has certainly put more emphasis on a well-trained ministry than many other churches in India; not only is there systematic instruction during their training, but evangelists must also take a yearly examination on a book of the Bible. Presbyters and deacons, too, have a considerable check on their competence as teachers and preachers during the years when they are on probation or under the supervision of a senior presbyter. Moreover, the Diocese provides a syllabus to aid evangelists in their sermon preparation. We found, however, that the evangelists in the Jangarai section were not using the syllabus.

In their preaching to non-Christians or teaching of catechumens, evangelists usually follow the method of 'lyrical evangelism'. They sing stories about the Creation and the Fall and about the main events in the life of Jesus (including a few miracles). Next they teach catechumens the Lord's Prayer, the Ten Commandments, the Apostles' Creed and some Christian lyrics. They have a strong tendency to teach memory lessons rather than to convey the meaning of what is being memorized, and they do not usually try to adapt the standard lesson to individual needs so that individuals might be challenged to a life of personal consecration and Christian witness.

The preaching of evangelists usually takes the form of comments on a passage of scripture. We found that a particular evangelist tends to refer to the same favourite passages or at least to the same kind of passages. In general, these are found among the following:

(*a*) the Christmas story in the Gospels,
(*b*) the miracle stories in the Gospels and Acts,
(*c*) the heroic episodes in the Old Testament,
(*d*) the moral exhortations in the Epistles.

Both the evangelist and his congregation like to hear stories that recount the triumphs of Christ and of other Biblical figures in the face of suffering, danger and death. The moral exhortations are also frequent, if less popular; one of the most frequent is the exhortation to liberality in giving.

The sermon summaries given in Appendix C indicate the effort that evangelists make to apply their message to the situation of their hearers and the use of Hindu religious concepts in their preaching. Sometimes the use of such terms as māyā reflects the evangelist's own understanding; at other times the evangelist (or presbyter) is consciously using a Hindu term which he thinks will be meaningful for village Christians. Certainly the evangelist often shares the village Christian's understanding of Christ as the bestower of material blessings. After hearing Sermon 4, the presbyter in charge of the pastorate made a statement to the congregation criticizing the evangelist's sermon for its failure to refer to salvation *from sins*. The fact that the presbyter would feel free to criticize the evangelist in front of his congregation illustrates the all too frequent attitude of presbyters towards their evangelists. The point of the criticism illustrates a principal difference between the village Christian and the educated urban views of the saving work of Christ. These beliefs will be discussed more extensively in Chapter 8 below.

The evangelists' understanding of sin and of salvation from sin seems generally much closer to the attitude of village Christians than to the evangelical theology the evangelists are assumed to have learned during their training. A number of evangelists interviewed in five different pastorates understood sin as lawlessness: 'not obeying the Ten Commandments or doing the things that we ought not to have done.' Evangelists demand that catechumens renounce idol worship, but this is presented as one of the Christian 'rules', with little or no explanation as to why idolatry is to be regarded as sin in the sense of separation from God. They put little stress on the need for repentance or for faith in Jesus Christ. When asked, 'What must you do to be saved?', most replied 'Follow the Ten Commandments, read the Bible, and pray to God; then you will be saved'. Only a few replied, 'Believe in the Lord Jesus'. To the question, 'Why should we give to God?', many replied, 'Because He has created us and given us many things.' Very few responded 'Because Christ has saved us from sin'. Most of the evangelists said that the doctrine of the Holy Spirit was hard for them to understand or to teach.

The preaching of both the presbyter and the evangelist takes place in the interaction between the theology of educated Christians derived from Western missionaries and the traditional beliefs and underlying assumptions of village life. The precise nature and results of that interaction depend not only on the level of general education and theological training the preacher or teacher has received, but also on his awareness of the thinking of his congregation and his sensitiveness and imagination in describing and expressing the Gospel for his hearers.

As we have noted in Appendix C, the topics—and even the texts— of the presbyters' sermons are often even more limited than those of the evangelists, because the specific object of the presbyter's visit is almost always to administer the two sacraments. Three of the five sermons preached by presbyters to village congregations which are summarized in the Appendix have the same text, 'Do this in remembrance of me' (1 Corinthians 11: 24). A third frequent theme of presbyters' sermons is Christian giving. At Christmas and Easter, seasonal themes are sometimes taken up. Especially is this true of the Christmas season, when both presbyters and evangelists preach on the birth of Jesus. The presbyters' sermons often contain much exhortation: to give more generously, to attend Christian worship more regularly, to refrain from traditional religious practices, to stand fast in the face of threats and persecution. The language presbyters use is generally more educated, sometimes to the point that the illustrations convey nothing, and the language itself is difficult to understand. Theological terms familiar to educated Christians may have no meaning at all, or a very different meaning, for village Christians. Presbyters sometimes feel that they can give only a 'simple' message to village Christians, and this feeling can well serve as an excuse for poor preparation of sermons preached in the villages. What is needed, however, is not this kind of 'simplicity', but a challenging relevance in both conception and expression. Sermons attract villagers most which are full of proverbial sayings and piquant analogies from the villagers' everyday life. It is necessary to have a sympathetic understanding of the pressing personal problems of the hearers, as well as of their traditional world-view and thought forms. But beyond this, it is necessary to become aware of the points where the Gospel most radically challenges the religious conceptions and social attitudes of the village.

F. *The Present Lack of Lay Responsibility*

The Diocesan constitution provides for the establishment of a 'Leaders' Meeting' in each local congregation, for the spiritual welfare of the members of the congregation and for the enforcement of church discipline. The members of the Leaders' meeting must be communicant members and should be elected by the communicant membership of the congregation on the nomination of the presbyter.[2] However, in the village congregations surveyed, such Leaders' meetings simply do not exist, and, at the time our study was made, there was no plan of the Diocese for implementing responsible and effective self-government in village congregations.

Each local congregation does have one or two elders (depending on whether or not there are more than fifty communicant members) who are elected by the communicant members and represent their congregation on the 'Pastorate Committee', which meets three times a year. The elders are expected to go to Wadiaram to attend these meetings and to assume responsibility for their respective congregations in matters of 'collections', discipline and pastoral care. The Pastorate Committee is supposed to be the body responsible for the pastoral and evangelistic work of the pastorate, as well as in charge of its finances. This body, unlike the congregational Leaders' meeting, does actually meet and has a definite membership, but in the Wadiaram Pastorate, and many other rural pastorates, it is still a long way from discharging its constitutional responsibilities. Many of the elders come to the Pastorate Committee meetings only after much persuasion on the part of the evangelists; sometimes they come largely to please their evangelist, and to save him from a warning or reprimand by the presbyter. Most of the talking in the meetings is done by the presbyter and those evangelists who are members of the Committee. The lay elders nod their heads in assent to what the presbyter is saying, but much of it they do not follow. Many of the elders remain silent throughout the meetings, and take little interest or responsible share in the deliberations. They are often equally inactive within their congregations, except in disciplinary cases, when it is customary for the members of the panchayat to be compensated for their services.

Only a few of these elders are the hereditary leaders of their clan or caste. In only one of the congregations surveyed was the traditional Madiga headman elected to the Pastorate Committee. The presence of the evangelist has tended to challenge or even displace the authority of the traditional Mala and/or Madiga leaders, and the official organization of the Church requires the local lay leadership to be chosen only by the communicant members. In all these congregations, however, only a fraction of the baptized adults are communicants, and they do not constitute a self-conscious *élite* within the larger Christian community. Most important, the members of village congregations have not felt any particular responsibilities to be theirs rather than the evangelist's, or that the discharge of their responsibilities could be led by their own chosen leaders. The evangelists generally regard any attempt at independent initiative with suspicion; they want the members of the congregation to contribute more liberally and they like the young men to call people to worship, but that is about the limit of their conception of lay responsibility.

The Diocesan programme of lay leadership training has stressed the village layman as an individual selected rather than elected, and trained as an unpaid substitute for the 'paid church worker'. To this training programme we now turn.

G. *Voluntary Church Workers*

The Diocese has been aware of the need for a larger number of ordained ministers to provide pastoral care and to evangelize; at the same time it has faced the difficulty of securing the necessary funds within the Diocese or from the Methodist Missionary Society in England to pay the salaries of these ordained ministers, as well as of the non-ordained evangelists. To meet this situation the Diocese has decided to recruit, train and ordain some competent and consecrated laymen who, while continuing in their various secular occupations, would serve as honorary (unpaid) deacons and presbyters. The scheme of V.C.W.s (voluntary church workers) is conceived as the first step in this direction.[3]

It is intended to develop a team of voluntary workers with 'bishops' licences' in every local congregation, both urban and rural, to exercise leadership and responsibility in the congregation's various activities. It is also planned to have at least one ordained minister without salary in each 'section' or 'parish' of a Pastorate. In 1954 a Diocesan Board on voluntary church workers was established, and in 1959 a senior presbyter was set apart for full-time work as Director of voluntary workers' training.

The scheme provides for training laymen with an elementary grade of education for rural churches, and laymen with a higher grade of education for urban churches. Both grades of voluntary workers are divided for training purposes into three types: 'servants of the church', lay deacons, and honorary ordained ministers. Three classes distinguished under the first type are (1) local preachers, (2) stewards, and (3) pastoral assistants. It is expected that these voluntary workers should be communicant members of good character and influence in their respective congregations. They should be inwardly called of God to this service, and should be nominated by the presbyter in charge of the pastorate and approved by their own congregation and the pastorate committee. Before taking the more specialized supplementary course, all the voluntary workers must take a course on the relation of Christian doctrine to witness-bearing, worship, the Bible and Christian discipleship. Those who successfully complete the prescribed courses are given a licence by the bishop, which can be renewed annually. (Details of the training programme are given in Appendix D.)

In 1959 there was only one licensed voluntary worker in the whole Jangarai section who had received training at the pastorate, regional, District Church Council and Diocesan levels. When asked about his licence, it became evident that he did not know for what type of work his licence was given to him, and that he did not receive the initial training in the village or the section, although such training close to home is supposed to be the indispensable first step in the training programme. When questioned about what he had learned, he showed that he knew the main events in the life of Christ (up to the resurrection) but he could say little about most Christian doctrines. He is helping the evangelist in worship services by collecting people for worship, leading the singing, praying and reading Scriptures. He was able to tell a simple story (the birth of Christ) to the congregation, but it became evident that he did not have a firm grasp of even that story. He can read the Bible for himself. Once or twice he accompanied the evangelist to Mallupalle and helped him in teaching the inquirers.

In Achampet, four young men attended the regional course held in Ramayampet two years ago, but they have not received bishop's licences. In all the other villages of the Jangarai section there are some literates, but they have not been given any training course in the congregation, section or in the pastorate headquarters. In 1959 no sectional or pastorate central courses specifically for voluntary church workers were held in the Wadiaram Pastorate.

The Diocese has been much more successful in its training of voluntary church workers than it has been in the other two main aspects of the New Pattern: self-support and evangelism. Although only a small fraction of those who attended one of the training courses have continued to attend and finally have been recognized with a bishop's licence, there are already a considerable number of licensed laymen, and some of them have taken courses for lay deacons. When they have attended two such courses, they will be given lay deacons' licences. After attending two additional courses, lay deacons may be ordained as deacons and then, two years later, ordained as presbyters. In 1961 no layman from the rural pastorates had yet received a lay deacon's licence.

While there has been progress in the training of voluntary workers, the rural pastorates have been much less successful in making effective use of these men after they have received their training licences. There have been some cases of misuse of their new position, e.g. by solemnizing marriages or keeping for themselves the 'collections' they raise. There are also instances where the V.C.W. becomes the spokesman for lay opposition to the established ecclesiastical order. Some complain, 'All the important services are kept for ordained people; we are given only the privilege of burying the dead!' Others ask, 'When we are serving the Church without any salary, why should you evangelists receive a salary?' Some assert their own power over against the evangelists by threatening to lodge complaints against them with the presbyter or the Diocesan authorities. A few have revolted against the established structure of the Church by joining the Pentecostalists and inviting the Pentecostalist evangelists to preach in their congregations.

There are other V.C.W.s who are fulfilling the expectations of the training programme. They have taken charge of congregations without a resident evangelist, and have managed not only to conduct night prayers regularly in their own villages, but also to visit 'second village' congregations and conduct worship there. Some receive the church offerings and take them once a month to the presbyter, carefully saving the receipts they are given by the presbyter.

The most serious problem, however, is the number of V.C.W.s who are neither using nor misusing their training, but doing virtually nothing in their new capacity. This is especially true if they belong to congregations with a resident evangelist; many an evangelist has made very little use of a V.C.W. who is in his congregation, whether from lack of confidence in his ability, fear that he might displace him (the evangelist) as leader of the congregation, or simply lack of imagination as to the tasks which the V.C.W. might be assigned. At one advanced course, the voluntary workers were asked what they had done during the past several months. The following were some of the replies:

> The evangelist is there, and he is doing everything.
> We have no chance to do anything.
> We sometimes conduct worship when the evangelist is away.
> Even when the evangelist is away, his wife conducts the worship.
> We help the evangelist in gathering people for worship and in taking the collection.

There were some V.C.W.s who reported taking full responsibility for a congregation; these were in villages where there was no longer an evangelist in residence.

It was clear from these comments and from other observations that whether the V.C.W. puts his training to work depends a great deal on the initiative and enthusiasm of the presbyter as well as of the evangelists, and too often the presbyter has not been aware of what the V.C.W.s were or were not doing, and has not been imaginative enough to break through the diffidence of the village laymen and the evangelists' vested interest in the absence of village lay leadership.

When the V.C.W. is actually working as the New Pattern envisages, he is taking over most of the evangelists' pastoral duties in his own congregation, thus freeing the evangelist for care of neglected congregations, teaching of inquirers, and evangelistic work among non-Christians. Yet this new type of lay worker encouraged by the Diocese is an assistant to or substitute for the evangelist, not a lay leader chosen by the congregation. Until the middle of 1959, it was the evangelist who selected the laymen who would be sent to the voluntary workers' training courses. The result was frequently that the congregation did not accept him, even if he completed the required courses and received a licence from the bishop. Since the middle of 1959, the congregation has selected those who are to be sent for training as voluntary workers, at least in theory, but the first two years under the new rules have not indicated much change in practice.

H. *The Experiment of 'Panchayat Committees'*

The author (P. Y. L.) happened to visit Achampet just after the resident evangelist (who was also the S.E. of the Jangarai section) had left to begin a year's course in Medak leading to ordination as deacon. The congregation had had a resident evangelist for many years and were distressed that they were now to be left without one. Some members complained, 'A congregation without an evangelist is like a *jathra* [Hindu religious fair] without a god!'

It was during this same summer of 1959 that the first panchayat board elections were being held in the villages of this area (see pp. 95–97), and the Christians in Achampet were keenly interested in the first exercise of local political democracy. The author suggested that they initiate a panchayat committee for the congregation along the same lines.

The Achampet Christians are all Madigas, belonging to three

vamshams (clans). Each clan elected three members to serve on the panchayat committee: an elder, a young man, and a woman. The congregation as a whole elected a tenth person to serve as chairman. This committee assumed responsibility for arranging for worship services, especially on Sundays and Christian festivals, and for collecting church dues, with the representatives from each *vamsham* responsible for the families in their *vamsham*. In addition, they have visited the sick in the families of their respective *vamshams*, settled quarrels arising between Christians, sent delegates to central meetings of the pastorate in Wadiaram, and entertained the evangelist from a neighbouring congregation or the presbyter whenever either of them comes to visit.

The panchayat committee worked so well that the Achampet Christians became quite enthusiastic about their own church affairs and gave up the idea of requesting another resident evangelist. The chairman acts as the liaison between the Wadiaram pastorate and the village congregation. He informs the neighbouring evangelist or the presbyter of their needs, and he receives word from the presbyter through the evangelist about various meetings in Wadiaram.

The committee appointed one of its woman members to sweep and clean the place of worship (the porch of the vacant evangelist's house) every Sunday. They promised her a sari at Christmas-time in payment for her services. The women on the committee are responsible for encouraging the women in their respective *vamshams* to attend the Sunday services. They succeeded in increasing the attendance of women. The young men on the committee are similarly responsible for stimulating the other young men to take a leading part in church activities.

The chairman is definitely accepted as the leader of the congregation, taking the place of the evangelist. The members of the congregation spent some time deliberating on whom they should elect as chairman. They finally selected one man by common consent, on the grounds that he could read well enough to conduct worship, that he was an older man, that he was patient and loving and not easily provoked, and that he was considered to have a good Christian family. They knew that he did not participate in non-Christian worship, that he attended Christian worship regularly and made regular contributions.

All the adult baptized Christians participated in the election, and no distinction was made between communicants and non-communicants with respect to the right to vote or the right to serve on the committee. It happened that the chairman and most of the members elected are communicants. While the author explained before the election the need for a local church panchayat committee, he did not suggest any name or otherwise interfere in the election itself.

Since the official government of the Church of South India is restricted to communicant members over twenty-one, this panchayat committee in Achampet had only an informal status; indeed its establishment was something of an experiment. The presbyter in charge of the Wadiaram Pastorate was informed of the election of the committee as a provisional arrangement. When the presbyter next visited Achampet, he sanctioned the continued work of the committee and exhorted its members to be faithful in the discharge of their duties. Moreover, the presbyter was so enthusiastic about the functioning of this committee that he asked for the author's help in setting up similar committees in a few other congregations in the pastorate, where there was already an active group of laymen.

In the Rayelli congregation in the southern section, there are also three Madiga *vamshams*, so the same procedure was followed. One of the members of this congregation, Daniel, a literate, had been elected chairman of the new panchayat board for the village, and we had expected that the congregation would elect him as chairman. Instead, however, they chose the Madiga headman (*Pedda Methat*) as chairman, and then elected Daniel as vice-chairman.

In the Gowlapalli congregation there are five clans, so it was planned to have a larger committee, with three representatives from each clan. However, in one of the clans there are two rival parties because of enmity between two of the older men. A compromise was reached by electing one elder from each party, a woman from one party and a young man from the Mala community who had just two months before been baptized. It proved impossible to compromise on the question of chairman, so this part of the election had to be postponed and the committee was unable to start functioning. Since there is a resident evangelist in Gowlapalli, both the members of the congregation and their evangelist find it difficult to see the point of such a panchayat committee.

The Ambojipet congregation includes Malas, Madigas and a few new converts from Sudra castes. Each of these major groups chose an older man, a young man, and a woman as their representatives. In spite of its multi-caste composition, the congregation chose a man from the Madiga community as their chairman and accepted his leadership of the congregation. (Ambojipet has had a rather inactive retired evangelist living in the evangelist's house.) What is even more remarkable is that the chairman was nominated by the man who had been the most active layman and was a member of the other major community, the Malas. Even though the chairman had previously been rather indifferent to the Christian faith and very inactive in the affairs of the congregation, the previous lay leader saw a real leadership potential in him. The new chairman, at least initially, fulfilled the expectations of his fellow Christians. Indeed, when we visited the congregation a few weeks later we were told, 'Saul has become Paul!'

These experiments in responsible government in village congregations produced initial results that were quite surprising, in view of the previous lack of a sense of responsibility on the part of the individuals and groups concerned. The Government's effort to introduce local political democracy (*panchayat raj*) provided a stimulus and a model for the electoral procedures. Account was taken of the various group-ings in the congregation, according to age, sex, clan and caste, but the chairman was elected by all the adult members of the congregation, without regard to their official ecclesiastical right to vote. Although the chairman has assumed some of the functions of the evangelist, he remains the congregation's own lay leader and its representative to the wider councils of the Church, rather than a substitute for the evangelist selected and trained by the official church structure outside or above the village congregation. We could also put the contrast in different terms: the chairman of the panchayat committee is primarily a 'ruling elder' rather than a 'teaching elder'. It is quite evident that his presence does not remove the need for lay teachers of the type trained as V.C.W.'s or for more skilled theological instruction by evangelists or presbyters. However, there is such a strong tendency for the official teacher of the congregation to function as its ruler that there are serious obstacles to having such an elected lay leader, as long as an evangelist is living in the midst of the congregation. On the other hand, a congregation that has long been without the presence of an evangelist is otherwise often almost totally neglected.

In order to develop potential lay leadership of the type represented by the panchayat committee, there seems to be the need of previous pastoral care by an evangelist who is willing to move out physically, but continue to come back and visit after moving to another village. Alternatively, a different evangelist who has not been in charge of the congregation previously could visit often enough to guide the lay leadership, especially in the matter of Christian teaching. To the extent that V.C.W.'s are trained as lay teachers, the role of the visiting evangelist will become less essential.

It has already been indicated that the panchayat committee was irregular from the standpoint of official church polity, especially in its ignoring of the distinction between communicant and non-communicant members. The problems created by this distinction will be treated in Chapter 10. We should note in conclusion, however, that it was only by ignoring this distinction that we were able to appeal to the only community of Christians that has some sense of identity and could exercise responsibility: the entire group of adult Christians in the village.

APPENDIX A: SYLLABUS OF THE MEN'S
TRAINING SCHOOL AT MEDAK

Prior to 1940 the following subjects were taught in the Training School for evangelists: Scripture, Christian theology, church history, pastoral theology, comparative religions, languages (Telugu and Urdu), teaching methods, and such miscellaneous subjects as hygiene, first-aid and social service.

From 1940 to 1955 the following general curriculum was followed:

1. *Theological training*: (a) study of the Old and New Testaments, with special emphasis on the application of Biblical teaching to the problems and needs of the Christian Church in India; (b) instruction in the major topics of theology and the foundations of the Christian Faith; (c) a general

outline of church history from apostolic days, with special reference to the heritage of the Indian Church; (d) instruction in practical methods of evangelism; (e) a general study of Hinduism and Islam, with methods of approach to caste Hindus and Muslims.

2. *Normal training*: study of the principles and practice of teaching in village schools, from nursery to the night school class, which involves a study of village script, arithmetic and the Laubach method of Adult Education.

3. *Training in practical service*: this includes a course in agriculture, carpentry, the work of the blacksmith, and building construction for village purposes; and elementary courses on economics, co-operative thrift and account-keeping; a course on personal and social hygiene, first-aid and the use of simple drugs; and a general course on the aims and methods of rural reconstruction.

From 1956 to 1959 the following syllabus was followed:

1. *Scripture*: introduction to the books of the Old and New Testaments; detailed study of O.T. prophets; the life of Christ, the Acts of the Apostles and the Epistles; studies in biblical theology; the theology of Jesus.

2. *Doctrine:* Campbell's *Theology*, Scope's *Catechism* (both in *Telugu*).

3. *Church History:* early church history; Indian church history; origin and spread of Christianity in Hyderabad; Christian martyrs.

4. *Pastoralia:* Christian ministry; content and methods of preaching; preparation for baptism and confirmation; Christian giving; keeping church rolls and collection books; the significance of statistics.

5. *Non-Christian religions:* Hinduism; modern trends in Hinduism; castes and tribes of Hyderabad; Dravidian gods, Hindu festivals; Islam and Christianity; Buddhism.

6. *Telugu and Arithmetic*

7. *Agriculture; health and hygiene*

8. *Music:* songs, *Burra Kathas; Kalaleshepams* and dramas with musical accompaniments.

APPENDIX B: THE RELATION OF THE BISHOP TO VILLAGE CONGREGATIONS

In the Church of South India, members of local congregations have a pastoral relationship, not only with presbyters, deacons and 'lay' evangelists, but also with the bishop of their diocese.

The bishop serves as a unifying figure in the diocese, and as a symbol of the larger Church beyond the local congregation and the pastorate. The actual contacts of the Bishop of the Medak Diocese with village Christians occur on the following occasions:

1. Confirmation services at pastorate headquarters. (Either the bishop or a presbyter may confirm candidates in the Church of South India, but it has been the practice for the bishop to do so as often as possible. Candidates generally come from their respective villages to the pastorate headquarters.)

2. Other visits to pastorate headquarters, especially for *jatras* (festivals or religious fairs).

3. Visits to a few village congregations for a special baptismal service, e.g. the baptism of a large group beginning a new congregation, or the baptism of the first Sudra converts in the village.

4. Contacts with village Christians when they come to the diocesan headquarters in Medak, especially during courses for voluntary church workers and at the biennial meeting of the District Church Council. (V.C.W.s who successfully complete the required course personally receive a licence from the bishop.)

The bishop is indirectly related to village congregations through his contacts with evangelists and village elders at the time of meetings, and his more direct relationship with the presbyters. His personal contacts with presbyters, apart from his visits to their pastorates, occurs during meetings of committees and church councils and at the annual retreat for presbyters. The presbyters sometimes have interviews with the bishop about special problems. If there is any question of disciplinary action against a presbyter, the bishop has the sole prerogative of initiating such action and hence must conduct preliminary interviews.

According to the C.S.I. Constitution, every bishop is chairman of his respective Diocesan Council and its executive committee, and he is a member *ex officio* of all diocesan committees and boards. According to the rules of the Medak Diocese, the bishop is not just a member but the chairman of all the boards and committees. There are fifteen boards and committees that meet annually for one or two days. Each year he attends the meetings of the three District Church Councils (three days each) and every other year the meetings of the Diocesan Council (three days) and the C.S.I. Synod (three days, plus two or three days' travel). Moreover, he participates in such interdenominational meetings as those of the Andhra Pradesh Christian Council.

At the time of our survey in 1959 there were forty-four pastorates in the Medak Diocese, thirty-six of them rural, the farthest more than two hundred miles away from Medak. In these circumstances it is difficult enough for the bishop to pay regular visits to all the pastorate headquarters, and virtually impossible for him to visit village congregations except for very special occasions. The Medak Diocese is too big for the bishop to be in a more personal sense the spiritual father to the more than a hundred thousand baptized Christians. This has long been recognized, and there have been numerous proposals to divide the Diocese. However, it may be that the primary problem is not one of size, but of the huge demands on the bishop's time by his complete involvement in a committee system of diocesan administration. In the Hyderabad Methodist District before Church Union, the Chairman of the District had extensive administrative powers, but the committee structure was less elaborate and all the committees met during the annual meetings of the Synod, which lasted a fortnight. The District Chairman was therefore much freer to visit the villages, and those visits are still remembered. The present elaborate system of boards and committees, each with a large membership, is the result of a gradual effort to democratize the Church. It appears, however, that the bishop and the senior presbyters serving on many of the committees are so bound by their administrative duties as to be seriously handicapped in fulfilling the more pastoral side of their vocation.

APPENDIX C: SUMMARIES OF SERMONS HEARD

Note: The following sermons were heard, not only in the Wadiaram Pastorate, but in the other Pastorates of the Diocese visited during the period of the study for purposes of comparison.

A. *Evangelists' Sermons*

1. *Lesson:* Matt. 25: 31–46—The Parable of the Separation of the Sheep from the Goats.

Summary: Our country is India. India was ruled first by Brahmini rulers, and at the time the Brahmins kept the Harijans away from the main village in a separate block. They were denied all privileges and education. Then came the Muslim rule. The Muslims defeated the Brahmini rulers with the help of the British. Then the British became the emperors of the world and ruled the earth. They, with the love of Christ, came here to us and lifted us up from our low state. Through Jesus Christ we have received salvation (*mukti*) and education. Salvation is to be found in the Bible, and now we are able to read it and tell others about this good news.

We have three stages of life—childhood, youth, and old age. God formed man of dust from the ground and breathed His breath into man's nostrils. Since then the world grew and mankind multiplied. Why did He create us? So that we may live knowing good and evil. When we die, God will separate us one from another as a shepherd separates the sheep from the goats. This is a world of illusion (*māyā*). We have not come here to be for ever in this world. 'Then the king will say to those at his right hand, "Come, O blessed of my father, inherit the kingdom".' Those who have done good deeds here in this world will be at His right side. Their souls will be rewarded in heaven (*Vaikunta*). To those at His left hand He will say, 'You who have blasphemed my religion, you who have not come to worship me, go into that hell of fire'.

O you young men, this is the world of illusion. When the evangelist preached the word of God, you did not listen, you did not receive baptism. Therefore you are consigned to hell. If we obey the commandments of God, then we will attain heaven.

O you, women and mothers, you know that women loved and served Jesus while on earth. Mary Magdalene went to the bazaar, bought a box of alabaster for Rs. 150, broke it and poured it on Jesus' feet to anoint Him. But Judas Iscariot said, 'These Rs. 150 would have been in my purse if this was not wasted here'. Dear women, if you love Jesus, you will likewise get His blessing.

2. *Lesson:* Acts 2: 14–36 (This was the lesson prescribed for that day in the syllabus.)

Text: Luke 4: 18—'The spirit of the Lord is upon me, because He has anointed me to preach good news to the poor.'

Summary: Jesus came to this world to preach the good news to the poor. The Church was built on the foundation of Jesus. He is the corner-stone. You believed in Jesus thirty years ago, and you were built on His foundation. Jesus appointed twelve disciples, and sent His Holy Spirit on the day of Pentecost and built His Church. On that day three thousand, hearing the word of God, believed on the Lord Jesus. The Church was built on Christ through the apostles' teaching. We have to preach Christ crucified.

Every individual member should witness to Him and fulfil His will. The burden of passing on His living sacrifice to others rests on us. Jesus became man, emptying Himself to save us from sin.

The Church built on the Holy Spirit and the apostles' teaching devoted itself 'to the breaking of bread and the prayers'. We have to experience salvation in our own lives and present it to others. 'And all who believed were together and had all things in common'. We have to keep everything at His feet and bear witness to Him. We have to surrender ourselves to the Lord, destroy the sins called the 'six enemies' (*ari shadvargams*) and live steadfastly in the Church. We have to stand firm in our faith and live a witness-bearing life. We should live together as one family for His sake.

3. *Lesson*: John 4: 4–26—Jesus and the Samaritan woman at the well.

Summary: The preacher described the conversation that took place at the well between Jesus and the Samaritan woman. He did not know the sequence of events and the various steps by which Jesus led the woman to know Him. He struggled for words and could not express himself properly. At the end of the study he drew three lessons: (*a*) there should be no caste distinction; (*b*) all need repentance and salvation; and (*c*) you should witness to Christ.

4. *Lesson*: Acts 3: 1–10

Summary: In the lesson just now read we find two names—John and Peter. In this congregation also, two men having these same names have laboured hard for this church. Because of them we are able to meet like this, and their names appear in the Bible. Are our names too recorded in the Bible?

Where do we usually find lame men? We find them begging by the roadside. But this lame man was being carried to the temple every day. As usual one day he went to the church and Peter and John also went to pray in the church. The lame man said to himself, 'Some strangers are coming today; I will get plenty of alms from them, and today my bag will be full'. But they said to him, 'O man, look at us here. We have no silver and gold, but we give you what we have; in the name of Jesus Christ of Nazareth get up and walk'. And immediately he leaped and walked, and entered the temple with them.

Look here, several times we have told you not to worship idols but you do not listen. Is there anybody who is healed in the name of gods and goddesses? Can you show me one man who could heal in the name of these local goddesses? But in the name of Jesus many miracles are being wrought. 'There is power in the word of God'. Because of Peter and John who led this congregation to the feet of Jesus, we are now able to walk. Peter faithfully worked for this congregation. Now he is dead, but his brother John is still with us as the elder of this congregation.

In those days you installed Jesus in your cattle-sheds, fields, and homes, but now you have forgotten Him. 'Children come, I am not here to punish you, but to love you,' says Jesus to you now; and He is stretching forth His hand to take you in His arms. You received lands through Him, you got rid of forced labour through Him, but you have forsaken Him.

Comment: The presbyter of this superintending evangelist, who listened to his sermon, remarked to the congregation: 'This evangelist said that you received lands, etc., through Jesus, but he did not say that you have received salvation from your sins through Him.'

5. *Lesson*: Acts 14: 19–23; and 2 Cor. 11: 23–30

Summary: When Paul came to Antioch, his enemies dragged him out of the city and beat him. Which Paul? Thota Paul? or Dumpala Paul? No, Saint Paul. On his return to Antioch from Lystra, Iconium and Derbe, he said to them, 'Through many tribulations we must enter the Kingdom of God'. We, who believe in Jesus Christ, must remain faithful till the end. Some people go back, in time of trouble, and lose faith in Him. But Paul said, 'Do not leave your first faith, but stand firm in it'. Paul was persecuted by his own men, by the Jews and others. He was taken in bonds to stand before the Caesar, he suffered difficulties on the sea, and was bitten by a snake. In the end he was cut into two pieces by a sword. We should not leave Christ but remain faithful to the end. We cannot enter into the Kingdom of God through our pretensions and hypocrisies but only through tribulations.

B. *Presbyters' Sermons*

Note: As the main object of the presbyters' visit to the village congregations is to administer the two sacraments, they very frequently preach on the baptism of children, basing the sermon on the story of Jesus blessing the little children, or they preach on the Lord's Supper, taking as their text, 'Do this in remembrance of me' (1 Cor. 11:24). Of the five sermons by presbyters to a village congregation which were heard, three took this text. They usually read for their lesson, Luke 22: 14–23 and 1 Cor. 11: 20–31. The third subject they deal with in the village is Christian giving, and their common text is, 'For you know the grace of our Lord Jesus Christ, that though he was rich, yet for your sake he became poor, so that by his poverty you might become rich' (2 Cor. 8: 9).

1. *Text*: 1 Cor. 11: 24—'Do this in remembrance of me.'

Summary: By way of introduction, the preacher described the scene in the Upper Room as found in the lesson, Luke 22: 14–23, and then took up the text.

The statue of Gandhi which is seen nowadays in the towns and villages reminds people of the great things done by him for the country—the political freedom he won. So also through this Lord's Supper we remember the great things done by Jesus for mankind. The preacher used two illustrations: (*a*) A mother had two children. One of them was a married daughter, and the other was a boy studying in school. After some time the mother died. One day the girl went to her mother's grave, plucked a little flower grown on her grave, and sent it to the boy in school in a letter. When the boy saw the flower, he remembered his mother's love. So also when we see the bread and the wine we remember Jesus' inestimable love for us. (*b*) The Christian parents of a boy taught him in his early days the Beatitudes, the Ten Commandments, and the two great Commandments. Before the parents died, they put a paper containing these passages in a clock and presented it to their boy, with prayers that in times of temptation and trial he might remember the things he had learned. So also God gave us Beatitudes, the Ten Commandments and the two Great Commandments, so that we may remember them and not yield to temptations or fall into sin.

2. *Text*: 'Do this in remembrance of me.'

Summary: The preacher started with an illustration, telling the congregation the story of a man who said to the village people, 'I am prepared to lay down my life for this village'. Then the villagers challenged him, 'All right, will you allow yourself to be burned to death ? We are going to do that now.' He replied, 'Oh yes, do it now—but on condition that you build a grave for my ashes with these words written on it, "In remembrance of Premaiah, who gave his life for this village".' So also in remembrance of Jesus, who gave His life for the whole world, we celebrate this Lord's Supper.

3. *Text*: 'Do this in remembrance of me.'

Summary: In the introduction, the preacher mentioned the two sacraments in brief, and traced the history of the Passover meal established in the days of Moses, and connected it with the Lord's Supper instituted by Jesus. Whenever we celebrate this, we remember the Lord, His cross and resurrection, till He comes back. We remember His love for us sinners, and the salvation He wrought on the cross. Like Sadhu Sundar Singh and St. Paul, we must appropriate that salvation and make it our own. In these days we Christians are called upon to face persecution, and to endure it for the Lord's sake. We have to stand firm in our faith, in the midst of troubles and hardships.

4. *Lesson*: Luke 7: 36–50—The woman anointing Jesus' feet in the house of Simon the Pharisee.

Summary: The preacher explained in graphic details (*a*) the sinful life of the woman, and (*b*) her repentance and gratitude to Jesus, shown in the act of anointing. Then he applied the story to the Christians: (*a*) If we repent and fall at His feet, Jesus will forgive our sins, and (*b*) we must show our gratitude to Him by loving Him. How can we love Him?

    (i) by taking part in the worship service regularly;
    (ii) by participating in the Lord's Supper; and
    (iii) by giving to God generously.
    (iv) We should not look back upon our traditional religion. We should not be like the man who put his hand to the plough and looked back. After believing in Jesus, we should not resort to traditional practices. If you do that, you are not loving Him.

5. *Lesson*: Mark 1: 40–45—Jesus healing the leper.

Summary: Jesus touched the leper and healed him. He touched Peter's mother-in-law and healed her; He touched Jairus' daughter and raised her up from the dead; He touched the blind Bartimaeus and gave him his sight; and He touched Samadanam eight years ago in this village and healed her. But Jesus does more than just giving physical healing. He touches and heals our sin, which is more dreadful than leprosy or any other disease.

6. A sermon preached by a senior presbyter at a Holy Communion service held during the monthly meeting with the evangelists.

Lesson: Psalms 19: 7–14; and 119: 1–16.

    Text: Psalms 119: 16—'I will not forget thy word.'

    Summary (1) *Introduction*: (*a*) Various names are given to the Bible in Psalms 119—law, way, word, precept, statute, ordinances, commandments. (*b*) The word 'Bible' is derived from the Greek word *Biblos*. (*c*) One of the greatest miracles is the miracle of the Bible, which took 1,600 years to prepare, and which is translated into 1,200 languages. The original language of the Old Testament is Hebrew, and that of the New Testament is Greek. (d) Covenant means agreement, promise. God's covenant with His people is 'I will be your God and you shall be my people'.

(2) The Old Testament was divided by scholars into: (a) first five books— The Law; (b) from Joshua to Esther—historical (c) from Job to Lamentations poetical (d) from Ezekiel to Malachi-prophetic 'Thus saith the Lord'.

(3) God revealed Himself fully and finally in Jesus Christ (Heb. 1: 1–3). The New Testament is divided into: (a) Gospel—Gospel means good news—these describe the life of Christ; (b) Acts—how Christianity spread— life for Christ; (c) Epistles—saints living in Christ—life in Christ; and (d) Revelation—life with Christ.

(4) Another promise God made—the 'blood of the new covenant'. 'Do this in remembrance of me'. Rev. 3: 20—'Behold I stand at the door and knock. . . .'

7. A sermon preached by a senior presbyter at an 'Agents' meeting' specially called for the investigator's interviews.

Lesson: 2 Tim. 2: 14–26

Text: 2 Tim. 2: 15—'Do your best to present yourself to God as one approved. . .'

Those of us who are called to the service of the Lord in the Church should at every stage examine ourselves, and see if we are acquitting ourselves worthily of the high calling to which we are called. If you want this New Pattern to be successful you should examine yourselves at every moment and 'present yourselves to God as one approved'.

1. '*Present yourself to God as one approved*'. Often we present ourselves not to God, but to the men above us, to our superior officers in the Church, so that we may appear to them as the ones approved of men. But are we worthy workmen before God? In my own experience, I have realized quite lately that all these days I have been doing merely a clerk's job, though I have been busy twenty-four hours in my office. Is that worthy of my calling? Paul is here giving kind and fatherly advice to Timothy, and warning him in these words; and these words come to us too as a warning.

2. '*A workman who has no need to be ashamed*'. When we examine ourselves and our work, we all have to feel ashamed of our failures and weaknesses. In these days we are having to face many troubles and persecutions. 'O Lord, I have not done my job properly; I feel ashamed of my own shortcomings' ought to be our confession, if we really put ourselves under His searchlight. Can God say to each one of us, 'Well done, good and faithful servant; you have been faithful over a little . . .'?

APPENDIX D: TRAINING COURSES FOR VOLUNTARY CHURCH WORKERS

Candidates for this training are nominated by their evangelist, or (more recently) their congregation, and, after an interview, selected by the presbyter. The stages supposed to be included in the training programme are the following:

1. training in the village by the evangelist;
2. joint training with other candidates of the section by the S.E.;
3. training at the pastorate headquarters by the presbyter (for men and women together);
4. training at a regional course, including candidates from several pastorates (separate courses for men and women), by the diocesan director of lay leadership training;
5. 'retreat' or follow-up course for each of the District Church Councils (men and women together), at the end of which bishop's licences are awarded to the successful candidates;
6. a recognition service in each congregation where a licensed V.C.W. is appointed;
7. follow-up courses for the newly licensed V.C.W.s at the village, sectional, pastorate, and regional levels;
8. three advanced courses, of a fortnight each, held at the Men's Training School in Medak for the Diocese as a whole;
9. after three years of satisfactory work as V.C.W.s, two courses, each lasting a fortnight, as preparation for recognition as a *lay deacon* at the end of the second course;
10. after one year as a lay deacon, two more courses of two weeks' duration, culminating in *ordination as deacon*; and
11. after two more years of training and practical work, *ordination as presbyter*.

It is the first seven stages which are as yet of practical significance in the Jangarai section. Stage 3 is expected to be a course for two complete days at the pastorate headquarters, at least once a year. Usually in the morning sessions there are three talks of one hour each, and practical work in the afternoon—story-telling, visiting nearby villages in groups, and conducting worship in a congregation. The regional course is held annually for three days. It includes the basic course and some supplementary courses, and concludes with interviews of all the candidates.

Unfortunately, both the original and the subsequent training at the village and sectional level are often skipped. This means that the V.C.W. has little instruction or supervised practice in his home village, where he is expected to serve, and also that the presbytery is frequently unaware of the obstacles to the effective functioning of a V.C.W. These weaknesses in the training programme then make it more difficult for the V.C.W. to overcome the difficulties of the congregation's reluctance to accept the leadership of a young man whom they have not elected as their leader, and/or the evangelist's unwillingness to utilize and train further a man who may be a threat to his continued leadership, or even his presence, in the congregation.

On the bishop's licences are written the specific type of work for which each V.C.W. has been specially trained: (1) local preacher, (2) steward, or (3) pastoral assistant. The presbyter makes a recommendation in the case of each V.C.W., after the V.C.W. has had general courses at the lower levels, consisting of instruction in the Bible and Christian faith; it is decided at the regional course for which type of work he should receive more special training. This differentiation of function may be justified by the various and varying abilities of those who come for training, but it does not correspond to the present situation in the village congregations, where the work that could be done by a V.C.W. is largely determined by the presence or absence of an evangelist in his village, as well as by the attitude of the evangelists and the presbyter in that particular pastorate towards V.C.W.s. As more laymen are trained in the same congregation, the value of some differentiation in their training will increase, but it is questionable whether the decision to train this man as a local preacher or that man as a steward should be made with so little reference to the needs and the wishes of the congregation itself.

F

CHAPTER 7

New Converts and Inquirers

A. *An Apparent Paradox: the Spread of the Gospel without 'Evangelism'*

The Medak Diocese has a strong interest in evangelism: in the preaching and teaching of the Gospel to non-Christians, with the aim of persuading them to be baptized and become members of the Christian Church. During the decades of the rapid expansion of the Hyderabad Methodist District through the 'mass movement', major emphasis was placed on evangelistic activity, not only by the English missionaries, but by Indian ministers, pastors and evangelists, and, in principle, by lay Christians as well. The accounts of the founding of the congregations in the Jangarai section (Chap. 4 B) indicate the extent of this interest and the fact that evangelists were sometimes inclined to stress the material and social benefits in becoming Christians. One traditional expression of evangelistic concern in the Medak Diocese has been the annual 'Week of Witness', when Christians would go in teams to non-Christians to preach the Gospel.

When compared to this 'official' emphasis of the Diocese, the interest and activity in evangelism on the part of Christians in the Jangarai section seem extremely slight. Christians are very much aware of the change in the political scene since Independence and the beginning of Congress Party rule. The material and social advantages, especially if one is an outcaste, are now on the side of remaining a Hindu. The Arya Samaj has even made some efforts in this area to persuade Christians to return to the Hindu community, and a number of Government officials, especially at the lower levels, have worked in the same direction through the way they have managed the various benefits for 'Harijans', a category that they restrict to non-Christian outcastes. The evangelists sense that the Church is shifting to a defensive stance, and some of them know that some Christian leaders in India believe it will be difficult enough for the Church to hold its own: if it is to survive as a small minority, it should not antagonize the Hindu majority by open efforts at 'proselytizing'.

Many of the evangelists feel that the era of evangelistic activity that they knew in their childhood and youth, the 'mass movement' in which all the members of one or both of the outcaste groups in a village became Christian at the same time, is definitely over, and that further 'witness' of the traditional type is quite useless. In some places they continue the annual 'week of witness', especially if the presbyter urges it. In the year of our survey (1959), the 'week of witness' was not observed by any of the congregations studied in the Jangarai section, though the evangelists in the section did pay a few visits to the new group of inquirers in the hamlet of Mallupalle. Moreover, many evangelists seem to share the view of caste Hindus that Christianity is a religion for outcastes; they find it difficult to believe that a caste Hindu would want to become a Christian, and they feel extremely diffident about presenting the Christian faith to him. We might say that the general lack of enthusiasm with respect to all their work affects the evangelists most clearly at this very point where they would need their utmost zeal to break the age-old barrier between outcaste and caste Hindus—and that, from the side of the outcastes.

In spite of the Church's emphasis on the evangelistic responsibilities of every Christian, most village Christians in the congregations surveyed think that the responsibility of presenting the Gospel to non-Christians belongs to the 'paid church workers': evangelists and presbyters. However, their indifference to evangelism is not simply a feeling that it is someone else's job. Like many of the evangelists, many village Christians are little concerned with whether someone is a member of the Christian Church or not. This is made evident by the marriage arrangements. Parents marry their children to members of different clans in other villages. Many of these are non-Christians. If a girl in the congregation marries into a non-Christian family in another village, she effectively leaves the Christian community, yet parents rarely make any special effort to avoid such matches. If villagers have something special on their minds, they are eager to share it with others. The fact that they do not engage in such sharing of their faith in Christ is a strong indication that they do not regard that faith as an exciting part of their lives. In the few instances where the Christians in these villages did become excited about some aspect of their Christian experience, they shared it with their non-Christian neighbours, often with dramatic results.

We noted in Chapter 4 that three of the five congregations specially studied were largely or entirely Madiga in background, and that the Malas in these villages have been unwilling to accept Christianity because they feared they would then have to live in the congregation with Madigas, accepting them as equals. The Malas in their villages claim to be unable to notice any difference in the conduct of the Madigas since they became Christian. Moreover, at the present time they fear that to become Christians would mean losing the benefits they have been receiving as Harijans.

The attitude of caste Hindus in the villages varies all the way from the few who are trying to reconvert Christians to Hinduism to the still fewer who are willing to listen to the Gospel and even to receive baptism. There are larger numbers whose attitude is somewhere in between. They may tolerate Christianity as a religion for outcastes but refuse to give the Gospel a hearing themselves, or they may have great respect for the powers of the Christians' God, 'Lord Jesus', but be unwilling to accept Jesus as their special 'Lord', or at least unwilling to join the community of Christ's followers.

In two of the five villages studied, there are a few Muslim families.

We noted in Chapter 3 that they are rather lax about their prayers and other Muslim obligations, but they think it inconceivable that a Muslim would break away from Islam. They are not really interested in converting others to Islam, though if any want to join their community, they have no objection and gladly welcome them. On the whole they are tolerant and friendly towards Christians, and, to a lesser extent, towards Hindus. Village Muslims say that Christianity and Islam are not poles apart; some doctrines are common to both. A few disgruntled Muslims, unhappy about both the Congress Government and the Communist policy since the end of the Nizam's rule, have turned to Christianity to find a new way of life and peace. But both Christians and Hindus assume that Muslims will always be Muslims.

In view of the generally unfavourable climate for evangelistic activity and the specific lack of interest on the part of both evangelists and lay people, it seems at first very surprising that the six months of our field survey (March–August 1959) included a number of decisions by Hindus in these villages to be baptized, and several other strong expressions of interest in the Christian Gospel. Among these were the baptism of two Bandela families in Jangarai, the first conversion of new families since the congregation's beginning thirty-two years before. In Gowlapalli there was the baptism of a Mala boy, the first Mala to join this congregation since its dramatic founding nine years previously. In the two of the five congregations where there have been both Malas and Madigas for many years, for the first time in their history (forty-six and twenty-seven years, respectively) caste Hindus (Sudras) were baptized and joined the congregation. It was only in Achampet, generally regarded as the 'best' village congregation in the section, where for many years the S.E. of the section has lived, that there were no baptisms from outside the existing community. It is curious, but perhaps finally quite understandable, that in this village, where the Christians have gone the furthest in developing a distinctively Christian community, there is the least interest in the Gospel on the part of Hindus and the most acrimonious relations between the Christians who are Madigas and the non-Christian outcaste group, in this village the Malas. Perhaps most remarkable was the united decision of the entire Madiga community of the hamlet of Mallupalle to become Christian, the first such group decision since that of the Madigas in Gowlapalli nine years before.

B. *The Influence of Sadhu Joseph*

During our three-week stay in Kondapuram, we noticed that a small number of Hindus from the Sudra castes were regularly attending the night prayers of the congregation. We learned that they had been to the healing services conducted a few weeks before (March 1959) by the Christian layman Sadhu Joseph. These services were held ten miles away, near Medak, and attracted thousands of people from many miles around. One Gowd (toddy-tapper) named Narsiah returned from the meetings convinced that he had been healed of his leprosy by the power of Jesus Christ. He told his friends and relatives this, and he started attending Christian worship. He and the others who had attended Sadhu Joseph's services had learned many lyrics and some of the miracle stories from the Gospels. They seemed more 'knowledgeable' about Christianity after attending a week of healing services than many of the members of the congregation were after a lifetime's exposure to their evangelists' teaching.

Narsiah Gowd believed in the power of Jesus as a miracle-worker and healer of physical ailments. Through conversations with the author (P.Y.L.), he gradually came to believe in Jesus as the Saviour who saves men from their sin, which is more dreadful than leprosy. When he had come to believe that Jesus had saved him from his sins, he confessed these at a family worship service held in his own house and committed himself to Christ. At Narsiah Gowd's express request, the author baptized him at a Sunday evening service of the congregation. In the following months Narsiah continued to be faithful to his new Lord and was much less ready to compromise with Hindu practices than the older members of the congregation.

The other Hindus attending Christian services in Kondapuram were from the Reddi (landowner) and Sakali (washerman) castes. They, too, believed that they had been healed of various physical ills by the power of the Lord Jesus at the healing services of Sadhu Joseph. They were willing to associate with outcastes, sitting together with them during Christian worship, and they joined enthusiastically in the Christians' praise of the Lord Jesus. However, they hesitated to be baptized, since this would mean a definite break with their own caste communities and complete social ostracism. The washermen have a tightly organized system in which each family works for a certain specified clientele. Since the caste council could assign this work to another family as a punitive measure, every family in the caste is completely dependent on the goodwill of the caste council for its livelihood. Moreover, the washermen have certain traditional duties to perform in some of the worship of the village goddesses, and the men who had been healed or helped by Sadhu Joseph's blessing in the name of Jesus Christ did not see how they could continue to perform these necessary caste duties if they committed themselves through baptism to the Christian community and its worship of Christ.

It is likely that for every Hindu who is baptized and joins the Church as a result of Sadhu Joseph's ministry, there are several others, like the Reddis and Sakalis in Kondapuram, who have been markedly affected in their attitude, not only towards Jesus Christ, but also towards the (outcaste) Christian community. Moreover, Sadhu Joseph's own story illustrates many of the striking themes in the village's understanding of Christ. For these reasons, therefore, in spite of the fact that his work has been outside the area of our immediate survey, we think it well to include some account of his life and work.

Botumanchi Joseph comes from a village in a pastorate of the Hyderabad Methodist District that is now part of the neighbouring Dornakal Diocese. His parents were members of the Christian congregation there, coming from the Mala community, and Joseph was baptized as an infant. Sadhu Joseph relates that he never attended school in his village and thus was illiterate. He absented himself from night prayers at the evangelist's house and says that he was completely ignorant of the beliefs and practices of Christianity. When he was about eighteen years old, he worked in Jalna for a year or two as a coolie for the army; he then returned to his village with a considerable amount of money with which he married a girl, Mary, from another village. Two sons were born to them, one of whom died.

When Joseph had been married for about five years, he contracted leprosy. His parents, relatives, friends and even his wife began to despise him and would not come near him. He was not allowed to touch anything in the house and was isolated from all contacts. His wife left him and went back to stay with her parents, taking their son with her. Joseph became very depressed because of his illness and the treatment he was receiving. He finally became so desperate that he decided to commit suicide: 'When all my relatives and friends forsake me, there is no use my living any longer in this world. I have enjoyed my life enough for the last twenty-four years. It is better for me now to put an end to my life.' Twice he tried to commit suicide. Once he fell in a pit of deep mud and quagmire, but to his surprise he found himself on the bank as if somebody had pulled him out of the mud, yet there was no one there. Then again one night in his parents' home when everybody was asleep, he locked the doors of his room from inside, put a thick new rope on a beam of the roof and tried to hang himself. However, he fell down on to the ground, and found that the rope was cut in the middle as if someone had sliced through it with a knife. He could not understand what all this meant, but lay flat on the ground weeping in utter despair. About midnight his room was suddenly flooded with bright light and he heard a voice saying, 'O Joseph, why are you weeping? Are you worried about your loathsome disease? Get up, I have healed your dreadful disease of leprosy. Now go in peace out into the world, take the Bible and heal all manner of sickness and diseases in my name.'

When he woke up in the morning he found that his disease had vanished; his sores and patches were healed. In great joy he left his house for good, took a Bible from one of his friends in the congregation and went out into the jungle to lead a Sadhu's life, spending his time in prayer and meditation and Bible reading. Miraculously, he relates, he was now able, for the first time in his life, to read the Bible and to pray to his Master. This happened in 1954 when he was twenty-five years old. Since then he has been going from place to place, camping in his tent (presented to him by an American missionary) on the outskirts of a village, and healing all kinds of diseases in the power and name of Jesus Christ. The news of this Sadhu soon spread far and wide. His wife joined him and began to help him in his ministry, no longer as his wife in the physical sense, but as a 'sister', living in a separate tent.

Sadhu Joseph eats no solid food but lives on milk and orange juice.

He has grown long hair and wears a cassock with a silver cross on a string around his neck. He fasts every Friday in remembrance of Christ's death on that day. He spends most of his time in his tent in prayer and communion with the Lord, waiting for His guidance in all that he does. He will not move to another town or village unless and until he feels that the Lord is guiding him to do so. He has felt guided by the Spirit to fix Sunday, Tuesday and Thursday as the appropriate days for healing services, and on other days will do no healing. The healing services always begin at 7.30 in the morning and, depending on the size of the crowd, sometimes go on until late in the afternoon.

Early in the morning on the 'healing days', those who plan to attend the service bathe in a tank or river and put on clean clothes. By 7.30 the crowds have gathered, whereupon the Sadhu's wife comes and teaches them songs. (Those who are able to read can get printed book-lets containing the lyrics sung at these services.) She sings one line and the audience repeats it after her; she goes on like this, line after line, until she finishes the whole song. For an hour she leads the crowd in singing one lyric after another. Then the Sadhu comes out of his tent and goes to the place that has been prepared for him. While the audience continues to sing, he kneels down and prays silently. When he gets up he is garlanded by many people; he collects the garlands and places them on the table.

After making any necessary announcements, Sadhu Joseph begins to read and comment on a passage of Scripture. For two hours he explains it verse by verse in his own simple village style. Usually he selects two or three chapters from one of the Gospels (a section containing a number of miracles) about which he has prayed and meditated the previous day. In his line by line explanation he gives numerous illustrations from the everyday life of his audience. The whole audience, which has sung in unison clapping their hands, now listens to him preach in pin-drop silence. There is no public address system to carry his voice to the crowd, but there are some volunteers who keep the audience quietly seated. At the end of the sermon, the Sadhu closes the first part of the service with the Lord's Prayer and a benediction.

The Sadhu has felt guided to determine that every person who comes for healing should bring a little castor oil in a bottle and a little sugar and honey wrapped in a leaf. After the blessing they should eat the sugar and honey and rub the castor oil on their body at the point where healing is needed. Barren women who want children are expected to bring a piece of fruit (an orange, mango or plantain), and after this fruit has been blessed, the woman and her husband should eat it. Each person (or family) brings as an offering one anna and a handful of rice, putting the coin in a collection box and the rice in a gunny sack.

After the first part of the service is concluded with a benediction, the audience comes to the Sadhu one by one in orderly fashion, or he goes to the members of his audience, who are sitting or kneeling in long rows. Placing the Bible on their heads and on the oil and sugar they have brought (or the fruit), he blesses them one after another in rapid succession until he has blessed everyone in the crowd. Many lepers come to receive the blessing, for they believe that Jesus who healed the Sadhu will likewise heal them.

In his preaching Sadhu Joseph emphasizes both the physical and the spiritual healing wrought by Jesus. He also describes the main events in the life of Christ, especially His death and resurrection, but he says very little about the Holy Spirit. He speaks about repentance in general terms but does not make it a condition for healing. He does not stress any moral requirements but exhorts people to worship Jesus and to give offerings to Him when they get back to their villages. He does not insist that those who accept his message should be baptized, but leaves it to their choice. He does not discuss other religions at all in his preaching, but urges his hearers to believe in the Lord Jesus Christ, and he presents the Gospel of Jesus to them in clear terms. He insists that everybody should listen to the word of God, which itself creates faith in them and aids in healing. He does not claim to possess any supernatural power himself, and he clearly tells people that he is just an ordinary person like anyone else. He says that it is Jesus and Jesus alone who heals them through their faith in Him and through listening to the word of God preached at the beginning of each healing service.

Sadhu Joseph works in co-operation with the church in the area, and has no intention of establishing his own separate church. He baptizes people at their request, in consultation with the local pastor— for many who wish to be baptized want the Sadhu, and no one else, to baptize them. However, he does not administer Holy Communion, but invites the local pastor to celebrate Holy Communion in his camp, and he receives Communion from the pastor.

In 1958, in a village in the Bodhan pastorate of the Medak Diocese, the entire Madiga community asked Sadhu Joseph to baptize them. The day before the baptisms he held a preparation service to which he invited the local presbyter. At the baptismal service he made the sign of the cross with oil on the forehead of each candidate and baptized them all by immersion in a nearby canal. The new converts took the initiative in building a prayer hall, and helped to build a house for the evangelist whom the presbyter stationed in their midst. They soon proved quite strong in their Christian faith and were more active than the older congregations in the pastorate.

The Sadhu's healing services have attracted thousands of people in all the places he has camped. He generally camps in one place for three to six months. Many people put up temporary booths near the Sadhu's tent and live there, and soon the place becomes a temporary village. Shops and restaurants are opened by local shopkeepers at this site of the Sadhu's healings. Between ten and fifty thousand people attend his services, yet he touches and blesses them all, one by one. Many of the people who have been to these services report that they have been healed, and that they have experienced the power and compassion and love of Jesus Christ. When they return to their villages, they spread the influence of the Sadhu's work among their relatives and other villagers.[1]

On the other hand, there has been strong and sometimes violent opposition from the Arya Samajists and some Congress leaders in many of the places the Sadhu has visited. In some places they have conducted rival meetings right beside the Sadhu's meeting, in which they have criticized and condemned the Sadhu's work and the Christian religion. In order to disturb his service they broadcast their speeches over a public address system. In some places hoodlums have been sent to the Sadhu's camp to beat up the Sadhu and his followers.

Just a few weeks before our survey of the Jangarai section began, on Palm Sunday, 1959, a group of men came out from Medak in a lorry to Sadhu Joseph's camp in a nearby village. After the healing service was over and the crowd had dispersed, they burned down his tent, destroying all his belongings. Sadhu Joseph himself, who was praying in his tent at the time, escaped unharmed. The first rumours to reach the villages in the Jangarai section (only ten miles away) were that the men were leaders of the Congress Party in Medak. It appeared later that men from both the Congress and the Communist Parties were involved.

Some weeks later Sadhu Joseph conducted healing services in the city of Hyderabad. When the meetings were interrupted by men who threw stones at the Sadhu and his audience, the commissioner of police ordered the services stopped, on the ground that they were disturbing the peace. However, the Andhra Pradesh Christian Council and the Roman Catholic Church, backed by public opinion, persuaded the Government to withdraw the injunction. The Christian spokesmen proved to the Government that it was not the Sadhu who had been disturbing the peace, but rather the ricksha drivers who were hired by the Arya Samajists to throw stones at the Sadhu, disturb the meetings, and distribute pamphlets condemning the Sadhu's work and Christianity in general.

In the face of such opposition and disturbance, Sadhu Joseph has carried on calmly with his work, apparently quite unperturbed. Indeed, after his tent was burned down, the Sadhu is reported to have said that the loss of his possessions was a judgment on him for having accepted personal gifts from some of his admirers.

The violence of the opposition to Sadhu Joseph on the part of some Hindus is itself an indirect indication of the extent of the Sadhu's influence in the villages, for undoubtedly many Hindus who once were indifferent to Christianity or even opposed to it have become much more sympathetic through their acquaintance with this Christian Sadhu, or even through hearing the good report about him that their fellow villagers bring back. Many have come to believe in the power of Jesus Christ, and, in varying ways, to accept the truth of Christianity. Moreover, the songs used in the Sadhu's healing services are on the lips of many villagers. Sometimes they are sung by men and women at work in the fields.

Sadhu Joseph exerts an influence on Christian congregations, both through those Christians who have attended his services and had their faith strengthened, and through those Hindus who now begin to join in the worship of the Christian congregation and brings their thank-offerings to Christ. This influence should provide the Christian evangelist with new opportunities for revival within the congregation and evangelistic outreach beyond it. In the area surveyed, however, church workers seem to be largely unaware of this new situation or unable to respond to the opportunities presented by the Sadhu's work.

C. *The Sudra Converts in Ambojipet*

On August 14, 1959, two families from Sudra castes were baptized in Ambojipet. The head of one of these families is Narayana Gowd, of the toddy-tapper caste. He first learned of Jesus Christ as a child, when he attended the evangelist's school. About three years before his baptism, cholera broke out in the village, and pressure was exerted on him to participate in the worship of the cholera goddess, but he refused to do so. That same night he had a dream in which he was wrestling with Satan, who was trying to strangle him to death because he refused to worship idols. Then Jesus appeared in white robes, killed the demon (Satan) and rescued him. Like all other villagers, Narayana regarded dreams as conveying a message from the world of spirits and divine powers, so he took this appearance of Jesus quite seriously, but for three years he took no outward steps to identify himself with the worship of Jesus.

In March 1959, Narayana's wife, Satyamma, became very ill as the time approached for the birth of her baby. When Narayana took her to the mission hospital in Medak, she was in a critical condition, but she had a safe delivery there and was blessed with a son, whom his parents immediately called Swamidas ('Servant of the Lord'). Two months later Satyamma developed a severe stomach pain, which the villagers tried to relieve with their traditional methods, but in vain. One night she had a dream in which she saw Jesus and felt Him touching her, putting His hand on the place where there was pain and then putting three pills into her mouth. The following morning her pain had disappeared.

After all these experiences Narayana and his wife decided to be baptized, even though that meant joining the Christian community in Ambojipet, which hitherto had been composed entirely of outcastes. Satyamma's parents, who lived two and a half miles away in the village of Maddoor, opposed their taking such a decisive step and tried to discourage them, but the young couple tried to refute their arguments and witnessed to them about their experiences of 'Lord Jesus'. Satyamma said to her father, 'You may sever all connexions with me; you may not allow me to go, if that is your wish, but I am not going to leave Christ in any case!' When they were baptized in August, Narayana was given the Christian name of Paul. He was soon recognized as one of the leaders of the congregation.

In November 1959, Paul (Narayana) took the author (P. Y. L.) to the house of his father-in-law, Posha Gowd, in Maddoor, and asked him to conduct family prayers there. A week before, Posha Gowd had been in the Sarojini Devi Hospital in Hyderabad; he gave the following account of his recent experiences:

> I had been suffering from eye trouble for nearly six months when one day the retired evangelist from Ambojipet happened to be here, and advised me to go to the hospital in Hyderabad for treatment. For some time I hesitated, until my son-in-law Paul visited us and pressed me to go to the hospital. Finally I decided to go to the city with my son-in-law, and we took the train. To my surprise and misfortune the train was derailed after two stations, but we were saved without harm. I thought that this was a bad omen and wanted to return home, but my son-in-law urged me not to believe in these superstitions but to trust in Jesus Christ and depend on His mercy. We reached Hyderabad very late in the night and the next morning I was admitted to the hospital. Since my youth I have been in the habit of doing *pujah* to my *Istha Devata*, and I continued that in the hospital, so that I might have a successful operation. However, my son-in-law, Paul, persuaded me to discard that idol worship and to believe in Jesus Christ, so I threw the idol out the window. That very night in my dreams Yesu Swami appeared; He came to my bed, patted me on the back and said, 'Don't be afraid; everything will be all right; I am with you'. When suddenly I opened my eyes, Yesu Swami disappeared. The following morning I had a successful operation. Now I know my son-in-law's Jesus is a true and living God, and I and my family have decided to believe in the Lord Jesus Christ and be baptized. There are another nine Gowd (toddy-tapper) families in this village. I do not know whether or not these families will follow my example, but whatever happens, my son and his wife, my wife and myself are going to be baptized, whether the other Gowd families allow us to mix with them or not. I have three acres of wet land and two acres of dry land, and I can live quite an independent life.

In spite of his striking experience and his bold resolve, however, Posha Gowd two years later was still putting off the decisive step of baptism, but he continued to be on friendly terms with his Christian son-in-law, Paul, and his own son started reading the Bible.

During the winter harvest at the end of 1959, Paul worked as a day labourer in the fields of the police patel of Ambojipet. When the paddy had been threshed and was ready for measuring, the patel asked one of the women who had been harvesting to estimate how much the paddy would measure; she guessed forty measures. Then he asked Paul the same question and Paul replied, 'In the name of Jesus Christ I predict that you will get sixty measures of paddy at this threshing floor'. When the paddy was measured the patel was astonished to find that it came to exactly sixty measures, just as Paul had predicted. Since then this patel and the other village leaders have started to respect Paul and to regard 'Lord Jesus' with some awe.

The other family baptized on August 14 had been strongly influenced by Paul (Narayana Gowd) and had had a somewhat similar experience. Five or six years before, the wife had gone to her parents' home for her confinement. She had previously lost three or four children, so she was very anxious to have a safe delivery. A young Christian teacher in the Government school in her parents' village had visited her parents' home and prayed with her. As he was leaving, he told the woman that if God blessed her with a son, she should give him the Christian name *Devadas* ('Servant of God'). She did have a safe delivery, and a son was born to her whom she named according to the instructions. The little boy has been in good health since his birth, but his Christian name was the only indication of the family's contact with Christianity. It was only five years later, through the influence of Narayana Gowd, that they considered becoming Christians at the same time as Narayana and his wife. When they attended some evangelistic services that the author (P. Y. L.) held in Ambojipet, they definitely decided to accept Christ and be baptized.

Just before the service in which these two caste families were baptized and confirmed, a young man named Vittal, a potter, decided that he wanted to be baptized along with the others. He got the permission of his parents and came to the baptismal service. He had had no baptismal instruction or other formal teaching about the Christian faith, but there was no doubt of his sincere desire to become a Christian. After a short interview with the lad, the presbyter decided to baptize him, but not to confirm him along with the other adults in the two caste families.

At the presbyter's specific request, the author preached a sermon to the candidates and baptized them. In the sermon he explained that the word 'baptism' is symbolic of the dipping under, or the forsaking, of the old life of traditional Hindu beliefs and practices, and of the old life of sin, and symbolic also of the rising up to newness of life in Christ. He gave a list of traditional practices which ought to be given up, one of which was participating in *Chirutala Ramayanam*, the dramatic dance based on the stories of the Hindu epic, the Ramayana.

After the service, Vittal (baptized John) came to the author with a troubled conscience, and asked him whether he could continue to take part in these Hindu dramas. The author emphatically warned him that it would be quite wrong for him to participate any longer.

John was the only one to come forward and ask this question, but there were also two other Christians who were members of a Hindu dramatic association in the village. One was Paul (Narayana), whose story was related above, who had just been baptized and confirmed in this same service. The other was Swamidas, a young man from a Madiga family, a lifelong Christian. Along with fifteen other young men (all caste Hindus), they had banded together to perform the *Chirutala Ramayanam* and had engaged a goldsmith named Vittal to teach them these dramatic dances. They agreed to pay him at the rate of two rupees per member at each harvest until they had finished learning. They pledged themselves not to leave the association under any circumstances. If anyone were to drop out, he promised to pay a fine of five rupees and to submit to ten beatings with a sandal as punishment.

John took the author's warning at his baptism quite seriously and talked the matter over with the other two Christians. The three of them came to the decision to leave the association, whatever it might cost, and Paul took the lead in explaining this to their teacher and the other members of the association. The other members, however, were quite unwilling to let the three Christians drop out, considering them indispensable to the success of the group. When they found that they could not persuade them to continue to take part in the Hindu dramas, they decided that they would give up these traditional themes and that they all would continue together, but now setting Christian lyrics and dramas to the old music and dances. The Hindu leader of the group seemed enthusiastic about this novel arrangement, proudly exhibited the talents of his pupils in performing two Christian songs he had already set to dance, during a visit of the authors. He begged to be lent some Christian plays, and when he received them he set to work trying to adapt his attractive and complicated tunes and rhythms to the words of Christian dramas. When Vittal had to leave the village and go to his relatives because of his wife's illness, a Gowd named Buchiah became interested in the job of fitting the Hindu music used by the group to Christian dramatic themes. With the help of a literate Christian (the son of the retired evangelist), he set the story of the birth of Christ to the traditional tunes and dances.

A few words in the author's baptismal sermon, the troubled conscience of a 'last minute' candidate for baptism, and the courageous stand of three young Christians—these were the outwardly visible factors contributing to the development of an unprecedented situation: a group largely composed of caste (Sudra) Hindu young men undertaking to sing exclusively Christian lyrics, and those in a traditional form extremely attractive to all the villagers. We were unable to follow this development closely after 1959, but we have heard that on December 10, 1961, four more people from Sudra castes were baptized in Ambojipet, and one of these was the goldsmith Vittal who led the *Chirutala Ramayanam* group.

D. *Recent Individual Converts among Madigas and Malas*

Since the baptism of the Madiga community in Jangarai in 1927 there had been no converts to Christianity from other castes. The evangelist and his wife who came to the village in 1958 started a night school for Christian children. Three lads from the Bandela caste attended the night school at the evangelist's house and learned to read; they also attended the nightly worship services of the congregation. (The Bandelas are a separate sub-caste, closely linked to the Madigas, who did not become Christians with the main Madiga community.) The evangelist gave Christian names to these three non-Christian boys and cut off their *zuttu* (the tuft of hair on the crown of their heads). He also took them to the training courses held at the pastorate headquarters in Wadiaram so that they might learn more about Christianity.

During the latter part of the author's (P. Y. L.) stay in Jangarai, he held evangelistic services each night to which many of the Bandela, Mala and caste people came. They listened eagerly to the Gospel message presented to them in their own thought-forms and idiom. Three days after the author left their village to go to Gowlapalli, he was invited back by the evangelist to conduct a service for the Christians in Jangarai and to baptize nine of the Bandela people, who had responded to the challenge of the Gospel message by deciding to be baptized. When the baptismal candidates were asked before the service why they had decided to become Christians, they answered. 'Now we have understood what the Christian Gospel is, and realized that Jesus is the only God who saves us from our sins.'

A Mala lame boy in Gowlapalli had been attending night prayers and night school at the evangelist's house along with another boy from another Mala family. This lame boy had no relatives and was working for a land-owner in the village. The evangelist had been teaching him now and then about Christian faith, and on the 1959 Jatra day in Wadiaram he was baptized at one of the services. He is now taking an active part in the life of the congregation.

E. *The Madiga Community of Mallupalle*

Mallupalle is a small hamlet administratively attached to the larger village of Shankarampet a mile away. A Madiga community of nine families (about eighty people) lives in Mallupalle. Since the larger group of Madigas in Shankarampet have the hereditary responsibility to officiate at village festivals and to perform *yetti* (compulsory service without wages) for the village, the Madigas in Mallupalle are free from these traditional duties. They are unusual Madigas in another respect: they own lands, so they are not compelled to be tenants or day labourers dependent on the wealthy landowners. They are thus both better off economically and more independent of the higher castes in the village than are most outcaste groups in this area.

Several years ago an evangelist in Ambojipet was temporarily dismissed from church service and therefore had to find another way to earn a living. He persuaded a number of men working on a road-gang to pay him four rupees a month each to be taught how to read. None of his pupils was a Christian, but his textbook was the Bible. One of the men was a Madiga from Mallupalle, who in addition to learning the bare rudiments of reading and writing developed some interest in the contents of his textbook, so that for several years he went occasionally to attend Christian worship in Wadiaram or Ambojipet. However, it was not until April 17, 1957, that he and his wife and grown-up son were eventually baptized in Jangarai, thus becoming the only Christian family in Mallupalle. At his baptism the man was given the Christian name of Yohan (John).

Two years later, in April 1959, the village officials started collecting money from each caste community (*kulam*) in Mallupalle to pay for renovating the shrine of the village goddess Poshamma. The Madiga community was assigned a certain share, which was then divided between the joint families. Yohan is one of four brothers all middle-aged men heading smaller joint families. When his brothers asked him to pay his share, Yohan categorically refused. To most villagers, including many Christians, it is a matter of social duty to contribute to the shrines or festivals of village goddesses. To the convinced Christian, however, such contributions may appear to be participation in idolatry. When Yohan refused to pay his share, his brothers felt quite justified in punishing him by denying his family fire from their hearths and water from the communal well.

Yohan was greatly troubled by these measures of ostracism on the part of his own community as well as by verbal abuse and threats of physical harm from many in the village. Nevertheless, he would not change his stand, and his family loyally supported him. One day his brothers heard him praying aloud, using phrases, *Sarva śakti-gala Deva* ('Almighty God') and *Pariśuddhatma śakti* ('power of the Holy Spirit'). His brothers caught the word *śakti*, used in Christian parlance in the generic sense of 'power', but having a number of specific and more emotionally charged meanings to village Hindus: it is the general name of the great feminine Divine Power (the consort of Siva) or of the local Powers (the village goddesses), but it is also used as a name for the specific mysterious power or powers invoked in performing black magic. Yohan's brothers feared that this was worship of a mysterious Christian Sakti in the interests of black magic, so they angrily interrupted his prayer: 'You are worshipping Sakti, and your *śakti puja* might bring disaster upon us. So you and your family had better leave this village and go to some other village. You must either worship our goddess and leave your Jesus Christ, or leave the village at once!'

Faced with this still more severe and immediate threat, Yohan walked over the mile and a half to the closest village with a Christian congregation to seek help. This was Gowlapalli, and Yohan happened to come during the week that the author was spending there. It was decided in consultation with the presbyter to meet with representatives of the Madiga community in Mallupalle to try to persuade them to stop their persecution of Yohan. This was the middle of the hot season, when most people were not busy in the fields, so on the morning of the sixth of May, the Madiga representatives met with the presbyter in charge of the Wadiaram Pastorate, some evangelists from the Jangarai section, a few Christian laymen from Gowlapalli, and the author (P. Y. L.), under the shade of a large tree just outside Mallupalle,

The discussion went on for much of the morning, without any resolution of the issue. Yohan's brothers and caste associates felt that they had been rather patient with Yohan's religious idiosyncrasies. They had permitted him to worship a foreign god as his *ishta devata* ('chosen or favourite deity') and to participate in the ceremonies of his special sect. Surely Yohan knew that support of the village goddesses was a collective obligation of everyone in the village, whatever his sect. Moreover, they were not asking him to do anything that Christians in the neighbouring villages of Jangarai, Gowlapalli and Ambojipet did not regularly do; they often contributed to such religious activities of the whole village. If Yohan were not willing to meet his basic religious obligations to his caste and to the village, he would simply have to leave. Not only would it not be fair if he did not contribute his share, but it might anger the goddess Poshamma and thus bring disaster to the Madiga community, or perhaps to the whole village.

Yohan, however, stood firm. He insisted that whatever the Christians in the neighbouring villages might be accustomed to doing, he and his family could not have any share in the worship of any deity but *Yesu Swami*. With the discussion at this impasse, the author proposed that he might undertake to persuade Yohan to contribute to the renovation of Poshamma's shrine, if the next day the other Madigas would help Yohan to build a prayer hall for 'Lord Jesus'. This unexpected application of the principle of group solidarity threw the Mallupalle delegation into some confusion. They announced that they would have to talk the matter over further among themselves and would come back to the tree after lunch. When they returned, Yohan's relatives and persecutors made a surprising announcement: 'Either Yohan must become like the rest of us and worship the village goddesses, or we must become like him and worship Jesus Christ. Since we cannot persuade him to fulfil his obligations to Poshamma, we shall all have to become Christians!'

There is nothing mysterious about the appeal to group solidarity in the community's reasoning, yet for the Christians present at this meeting, most of all for the persecuted Yohan and his family, this sudden reversal of community sentiment was nothing short of miraculous. Indeed, nothing that happened during the period of our survey more clearly suggests to the eyes of faith the working of the Holy Spirit. However, this was not the dramatic and successful conclusion of a short story, but only the close of the first chapter in a history that is still going on and has already included several striking developments.

The community was serious about its decision to join the Christian Church, and its adult members officially requested the presbyter to baptize them by affixing their inked thumbprints to a document that sets forth their promise to accept Christ as their Saviour. The presbyter then initiated the steps to prepare the community for baptism and the founding of a new congregation. First a full list of baptismal candidates or 'inquirers' was prepared, giving all the proposed Christian names, family by family. In each house a list of the new Christian names of all the members of the household was written on a piece of cardboard and hung on the wall. The presbyter instructed the evangelist in Gowlapalli to visit Mallupalle and to give the group systematic instruction. There were already three or four literates among the inquirers, and they bought Bibles from the presbyter to use in the new congregation.

For two weeks in May there was intensive instruction for baptism. One week four evangelists from the Dharmavaram section of the Pastorate spent their annual 'Week of Witness' in Mallupalle, teaching the Christian faith to the inquirers. The following week the four evangelists in the Jangarai section came for the same purpose. However, the presbyter was able to be with them only one night, and in the next few months he paid only two brief visits along with the authors. After the initial flurry of activity in May, the Gowlapalli evangelist and his wife seem to have made only three visits of one day each in the five months that followed. The evangelist taught the older children, while his wife taught the women and younger children. The young men and women and some of the children learned to say the Lord's Prayer, to recite and sing the Ten Commandments, and to sing a few Christian lyrics. They learned their Christian names, which the evangelists used, but they did not use these new names in talking to one another. In the first five months after the May decision, the older men largely responsible for that decision received very little instruction in even the rudiments of Christian faith and life.

It is true that the Gowlapalli evangelist was ill for a month and that the unusually heavy rains made it necessary for several weeks to make an extra mile and a half detour between Gowlapalli and Mallupalle, but this hardly excuses the almost total lack of instruction and pastoral visitation by either the presbyter responsible for the pastorate or the evangelists working in the section in the crucial months between May and October. Mallupalle is only about a mile and a half from three of the villages in the Jangarai section with Christian congregations (Gowlapalli, Jangarai and Ambojipet), and only a mile away from the main road at Shankarampet, along which comes the bus running between Wadiaram and Medak. Mallupalle is therefore considerably more accessible than many of the villages in the pastorate.

While the official representatives of the Church seemed almost to have forgotten the Madiga community, the Hindu leaders in Shankarampet and Mallupalle certainly had not. Some made crude threats, such as, 'If you become Christians, your houses will be burned down, just as was Sadhu Joseph's tent.' More significant was the argument that we have already encountered: if they became Christians they would cease to be Harijans, and would therefore not receive any of the special Harijan benefits, such as the well for which they had already applied under the Harijan Welfare Scheme.

The most effective deterrent of the Hindu officials and landowners, however, was their control of land registration. For about twenty years the Madigas had been cultivating certain Government lands and had spent a good deal of money to improve them, but they had never been given formal title to these lands. Several months before they had applied to the Tehsil office in Medak through the village officials of Shankarampet, whose 'expenses' in forwarding and recommending the applications they had been obliged to recompense liberally, to have these lands formally registered in their names. Prior to their decision in May to become Christians, they have been assured that their applications would be approved. After that decision, however, the village officials told them that if they were to become Christians, the lands would certainly not be registered in their names. Indeed, if they persisted in their folly, the lands would be taken way from them and given to others.

Such a transfer would have been quite illegal, for the law under which the Mallupalle Madigas applied for registration of these long-occupied lands is of general application. It is certainly not restricted to

Harijans, still less to Harijans interpreted as only outcastes who have remained Hindus. These Madigas, however, did not know the specific provisions of the law, had no influence at the Tehsil office, and had little money to engage a lawyer to plead their case, especially since they had already given such large sums to the Shankarampet officials. In the face of this threat of being deprived of their most precious possession, their lands, the Madiga community decided to reconsider their decision for baptism or, more precisely, to postpone a final decision as to whether or not to become Christians. Early in October 1959 they asked the Gowlapalli evangelist to pay them no more visits.

The community remained in this undecided state for another two years. Yohan and his family were the only Christians, but their relatives tolerated their religious affiliation, and some of the group wanted to become Christians, if the threat of persecution could be lifted. By this time it had become clear to the higher caste Hindus in Shankarampet that the mild and unassuming Yohan, who in most matters deferred to his more aggressive brother Paul, was nevertheless the leader of a movement that could seriously disturb the *status quo*. Yohan was frequently held up to ridicule by the higher caste Hindus of the village. On the pretext of a land dispute, they subjected him to more direct persecution, and once they beat him badly enough to necessitate his going to Medak for treatment in the Government hospital.

In May 1961 a new presbyter was appointed to the Wadiaram Pastorate. He heard the story of what had happened in Mallupalle and made repeated visits to the Madiga community there. Since the new resident presbyter was still a 'junior presbyter', a more senior presbyter had been appointed as superintendent, and he, too, was keen to seize on all the evangelistic opportunities which the preliminary draft of our report indicated as present in the Jangarai section. He designated Mallupalle and several other villages without congregations as areas for extension work, which meant that the evangelists and their wives were to visit these villages, both individually and in teams. He also had some of these villages, including Mallupalle, recognized as extension areas by the District Church Council, and this meant that additional funds were available for placing evangelists in 'new villages' (i.e. villages where it was hoped a new congregation would develop).

By November 1961 the Mallupalle families had learned more about their legal rights, and had succeeded in getting the lands they were cultivating finally registered in their names. After that about half of the families decided to be baptized. The other families were reluctant to make any such drastic change in their lives, and were afraid of what the higher caste people and especially the village officials might do to them. They were not really opposed to the decision of the others, but they wanted to wait and see how their relatives and caste associates fared once they had become Christians. Thus what had begun around the issue of community solidarity finally led to a decision that cut through that solidarity, though it certainly did not destroy it.

Once some of the families had expressed their renewed desire to become Christians, the resident presbyter took up the task of preparing them for baptism as quickly and as thoroughly as possible. Both he and the evangelists paid them regular visits. When they sent word that they wanted no more visits from the Gowlapalli evangelist because his wife had quarrelled with them, the presbyter arranged for other evangelists to go instead. For the week just before their baptism, students from the Men's Training School in Medak came and helped with the instruction. It is difficult to assess the effects of this process of preparation, for the more significant results in the deepening of faith and the increase of moral sensitivity are not immediately evident. The older people still did not get much instruction. The children and young men learned some songs and some stories about episodes in the life of Jesus. As we have already noted, they were taught the Lord's Prayer and the Ten Commandments.

The baptismal service finally took place early in 1962, with the students from Medak, all the evangelists in the pastorate and some laymen from Jangarai and Gowlapalli present. The congregation sat in the shade of a tree and the ministers under a small pandal. Baptism was given by the superintending presbyter and the author (P. Y. L.), while the candidates sat in rows. (Some thought was given to the possibility of baptism by immersion, which is permitted by the Church of South India and preferred by some presbyters for the baptism of adults, but at that time of year there was no nearby canal deep enough.) The service included a triumphal procession through the village.

After the baptismal service, the resident presbyter made plans for evangelists to continue regular visits and promised to build a prayer hall if the new Christians donated a plot of land. The Christians asked that an evangelist be stationed there. The evangelist in Jangarai started coming twice a week and every other Sunday evening to conduct worship. On the alternate Sundays Yohan led the worship service. Since the new Christians were baptized but not yet confirmed, Yohan and his family were the only communicant members.

The formal beginning of a Christian congregation did not cause any break in the social relationships within the Madiga community, nor did it make any immediate difference in the association in traditional religious rites. The majority of the baptized Christians still joined with the other Madigas and the rest of the village in participating in Hindu festivals and other religious observances. In this respect they conformed to the general practice of the other Christians of the area rather than to the lonely stand of Yohan's family.

The presbyter saw as the two important tasks ahead of him the persuasion of the rest of the Madiga community in Mallupalle to receive baptism, and the preparation of the newly baptized converts for confirmation and the effective organization of their local congregation. He also saw to it that this community is closely linked to the larger Madiga group in the main village of Shankarampet. The traditional headman respected by the Madigas in Mallupalle lives in Shankarampet. There is bound to be influence back and forth, and the new presbyter was concerned that it be Christian influence extending from Mallupalle to the main village. He and his evangelists therefore went to

Shankarampet and held evangelistic meetings in both the Madiga and the Mala *palems* (sections of the village). They received a friendly welcome and were asked to visit more often.

This unfinished history is full of light and shadow, not least about its principal actor, Yohan. After the baptismal service, a quarrel developed between Yohan and his brother Paul, which probably had as one underlying cause that the new developments had threatened Paul's role as the leader and spokesman for the community. Yohan now received support from an unexpected quarter. The caste people, who a year before had persecuted Yohan and even beaten him, came to realize that he was innocent of the land encroachment of which they had accused him. They realized that they had been at fault and they came to respect him. When Yohan became involved in a quarrel with his brother, they took Yohan's side. If Yohan's humility and sincerity should change the attitude of the Mallupalle and Shankarampet landowners towards Christianity, a still more significant chapter may later be added to the Mallupalle story.

CHAPTER 8

The Meeting of the Gospel with the Village Mind

A. *The Persistence of Village Religion in the Christian Community*

At the pastorate headquarters in Wadiaram is a little shrine of the local goddess, Mankali; it stands inside the compound behind the church hall. At this shrine the villagers offer sacrifices to the goddess on a few special occasions, and they call the entire church compound the 'Mankali Compound'. This churchyard with two names is symbolic of the spiritual condition of village Christians in the pastorate; both Christian and traditional beliefs and practices exist side by side.

Most Christians have a Hindu or Muslim name as well as a Christian name. Some tie a cross round their necks, and on the same thread put a Hindu charm or talisman. Once when the author (P. Y. L.) was invited into a home to pray with a woman in acute pain, he found the sacred ashes of Kamudu (kept from the bonfire at Holi) smeared over her body in order to ward off the evil spirits. Christians give thank-offerings to Christ, and also pay considerable sums to the wandering religious mendicants of their own caste. They meet regularly to worship Christ, but also on occasion sacrifice a chicken to Poshamma, the goddess of smallpox. They respect their presbyter and sometimes bring him through the village to the evangelist's house in great procession, yet they consult a Brahmin about auspicious days and hours and ask him to draw up horoscopes for various purposes. They keep a picture of Jesus Christ on the wall of their houses, but in a niche in the same wall they have a little image of their household goddess, Balamma or Ellamma. They want the blessings of 'Lord Jesus' without incurring the displeasure of any of the village goddesses. Each year many of them celebrate twelve or thirteen Hindu festivals and one Muslim festival (*Muharram*) as well as the two Christian festivals of Christmas and Easter. In Kondapuram, the washerman who came back from Sadhu Joseph's healing services and started attending Christian worship said that he could not possibly be baptized because of the religious duties he had to perform for the whole village. To this an elder of the congregation replied, 'It does not matter. You can do both. We are doing both and yet we are Christians. We carry out our traditional duties at the village sacrifices, except that we do not eat the meat offered to idols.'

Most Christians in the Jangarai section participate in the various forms of non-Christian rites described in Chapter 3. By *participation*, we mean both (1) that they *perform* or *contribute* to the performance of these rites, and (2) that they *believe* in the efficacy of the rites and in the divine or demonic powers to whom or against whom the rites are directed. In four of the five congregations specially studied, all but a few families thus generally participated. In the three 'second village' congregations of the section where there has not been a resident evangelist for many years, there is not a single family that does not participate in all the Hindu rites.

They celebrate the calendar festivals in the same way and with the same motives as other low-caste Hindus. If they own land, they observe the agricultural festivals. They visit shrines in nearby villages and attend the festivals at those shrines and other religious fairs, in order to gain some 'blessings' of health or wealth. They keep little images of Balamma and Ellamma in the niches of their houses, and worship them in times of illness or distress, whether as a family or as individuals. They pay their assessments for the animal sacrifices to the village goddesses, in the belief that these will placate the local goddesses or send away the 'foreign goddesses', and those families which have traditional duties to perform, carry out those duties and eat the food endowed with a share (*amsham*) of divine power by being sacrificed to a goddess. They use amulets, talismans, and other charms to keep away evil spirits. They observe all the domestic ceremonies connected with the life-cycle: birth, coming of age, marriage, and death. Christian married women wear *bottu* (a vermilion or saffron coloured dot on the forehead) during all religious festivals and ceremonies and at every stage of marriage negotiations and the wedding. Out of deference to the evangelist's views, they do not wear *bottu* when they go to Christian prayers. Christian men continue to wear *zuttu* (a tuft of hair on the crown of the head). Christian young men take part in the singing and dancing of stories from the Hindu Epics and Puranas. Occasionally a Christian woman becomes possessed by a god or goddess and performs soothsaying, while in a trance.

The few families who do not participate to such a large extent in these Hindu rites do not join in celebrating the calendar festivals, but if they have land they may take part in the agricultural festivals. The men do not wear *zuttu* nor the women *bottu*, and they do not keep images of Ellamma or Balamma in their houses. They do wear talismans and other charms. They pay their subscriptions for the sacrifices to the village goddesses out of solidarity with their community and fear of social sanctions, but they take no further part or interest in these sacrifices. They perform the Hindu ceremonies connected with the life cycle, but they do not give their children Hindu names. The marked distinction in this regard between these families and the rest of the congregation does not correspond to the distinction intended by communicant membership. There are full and 'trial' members (non-communicants) in both groups. Neither are the members of this minority always known as 'good Christians'. For example, a girl in one congregation who had stood out against joining in the celebration of the Holi festival was living in adultery.

The situation in Achampet congregation is somewhat different, because of the influence of a group of young men on the rest of the congregation, and the influence of two families who have moved away to the city but come back to the village during vacation periods. Here we found three distinct groups: the few families not influenced by the young men, the majority who are somewhat guided by the young men's teaching and example, and the young men themselves.

Except for the caste headman, who has the duty of killing the sacrificial buffaloes, and the few families who have the duty of beating the drums, the Achampet Christians do not participate in these sacrifices apart from paying their caste assessment, and only the first group celebrates a few of the calendar festivals. These families still share the beliefs underlying the rites, but they now refrain to some extent from practising them, because the young men insist that it is wrong for Christians to join in the ceremonies of non-Christians. Families in this first group still retain their worship of household deities. The second group has been further influenced by the young men and has also given up the household rites, and many of them have stopped giving Hindu names to their children, but still use amulets and other charms.

The young men themselves have given up such charms, but they, too, continue to observe the traditional ceremonies of the life-cycle, though they have made certain Christian adaptations (see section D, below). The conduct of weddings, for example, is not in the hands of the young men. During the author's stay in the village, one of them was married with traditional ceremonies to a girl and at the same time to her sickly elder sister (the custom of 'treading on the feet' described on pp. 13, 47). The older men in the congregation wear *zuttu* and all the women, including the wives of the young men, wear *bottu*. The older people who arrange and conduct the marriage ceremonies all regard *bottu* and *bashingalu* as indispensable to an auspicious wedding and a successful marriage.

The young men have been influenced by the view of the Christian families from the city and also by the teaching of an evangelist who worked in the congregation several years ago (now a presbyter working in another part of the Diocese). First, their belief in the deities and demonic spirits of the village has been greatly weakened and perhaps in some cases even destroyed; second, they have gained a heightened sense of the distinctiveness of the Christian community, and feel that they should distinguish their life from that of their non-Christian neighbours. An additional circumstance which may be either a contributing cause or an effect of the second factor is that there is a sharper barrier of distinction and ill-feeling between the Christian Madigas and the non-Christian Malas in this village than is the case in the other four villages.

The persistence of these village religious practices is certainly due in part to social pressures, in some cases economic or even physical coercion and to such subtler pressure as the desire of Christians to enjoy themselves and provide their children with a feast and clothes at the same time as their non-Christian neighbours enjoy a festival. There is also a sense of solidarity with the rest of the village, especially in warding off a calamity affecting the whole village. But even this sense is not purely social, for there is the vague feeling that the village is bound as a unit to certain divine powers, and most Christians are convinced of the reality and power of the divine and demonic spirits inhabiting the village and the region. It is clear that the rites which persist most among these Christians are those which are considered to be fitting or auspicious. Failure to perform them may evoke the wrath of specific deities, but even if the village deities are no longer believed in, there is a feeling that some calamity will befall if these traditional rites are not performed, especially the rites accompanying various points of transition and crisis in the life-cycle.

The general pluralistic attitude of the village towards rites and deities makes it easy for Christians to reconcile their participation in Christian worship and their joining in other rites. Each sect may have its own *ishta devata*, favourite deity, but it tolerates to some extent the presence of other sects, and the less zealous members of the sect venerate the gods of the other sects as well as a whole host of lesser gods and spirits. This 'hospitable' attitude and tolerant spirit of village Hinduism made it much easier for the Gospel to gain a hearing and for Christianity to become one of the *matams* (religions or sects) of the village.

It is not the presence of these village religious practices and their accompanying beliefs among the Christians which constitute the Church's problem, but their persistence with little or no change for two or three generations. If these practices continue within the congregation, it might become an even less distinctive community than that of the village Muslims, approaching the status of the Saivite Baljis or the Vaishnava Visva Brahmas. Lack of systematic teaching by presbyters and evangelists is a major cause for this persistence of 'pervasive Hinduism' or 'village religion'. What is still more important, however, is that such teaching as there is sets forth a new 'law' which the village Christians are exhorted to follow, without the exhorter having much confidence that they will actually do so. Presbyters and evangelists tend to regard members of the village congregations as poor Christians, because of their extensive participation in non-Christian rites and their other failures to live up to the norms of educated Christians. This disapproval is often plainly expressed, but sometimes evangelists are reticent about expressing their disapproval, lest the members of their congregation stop coming to worship or giving 'collections'. Only rarely is the Gospel communicated with such power as both to convict Christians of sin and to give them a new freedom to reorder their lives. Consequently most village Christians do not feel the serving of other 'lords' besides Jesus Christ to be sin. They know that the ministers of the Church disapprove of village rites, but most of them do not feel such disapproval in their own consciences. Most important, it is only in a few exceptional instances that the Gospel has worked in their minds with such liberating and creative power as to suggest to them what in the various cycles of rituals can be wrested from the other 'lords' and 'powers' of village existence and taken captive for 'Lord Jesus'.

B. *Village Christian Understanding of Christian Doctrines*

It happens that the area chosen for this study is one in which there is more Hindu influence upon Christians than is generally true in South India, but perhaps also more influence of the Gospel upon village Hindus. The area was certainly not selected for study with this fact in mind; indeed it has been somewhat embarrassing that such has proved to be the case. Just because of this high degree of mutual influence between Hindus and Christians, however, one can see more clearly certain features of the present encounter between the Christian Gospel and the traditional beliefs and attitudes of the villager than would have been possible had the study been of a more 'typical' Christian community, which was more separated and distinct from its village Hindu environment.

It was most difficult to gain a clear picture of the beliefs of the Christians in the Jangarai section, for they do not readily articulate their fundamental conceptions and attitudes. Many of the statements of belief obtained are repetitions of the phrases of the evangelist or presbyter, which as such furnish little clue as to whether those particular Christian teachings have been inwardly appropriated. Since the topic is central to our study, we are presenting the picture as we are able to draw it, fragmentary as it is, along with a number of somewhat speculative generalizations.

In the first section of this chapter we discussed the large extent to which these village Christians share the traditional world-view of the rest of the villagers, and participate in the traditional religious practices. This section and the following one are concerned with the other side of the same picture: the extent to which Christian ideas have penetrated the minds of both Christians and non-Christians in these villages, and the way in which these ideas have combined with or reacted upon the traditional beliefs of the village. Some of the factors contributing to this two-way traffic between Hinduism and Christianity have been noted in previous chapters. Perhaps the most important factor on the ideological level is the 'both . . . and' attitude toward different sects and traditions; the most important sociological factor may be the high proportion of intermarriage between Christians and Hindus in this area, which will be discussed in the next chapter.

Most of the Christians in the Jangarai section know a few of the miracles of Jesus, a little about Christ's birth, and the fact that He was put to death on a cross. Many know nothing about the Resurrection, Ascension, or Pentecost, or the promise of Christ's return.[1] When asked what happened after Jesus died, some replied, 'Nothing happened. He died like us, was buried and came to an end'. They regard Jesus, like Krishna and Rama, as a human incarnation (*avatara*) of God. 'He was incarnate in a form like ours'. This does not mean, however, that they cannot conceive Jesus as a present reality. They believe that, like the air, 'God is everywhere', and similarly, 'Christ is everywhere'. Many know of the Virgin Birth, but some of the older people do not. Those who have attended the evangelist's night school classes know some stories from the Acts of the Apostles (on which they must take an examination); they are especially fond of the story of Stephen and the conversion of St. Paul.

Both Christians and non-Christians listen very attentively to the Passion story, and sometimes the women shed tears during the preacher's narration. Any story of a person being persecuted and going through suffering arouses their sympathy. A notable example is the story of the martyrdom of Hassan and Hussain recounted by the Muslims at Muharram. Christians feel sorry because of Jesus' innocence. 'Wicked people killed Jesus without realizing he is God'. For the majority of Christians, the death of Jesus is without sacrificial significance. The young men and women who have attended the evangelist's night school classes or who have attended short courses in Wadiaram or Medak are familiar with the formula, 'He died for our sins and rose again'. Both they and their teachers attempt to give these words meaning in more familiar terms. e.g. 'Gandhi's death was for the sake of the country, but Jesus' death was for our sakes'. What 'dying for our sins' means is not at all clear to them.

There are two Hindu conceptions of sacrifice with which they are familiar, and in terms of which they try to understand the sacrificial significance of Jesus' death. One is the philosophical and ascetic notion of *tyāgam*, the renunciation or 'self-denial' of the ascetic, or even some less sweeping renunciation of an ordinary person. This idea is familiar, but not of central importance for villagers of the lower castes, and in any case it does not seem to fit what they are taught about the sacrificial death of Jesus. The other familiar notion is the village Hindu conception of animal sacrifice, *bali*, but this also seems very far away from what they are taught. The young people who have been to night school or gone to special courses outside the village are familiar with the phrase, 'The blood of Jesus cleanses us from sin'. They sense a vague connexion with the familiar notion of *tirtham*, the cleansing with water in a sacred bath, and they have some sense of a purificatory power in the blood of Jesus.

Villagers believe in offering to the goddesses or demonic spirits, in order to please or placate them, the blood of a chicken, goat, sheep or buffalo. (Cows are not killed, and pigs are not slaughtered but buried alive.) When the animal is killed, the blood is poured out before the goddess and the meat is eaten by the worshippers. It is especially the blood that is considered the sacrificial offering, although the wing of a chicken or the foreleg of a sheep or goat is also sometimes left as an offering. Many other offerings are also presented, such as saffron coloured rice or coconuts. Indeed, there is a strong feeling that the goddess should not be approached with empty hands, so the worshipper always brings some offering, which can also be a flower or a piece of fruit. The best possible offering, however, is the blood of an animal, for the goddesses like blood very much. There seems to be some recognition that in offering blood, they are offering the most valuable thing they can: life itself. Yet though they share the meat of the sacrificial victim, they do not seem consciously to identify themselves with the sacrifice, such as participants in many sacrificial cults in other parts of the world have done, including that of the Old Testament.

When Christians slaughter a goat for a marriage or some other feast, they like to slaughter the animal near the evangelist's house (which is usually the place of worship), and they invite the evangelist to come and pray. Later they send some of the meat to the evangelist. Non-Christians who are naming a child after 'Lord Jesus' like to slaughter a goat near the Christian Church (often the evangelist's house) and have a feast there. If they are not permitted to slaughter the goat in the church compound, they do so at a distance, but face the goat towards the church. They expect that this will please Jesus.

On the whole, however, animal sacrifices are associated with the village goddesses and demonic spirits. Animal sacrifices are not offered to the Hindu high gods or their incarnations; nor do any of these gods sacrifice themselves for any of their devotees. Since Jesus is usually conceived as a 'Lord' or 'incarnation' it remains extremely difficult for even the better educated village Christians to understand what the sacrificial death of their Lord Jesus could mean. The least educated Christians tend to think of the shedding of Jesus' blood as the placating of Satan (they use the Muslim word *Shaitan*), not of an angry God. Both the influence of Islam and the emphasis in the evangelists' teaching lead them to believe in Satan as a power responsible for evil, who tempts people to do evil. Satan is thus the special kind of *dayyamu* (demonic spirit) recognized by Christians, and since blood is shed to placate such spirits and the local goddesses, rather than as an offering to the Supreme Deity, it is quite natural for some Christians to conceive of Jesus' blood as being poured out to Satan.

Not only the 'sacrifice' of Christ but also the 'sacrifice' expected of the Christian are hard for the Jangarai Christian to understand. For the latter the evangelist uses the term *samarpana*, which means 'complete offering' or 'self-dedication' in high Sanskritic Telugu and is also a term borrowed from Hindu cult language, but this is the language of the ancient Vedic ritual, which means nothing to villagers of the lower castes. The evangelists do not use the term *tyāgam*, with which villagers are acquainted, whether for fear it will suggest too much of the content of Hindu asceticism, or simply because it was not what they were taught.

The many Christians who are ignorant of Jesus' rising from the dead celebrate Easter at the urging of their evangelist, but without understanding or enthusiasm. They take Christmas much more seriously than Easter, though some seem to look forward to Christmas with less enthusiasm than to some of the Hindu festivals. *Kristu Jayanti*, the birthday of their special god, is analogous to the birthdays of the Hindu gods, such as *Krishna Jayanti*, the birthday feast of one of the most important incarnations of Vishnu.

Those who have studied in the night school know of Jesus' resurrection and have some idea of its significance. They say, 'No other god but Christ ever rose from the dead'. It is the uniqueness of Christ rather than His victory over sin and death that impresses them. They do use the word *jayam* (victory) a great deal in their hymns, but there too, it seems to mean to them that Jesus is a better or more powerful god than the other gods. Even the better informed and more thoughtful Christians see the meaning of the Resurrection in terms of its demonstrations of the power of Jesus as God. Perhaps the underlying reason for the lack of significance attached to the Resurrection is that the *humanity* of *Yesu Swami* remains somewhat vague and uncertain for these Christians, like that of the human incarnations of Vishnu, who are regarded by some Hindus as having been genuine men and by others as having adopted a human form only as a temporary disguise, or even as an illusive appearance. The evangelists were trained by Posnett to put a great deal of stress on the events of the human life of Jesus, but in the prevailing village climate of thought, this has generally meant an emphasis on the miracles of Jesus as signs of His Divine power and has not impressed village Christians with Christ's genuine humanity. If the Resurrection is not of a man who really died, it loses the meaning which it has for Christian faith, and there is nothing in their particular pre-Christian background which would lead them to give it any other meaning, such as that of a dying and rising god who reactivates the cosmic cycle every spring.

Even the Christians who know the phrase in the Creed, 'He shall come again . . .' do not appear to wonder what it means. There seems to have been no teaching on this subject by evangelists or presbyters for many years. Evangelists are familiar with the expectation of Christ's return, but do not concern themselves about it. Consequently none of the village Christians has any idea about Christ's Second Coming and the establishment of the Kingdom of God on earth. It is of interest that most village Hindus in this area are not familiar with the belief in Kalki, the avatara of Vishnu, who will come to restore righteousness at the end of this evil age. This belief seems to be limited to the few educated Hindus, especially the Brahmins, and to the high-caste devotees of Vishnu. However, all Hindus in this village expect the return of Virabasantarayyadu, a Hindu saint who stated just before he died that he would come again.

The usual name for Jesus is *Yesuswami*. *Swami* is used here with the meaning 'Divine Lord', the same sense it has when applied to the incarnations of Vishnu. Villagers also, however, use *Swami* in addressing or referring to a saint or sadhu. (Sadhu Joseph is called *Swami*.) The term can therefore signify either God in the form of a man or a man with the power of God. Village Christians believe that if their 'Lord' Jesus is worshipped, He will heal the sick, bless their family and keep it from all troubles and misfortunes, bless their crops and livestock abundantly, and give success in all their undertakings. But if they fail to see such *barkat* (material blessing) in those families which are faithful to Christ, they sometimes begin to doubt the power and effectiveness of Christianity and ridicule other Christians who remain faithful in the face of misfortune. (Cf. the experience of Nathaniel of Gowlapalli described in Chapter 9 below.)

It is also said, 'Through *Yesuswami* we have received *telivi* and *barkat*'. *Telivi* is literally 'knowledge'; it includes for these Christians the knowledge of reading and writing (possessed by a few members of the group and their teacher, even if not themselves), the cultural advancement and widening of intellectual horizons which they have experienced since becoming Christians, and for some, the knowledge of the Bible. However, this term does not seem to include the sense of orthodox Hindu *jnana* knowledge, leading to salvation. The 'gift of the Bible' has been granted by Jesus; this means that like the Muslims and higher caste Hindus, they now for the first time have their own special Sacred Scriptures. They believe that Jesus frees them from the caste people's 'yoke of oppression', and gives them the privilege of reading and writing, which the higher castes denied them; He gives them the free access to the Sacred Scriptures, from which they were excluded as low-caste Hindus. Their understanding of the blessings Christ has brought them is reflected in the evangelist's sermon summarized in the Appendix to Chapter 6 (Sermon 4): 'You received lands through Jesus; you got rid of forced labour (*yetti*) through Him'. Jesus is thus mainly regarded as a wonder-worker and a bestower of blessings, though there are a few who regard Him as the Saviour who suffered on the cross to save men from sin, and they compare that suffering on their present situation: 'As Jesus suffered, so we are persecuted by the landowners'. These few may also say, 'After death we shall go to Jesus and be with Him for ever'. Although most of the Christians believe it necessary to worship local spirits and placate demonic spirits in addition to worshipping *Yesuswami*, there are a few who say, 'Demons need not be feared, for the Lord Jesus is stronger than demons'.

Many use the terms 'sin', 'sinners', and 'forgiveness of sins' in their prayers. They generally consider the same acts as sins as do non-Christians: adultery, murder, stealing, lying, and 'breaking the commandments'. They generally do not regard idolatry as sin. There is little understanding of God's forgiveness of sins, or of Jesus' forgiving His enemies while on the cross, and there is little willingness on their part to forgive others. Only a few have much understanding of 'repentance'.

The term 'Holy Spirit' is used in prayers, but most Christians seem to know nothing about the Holy Spirit or His work. At a convention in Medak at which a number of neglected doctrinal topics were discussed, a number of evangelists from different pastorates said that this was the first time they had learned of the work of the Holy Spirit. One said, 'Until now I never depended on the Holy Spirit'. These evangelists have all been taught something of the doctrine of the Holy Spirit during their years of training, but apparently for many this teaching has not become a vital part of their Christian understanding. While they have accepted the Holy Spirit as one Person of the Trinity, they have communicated nothing about the nature of work of the Holy Spirit to members of their congregations, to whom the Christian Telugu term *Pariśuddhātmā* meant even less than it did to them. Both *pariśuddha* ('holy') and *ātmā* ('inner self' or 'Spirit') are Sanskrit terms familiar to the educated Hindu but holding little meaning for most villagers. They consider *pariśuddha* a synonym of the ordinary word for 'clean'.

Some Christians use the term *śakti* for the 'power' of God, meaning active, immanent Divine power. For village Hindus the word also is a general term for goddesses, ghosts or demons who embody divine or demonic powers. The Christian usage is sometimes confusing or alarming to non-Christians, as Yohan of Mallupalle found to his cost (see p. 159), but Christians themselves seem quite able to use *śakti* in a distinct sense for the power of God in Christ, and it may be that they thereby understand more of the significance of the Holy Spirit than by the use of the 'proper' term in the Telugu Bible translation. (A similar situation now exists in English with 'ghost' and 'Holy Ghost', where a radical distinction in meaning has developed, which is simply taken for granted by instructed Christians but is sometimes confusing to non-Christians.)

The Christians in the Jangarai section seem to have been ignorant of the idea of the Trinity (*tritvam*). The young men going to the courses for voluntary church workers say that they there have heard the word for the first time. However, the Arya Samajists are now questioning the Christians about their belief in the Trinity: 'It is not true that you believe in only one God. Actually you believe in three Gods. If you say these three are one, then we also believe in one God. Our *Trimurti* [Brahmā the Creator, Vishnu the Sustainer, and Siva the Destroyer] is One'. Village Christians are quite baffled by this attack on the distinctiveness of a Christian doctrine of which they are not even aware, and the evangelists are unable to help them.

The general term for 'God' used by Telugu Christians is *Devudu*. In classical Hinduism the ancient Vedic *devas* have descended to quite a secondary status in comparison with the 'High Gods' or 'Universal Lords', but in Telugu the term has kept the generic meaning of 'deity'. *Devudu* is the Telugu masculine form of *deva* and can be used in the village to refer to any god, including that of the Christians, but not to one of the goddesses. It is also used as a general vague term ('deity-in-general') corresponding to *Bhagavantudu* ('Adorable Lord') as a name for the Supreme Deity. Bhagavantudu and Narayana are names given by worshippers of Vishnu to God in His supreme personal form as Creator, Sustainer and Destroyer of the universe, comparable to the title *Parameśvara* ('Supreme Lord') for the devotees of Siva, but in these villages it is particularly the Vaishnava names for the Supreme Deity that are used by all the villagers without sectarian connotations. Less frequently they use *Parameśvara*, which they shorten to Isvara, and occasionally the more philosophical *Paramātmudu* ('Supreme Self or Spirit'). When the villagers go to sleep at night and awake in the morning, and when they sneeze, they often say, 'Narayana' or 'Swami'. They also cite the verse,

> 'Where three or four are gathered, Narayana is present;
> Where ten are gathered, Paramātmudu is present.'

No contrast is here intended between the two names for the Supreme Deity used in parallel. God is understood to be transcendent, yet in some sense He pervades the whole universe with His power and is concretely present in certain forms.

Christians understand *Yesuswami* to be the *avatar* of *Devudu*, the Supreme Creator, that is to say, the form of God which is present and active within this world. When asked to describe God, these village Christians answered, 'God is spirit and omnipresent'; 'God is the creator of heaven and earth'; and 'God is love'. Christians who can read the Bible and have attended study courses also say, 'God is holy and eternal'. Describing the presence of God, many of these Christians say, 'He is everywhere, in the wood, in the wall, in everything. He is present like air; we can't see Him'. Yet there are certain forms in which God's power is especially present. The cross, the Bible, and pictures of Jesus are representations which have power to ward off evil, but a clear distinction is made between them and idols (*vigrahalu*), which are considered to be concrete embodiments either of some visible form of the Hindu high gods or of one of the local goddesses. The Christians' *Devudu* has no such 'incarnation' in an image.

The understanding of the Christian sacraments reflects varying combinations of the Church's teaching and traditional ideas. Such combination is symbolized in the new word these Christians have coined by mispronouncing *baptismamu*. They say instead *baptirthamu*, thinking of *tirtha*, a sacred bath, or sacred waters in which such a bath takes place. Even more important than the association with sacred bath, however, is that with the naming ceremony of *purudu*. Baptism thus signifies the receiving of a distinctive name associated with the Christian community and the Christian God, and is also considered an act of ritual cleansing.

Some very ignorant Christians use the term *baptirthamu* for Holy Communion as well, making no distinction between the two sacraments. Most Christians, however, think of Baptism as a distinct rite of entry into the Church, whereas they consider Holy Communion a part of the Christian worship service in its fuller form. They usually conceive Communion to some extent in terms of the Hindu *prasādam*, divine 'grace' or power concretely present in flowers, fruits or other food which has been offered to a deity and then returned to the worshipper. Such food is not eaten at the temple but is taken home (especially saffron rice) and distributed to other members of the family, and the consecrated flowers are sometimes kept for a time in the house. Some village Christians actually call the Communion elements *prasādam*, and the idea is influential even when the word is not used. After a communion sermon on the usual text, 'Do this in remembrance of Me,' the preacher asked a faithful woman in the congregation, 'What are these elements for?' She replied, 'Jesus gave them to us so that we may keep them in our pockets to remember Him by'. The preacher thought that the woman had not been paying attention, but actually she had been listening only too well! The exclusive mention of the memorial aspect of the Communion elements was associated in her mind with the remembrance aspect of *prasādam*, and so she answered, to 'keep them . . . to remember Him by'.

Christians consider the celebration of the Lord's Supper to be a special duty of the presbyter and an integral part of his visit to the congregation. They know that the Communion elements are given to only a few people, but they do not know why Communion is given to some and not to others. Some people who want to receive the elements are told, 'This is not meant for you'. Sometimes Hindus present at the service come forward to receive this Christian *prasādam*, but they are sent back by the evangelist. The villagers in general understand Holy Communion as a special *prasādam*, distinguished by being given by the Christian priest and given only to a few, instead of being distributed freely, like the usual Hindu *prasādam*. While some in the congregation take part in the service with understanding, others are simply directed by the evangelist as to what they should do. Some do not know what is expected of them when the presbyter places the bread in their hands. On the other hand, some Christians consider Communion as a very distinct rite connected with the crucifixion of Christ, and with His body and blood. While this deeper understanding is particularly characteristic of V.C.W.s and others who have gone outside the village to training courses, it is shared by a few who have gained such understanding within the congregation by regular attendance at the Communion services and listening to the presbyter's sermons.

Another reflection of the ideas of *prasādam* (associated chiefly with Sanskritic deities) and *amsham* (literally 'share', associated with sacrifices to village goddesses) is seen in the custom of many Christians who, when they give an offering of grain, take a few kernels back again. They do this because they believe that they will share in the Divine power if they share in the things offered to Christ. Evangelists and presbyters are therefore now in the habit of putting a few kernels of grain back in their baskets after they have made their offerings. The Christians call this returned grain *lābham* ('gain'); they do not use the words *prasādam* or *amsham*. The direct use of the term and practice of *prasādam* during Christian *jatras* will be discussed in Section D below.

Christians use some distinctive terms even when there are apparently appropriate Hindu words available. Villagers are familiar with the practice of *gurudakshinam*, gifts to visiting religious teachers by their followers, and with the custom of *patti*, the compulsory tax levied on all groups in the village to build a shrine or to pay the expenses for a sacrifice in which the whole village must share. Christians, however, have long used the term *tsanda*, 'voluntary collection' or 'subscription', whether their gift is an ordinary harvest offering, a special thank-offering given to the evangelist, or some other special offering for the presbyter or the bishop. Because *tsanda* has the connotation of an obligatory collection or a subscription to a club, the Diocese has tried to replace it with *kānuka*, 'gift', the word used in the Telugu Bible for the gifts offered by the Wise Men. While *kānuka* is the official word in the Christian service, it is not very familiar to these villagers, and Christians continue to use the term *tsanda*. Most village Hindus have no special word for gifts to the gods; they use the verbal noun *pettuta*, 'what is placed or set down'.

The non-Christian guru chants a sacred verse (*mantra*) and raises his hands with palms outstretched over his followers in blessing. High-caste Hindus use the word *āśirvādam* for this blessing; other Hindus call it *dīvena* or *barkat*. Both the noun *āśirvādam* and the derived verb are regularly used to mean 'blessing' in the Telugu Bible, and some Telugu Christians use the word to refer to the benediction or blessing at the end of the worship service. These Christians, however, do not consider the presbyter's benediction as such a powerful 'blessing'; it is simply another prayer. Similarly they ask for 'prayer' for a sick person, not for 'blessing'. They believe that when the presbyter touches a sick person or places a Bible on his head, while praying for him, it increases the sick person's faith but does not itself bring 'blessing'. They refer to Sadhu Joseph's services, however, as *dīvenalu*, and they believe that Sadhu Joseph uses the touch of the Bible or the eating of sugar and honey to convey the *dīvena* of healing.

While presbyters and evangelists use the term *guru* ('religious teacher') as a title for a presbyter, village Christians do not use this honorific in addressing the presbyter. Local Brahmin priests are also not usually addressed as guru; the term is reserved for the travelling Hindu priests who are considered to possess greater religious authority; they have jurisdiction over several villages (like the presbyter) and they are believed to possess real power in their blessing (unlike the presbyter). Christians therefore do not use the term *guru-bhakti* ('devotion to the guru') to describe their regard for the presbyter. They only rarely wash the presbyter's feet and garland him only when he visits a congregation for the first time. It sometimes appears that they go to non-Christian gurus for 'blessings', and go to the Christian presbyter with requests for help! This is not very flattering to the presbyter, especially if he considers himself a Christian 'guru', but the Christians' general refusal to accord the presbyter the title and honours appropriate to a Hindu guru reflects both a realistic and a theologically defensible conception of the Christian presbyter: he is not a mediator of 'blessing' or 'salvation'.

For village Hindus, the conception of salvation or the supreme goal of human life ranges from the philosophical concept of *moksha* (release from the cycle of empirical life and entry into a state of transcendental knowledge and bliss), on the one hand, to the notions of *śubham* (all that which is auspicious, good or happy, or contributes to welfare) and *barkat* (material blessings), on the other. The philosophical concept of *svarga* (heaven) is in between, since it is a continuation of worldly happiness after death, but for a limited time. Most villagers, however, do not distinguish between *svarga* and *moksha*, conceived as the state of eternal personal communion with one's chosen Lord.

Most villagers, including the Christians, express their understanding of life after death something as follows: 'We do not know what happens after death. We only know that we go to *svarga*, which is a pleasant place. Bad people go to *Yamalokam* (Hades, literally, 'the world of the Lord of the dead').' Villagers fear stories about Yama's coming to take someone's life, but they have no fear that they will go to hell. They see representations of heaven and hell in pictures and dramas, but they have no clear idea about them. There seems to be little Christian preaching about life after death, and little reference to hell.

Christians in this area call heaven *moksham* and use its synonym *mukti* to mean salvation. They also use the term *Vaikuntam* which for Vaishnavas means the eternal abode of Vishnu and His devoted attendants. *Paralokam* ('higher or supreme world') is another synonym more extensively used by Christians than by village Hindus, but the most common term is *moksham*. Salvation in the future life is conceived by some Christians as the state of eternal personal communion with the Lord Jesus.

For most Christians, however, it is the this-worldly aspects of 'salvation' or Divine favour that loom the largest, just as it is present misfortune or the threat of calamities in the near future, within this earthly life, that weigh most heavily upon them. Christians share this village outlook, and it is therefore not surprising that their conception of Christ's blessing should be strongly influenced by the village notion of *śubham* or *barkat* (an Urdu word of Muslim background that is more popular in these villages than the standard Telugu word *dīvena*). The influence of the idea of *śubham* is only indirect, because the auspicious state is still so largely associated with Hindu deities. Christians share with most Hindus and Muslims in these villages the idea that Divine blessing is expressed in very tangible or material ways.

The 'official' Christian word for salvation is *rakshana*, a theistic Hindu term signifying both the present 'protection' of the Lord in this life and His 'rescue' of the soul from worldly existence to the eternal joys of His trancendental abode. We do not know whether *rakshana* was chosen as a translation of 'salvation' because of this happy combination of mundane and supra-mundane connotations, or because it lacked the undesirable associations of other Hindu expressions for 'salvation'. In any event, *rakshana* is another Sanskritic Telugu word in the official Christian vocabulary which has little or no meaning in ordinary village parlance. There is a word for sandals, *padarakshalu* ('foot protectors'), but even this is a high Telugu word not used in these villages. There is also a verb, *rakshintsuta*, which means 'to rescue' in high Telugu, but this is not used in the villages. Consequently when these Christians are asked what *rakshana* means, they either can make no reply or repeat the phrase they have learned, 'Jesus is my *rakshakudu* (Saviour)'; but it is doubtful whether *rakshakudu* means any more to them than *rakshana*, except as it acquires its content from Christian teaching. The same is true of another common Christian term, *nityajīvam*, 'eternal life'. It is Sanskritic Telugu, virtually meaningless to most villagers. This does not mean, however, that there is nothing in village Christians' experience or their understanding of the Christian faith which in any way corresponds to 'salvation' or 'eternal life', and it is these various shades of meaning which we have tried to explicate above. One element clearly missing in their conception of 'salvation' is salvation from sin. Even in educated congregations there is little recognition of the seriousness of sin, and if anyone preaches on that subject he may be accused of having become a Pentecostalist.

There is little emphasis in the preparation of presbyters and evangelists on their witnessing to the experience of salvation from sin.

C. *The Influence of the Gospel on Village Hindus*

Since our study was limited to the Christian communities in a small group of villages, we have no accurate way of assessing the influence of Christian ideas and practices on others in the village. However, we found considerable evidence that suggests that the strong village Hindu influence on Christians has its counterpart: there seems to be a vigorous two-way traffic in a number of aspects of village religious life.

We have just noted the fact that almost the entire Christian theological vocabulary is composed of Hindu terms. Many of the official terms are Sanskritic Telugu which might convey more meaning to educated high-caste Hindus than to most village Hindus. There are also a few Muslim terms, as well as some village Hindu words, which are incorporated in the actual Christian vocabulary of the village congregation.

The problem with terms like *Pariśuddhatma, rakshana,* and *baptismamu* is that they are simply words in a foreign language until they have been explained and brought to life by Christian teaching. The opposite problem exists with words like *Devudu, Swami* and *śakti,* which already have definite religious meanings familiar to Christians that may be both a help and a hindrance in understanding the Christian faith. These 'bridges' of meaning may contribute to a partial or distorted understanding of the Christian message if the concepts are not reinterpreted in regular Christian teaching, but whatever their dangers, they do make it easier for non-Christians to come to some understanding and even acceptance of Christian ideas. This is especially possible in the intellectual atmosphere in which the beliefs and practices of potentially or actually rival religious groups are accepted simultaneously. This atmosphere restricts the range of the encounter within the mind of the village Christian; there seems to be very little meeting between the Christian and Hindu ideas of sacrifice, for example, because they belong to different cultic systems, even though the Christian may still participate to some extent in both systems. There seems to be greater interpenetration of ideas relating to the nature of the divine powers. It is not difficult for the village Hindu to accept Jesus as one among many 'Lords' or 'incarnations' of the Supreme Creator, to all of whom he ascribes about the same nature. It is always possible, however, for such a belief to develop into the view that Jesus is the most powerful, or even the only genuine *Swami* or *Avatar,* and that the Supreme Creator has the nature which the Christian Scriptures attribute to the Father of Jesus Christ. In this section we shall discuss the Christian ideas which are at least partially understood and accepted among village Hindus, and the occasional development of such germinal beliefs into a genuine faith in Jesus Christ.

Hindus in these villages do not distinguish between *Bhagavantudu* (*Narayana*) and *Devudu,* between the Supreme Deity as they call Him and the Christians' God. They believe that there is one Supreme God who may be called by all sorts of names. God has many incarnations or *avatars*. Jesus (*Yesuswami*) is not one of the ten recognized avatars, but He is like them, and some of those Hindus who have had a personal experience of the power of *Yesuswami* would be prepared to say, not only 'I believe that Lord Jesus has blessed me', but also 'I believe that He is the most powerful "Lord" (*Swami*).' After hearing Christian preaching and teaching, a few come to believe that the Supreme God (*Bhagavantudu*, etc.) has descended in the form of Jesus. When they learn the qualities of the Christians' God, they attribute them to the Supreme Deity or Creator, so that they can say, 'The Supreme Creator is loving Father'. (There are many Christians who can say nothing more of the qualities of God than that He is the 'Creator'. While the evangelists know the Christian doctrine that God created the universe out of nothing, and know that this belief is different from the Hindu doctrine of Creation, they do not teach this Christian doctrine to their congregations.)

There are many Hindus in these villages who accept Jesus Christ as a *Swami* who can work miracles of healing and bestow material blessings. The healing services of Sadhu Joseph have probably still further heightened this belief. In some villages near the area studied, non-Christians say when the crops fail, 'There is no *Yesu* for the harvest', thus identifying the name of Jesus with *barkat*, or material blessings.

Some Hindu parents name a child after Jesus (e.g. *Yesudas*, 'servant of Jesus') and then bring a thank-offering to the Christian evangelist. This may happen because the name of Jesus was included in the list of divine names repeated before the child's birth and happened to be the one uttered at the instant of birth. It also sometimes occurs that Hindu women come to the Christian hospital in Medak for their confinement and make a vow that, if the baby is a boy or if the mother has a safe delivery, the child will be named after Jesus, or the presbyter will be asked to give the child some 'Christian name'.

Hindu women sometimes spend a night in a temple or shrine in order to pray more effectively to the resident deity for the blessing of a child. Some women visit a number of temples in the area in this way and include the cathedral in Medak. A Hindu woman from another section of the Wadiaram Pastorate who came to Medak to go to the hospital first spent a night on the porch of the cathedral. She was impressed by the stained glass picture of the Crucifixion. Later, while she was in the hospital, she had a dream in which Jesus appeared to her and told her that she would soon conceive and bear a son. Soon after she went home she became pregnant and in due course bore a son, whom she insisted should be called Yesudas, in spite of the fact that her husband was a village official and that the only Christians in the village were outcastes.

If the Church permitted, the parents would allow such a child to be baptized, since they consider this to be part of the Christian naming ceremony, but they are not willing to be baptized themselves. It is the parents, not the child, however, who thereafter discharge the ritual obligations to Jesus, just as they would to any other deity after whom their child was named. The parents come once a year to make an offering to *Yesuswami* (represented by the presbyter at the place where they made the vow). However in addition to going to the annual *jatra* in Wadiaram, if they made the vow there, they go to the Christian *jatra* in Medak, for they believe that they should visit the 'chief shrine' of *Yesuswami* in the area, which is the cathedral in Medak. They make the offering to fulfil their vow and so that no harm may befall the child, and they continue this practice until the child is grown up or leaves their charge. At the time of marriage, on the advice of a Brahmin, the child may be given a second name considered more favourable to his horoscope. Even if the Christian name is retained in adulthood, the person bearing it feels no obligation towards *Yesuswami* or His community.

We have described in the previous chapter how a few village Hindus had come into touch with some of the congregations studied, some attending Christian worship regularly and others being willing to acknowledge Jesus as their special 'Lord' in baptism, thus joining the Christian Church. Some of these new converts are from the Sudra caste; they have joined congregations previously consisting entirely of outcastes, and they have sometimes had to face ostracism and persecution. Two factors in their interest and/or their decision to become Christians are quite clear. The first is a striking Divine blessing, usually the blessing of a child or a miraculous healing, while the second is a dream, which sometimes accompanies or foretells a miraculous event. Apart from the rather exceptional case of Sadhu Joseph, the most striking instances of Jesus appearing in dreams come from Sudras who have had some connexion with the Vaishnava sect and are familiar with stories of the appearance of an *avatar* of Vishnu (Krishna or Rama) to a devotee in a dream. Paul (Narayana Gowd) of Ambojipet, his wife, and his wife's father all had dreams of Jesus in connexion with the healing of some illness, but the visions and healings did not immediately lead any of them to join the Christian Church. The villagers who take that further step usually have some contact with Christians who are knowledgeable enough to discuss the Christian faith with them and concerned enough to try to persuade them to be baptized and join the Christian community.

When an individual who has had a vision of Jesus and/or has experienced an event that he interprets as the act of *Yesuswami*, he sometimes persuades a number of his relatives or his whole caste group in his village to become Christians. This was true of Yesudas, who attributed his healing from leprosy in the Christian sanatorium in Dichpalli to the action of Yesuswami, and whether from gratitude to Jesus or fear of divine judgment for pretending to be a Christian in order to gain admittance into the sanatorium, persuaded the entire Madiga community in Gowlapalli to become Christians.

Another factor in Christian influence is the attendance of Hindus at Christian worship services. While there are relatively few evangelistic meetings directed entirely to non-Christians, there are special meetings of the village congregations and the annual *jatra* at the pastorate headquarters at which non-Christians are welcome and during which various means are employed to present the Christian message in terms intelligible to villagers. (The *jatra* will be described in Section D below.)

The healing services of Sadhu Joseph offer a unique combination of the factors already mentioned; in addition, they include a special instance of a fourth factor: the concern of individual Christians, many of them village laymen, for the total welfare of their Hindu and Muslim neighbours. Closely related to such concern is the courageous witness of small groups of Christians who stick to their Christian convictions in the face of opposition or even persecution. When one compares the developments in Mallupalle with the other experiences of new converts, one is struck by the complete lack of visions or miraculous healings. The only 'miracles' in the situation were Yohan's courage and the sudden decision of the Madiga community to follow his example in becoming Christians.

The observable influence of Christianity on the village religious scene does not include the change of Hindu ideas and practices under Christian (or Western) influence that is apparent among urban Hindus, especially those given a Western education in Christian schools. Our picture is obviously one-sided, for it is largely limited to the experience of those Hindus sufficiently attracted by the figure of 'Lord Jesus' to come into relation with the Christian community, but it is still significant that the influence of Christianity on the village mind has not been that of ethical principles or theological concepts, but rather the addition of a new divine figure to the village pantheon: *Yesuswami*.

Perhaps the most remarkable instance of a dream of Jesus which has come to our notice occurred a few months after the close of the period of investigation in another part of the Diocese. A young Sudra named Venkatesvara had a dream in which he thought he saw Krishna, who commanded him to accept the next marriage proposal received in the mail. A few days later such a letter did arrive, but it was from a Christian who wanted to find a husband of the same caste for his daughter, provided the young man would first become a Christian. The boy finally agreed, although this offer was less attractive financially than others he had previously received, because he came to believe that the figure he had seen in his dream was not Krishna but Jesus Christ. He was instructed in the Christian faith for several weeks by his prospective father-in-law, a landowning farmer who had himself become a Christian several years previously as the result of a miraculous healing.

This farmer had been a staunch Hindu who never listened to Christian preaching and had once beaten a Christian evangelist who had come to his village to preach. At one time he developed a chronic abdominal pain which he vainly tried to cure with various medicines. He also went to the hospital for treatment but secured no relief. One night in his dreams he had a vision of Jesus Christ, who told him that by a certain date he would be well. To his surprise, on exactly that date he felt perfectly all right. After this experience he became interested in the Christian Church and was subsequently baptized. Later he began to effect healings through prayer in the name of Jesus. According to his own report, his young son once became ill and actually died, but after he had 'prayed with tears' at his bedside for two hours, his son came back to life. He is said to have healed many people in his locality through prayer.

After this instruction from his father-in-law, Venkatesvara was baptized with the name of Christopher Dayanand and soon afterwards married. Then he decided that he wanted to learn more about Christian faith, and enrolled in a one-year course at Medak. Before the end of the year he decided to offer himself for the Christian ministry and take a three-year course in a theological college. Soon after coming to Medak, Christopher entered into regular conversations about Christianity with a group of young men of a landowning caste in a village near Medak, where the Sudras had never previously shown any interest in the Gospel already accepted by the outcastes of that village. This is an actual occurrence, but it may also be a symbol of great significance: the attribution to the Lord Jesus of the power and the presence which have previously been ascribed to Lord Krishna or the other 'Lords' of the village mind.

D. *Christian Adaptations of Village Hindu Practices*

Among a group of Christians who are still so completely involved in village society and religion, it might be expected that there would be frequent and far-reaching adaptation of traditional practices in order to utilize them in the service of the Church. So far, however, no such extensive Christian adaptation is taking place, precisely because Christians are so involved in village religion that they generally accept Christian rites as a new addition to their religious life or at most a partial substitution for some of the old rites, not as a replacement of the old practices, still less as their fulfilment. The new Christian forms are felt to be novel and foreign by village Christians as well as by Hindu onlookers, but this is not usually considered a drawback; sometimes it is even an added attraction. If one follows a 'foreign religion' like Islam or Christianity, then he must expect to have 'foreign religious practices.'

Nevertheless, there is a certain amount of adaptation going on, both spontaneously and at the suggestion of the presbyter or of some committee of the Diocese. It is significant that the most spontaneous adaptation is going on in Achampet, the one congregation in the section which is beginning to see the Christian way of life as an alternative rather than an addition, but an alternative that can utilize the traditional religious practices for its own ends or can at least partially Christianize them.

The spontaneous adaptations by village Christians are largely in the use of Christian symbols as embodiments of the power of Christ and effective means to ward off demonic powers. Crosses are sometimes tied around the necks of children to ward off evil spirits. In Achampet many families paint a cross in red on the outside walls and door-posts of their homes to show that they are Christians. At the time of the Police Action in 1948, Christians in many villages painted crosses on their houses, so that they would not be molested by the Muslim Razakars terrorizing Hindus or by Hindus retaliating against Muslims, or, in the first several months after the entry of Indian government troops, by Communist armed bands. In the years since, the custom has been continued in some villages. The cross painted on the house is for the Achampet Christians both a sign of their distinctiveness as a religious community and a means for warding off the demons. In all of these congregations, many homes have pictures of Jesus placed over the doorway, to ensure the presence of Jesus in the home to protect the family against evil and to bring it *barkat* (material blessing). The pictures are often Roman Catholic pictures of Christ on the Cross and Christ with the Sacred Heart. On the pledge cards recording the family's annual pledged contribution is a picture of Christ. These cards are hung up in the home in the same way.

In one marriage according to traditional rites observed in Achampet, the Bible replaced the earthen pot containing porridge in the ceremony of the welcoming of the bride; the Christians carried the Bible in a procession from the evangelist's house to the place where they welcomed the bride's party. In another village, Christians used the Bible and the cross in a funeral ceremony. The son performing the last rites for his father, instead of carrying an earthen pot containing fire, carried the Bible in one hand and a wooden cross in the other as he walked at the front of the funeral procession.

Another type of adaptation is the practice in many congregations of singing Christian songs in village Telugu (composed by various evangelists in the Diocese who have this gift) instead of the hymns in the Andhra Lyric Book, which are written in high (Sanskritic) Telugu. It is these more popular Christian lyrics that are included in Sadhu Joseph's Lyric Book and are sung at his healing services. These lyrics are set to village tunes, the same tunes used for Hindu ballads and wedding songs, as well as for the songs sung during daily work, as when grinding grain. Sometimes these village tunes are also used to sing the more official hymns of the Andhra Lyric Book, instead of the unfamiliar and more complicated tunes there indicated.

The other adaptations were not initiated by village Christians but introduced by evangelists or presbyters, usually with the encouragement of the Diocese, which for many years has been more actively and positively concerned about Christian adaptation than most Protestant Churches in India. Most of the adaptations have been adopted readily and sometimes enthusiastically by village Christians. Among these are the processions which the evangelist arranges on Christian festivals or other special occasions, on the model of the village processions during Hindu festivals. On Palm Sunday and again on Easter, some of the Christian young men, women and children in Jangarai went in procession through the village with drums, and 'sang' the congregation to the place of worship; other Christians, and some Hindus when they heard the singing and playing of drums, came out and joined the procession. They all walked around the place of worship three times, waving palm leaves and other branches and singing the chorus, 'Victory, victory, (*Jayam, jayam*) Hallelujah; Victory, victory, to our Jesus right now!' Then they entered the church for worship.

When the presbyter visits a congregation for the first time or when the bishop or some guest of the Diocese pays a visit, the evangelist very often arranges for the visitor to be greeted with the honours accorded to a Hindu guru. (While Western missionaries are always given a guru's welcome, Indian presbyters are not regarded as gurus simply by virtue of their office. Christians in these villages esteem as real 'gurus' only those presbyters whom they genuinely respect and whom they believe to possess some spiritual power.) Members of the congregation come in a group to the village boundary and lead the presbyter or other visitor in triumphal procession through the village, often with drums beating. In Achampet some of the Christian young men lead the way in a small band playing flutes, drums, and cymbals. They call to the non-Christians, 'Our Guru has come', and they proudly introduce their Guru to the village officials. Some Christians also follow the traditional practice of touching the 'guru's' feet, or washing them when the presbyter or other official visitor enters their home, as a mark of reverence or in order to secure his blessings.

On *Ugadi* (Telugu New Year's Day in April), the Christians in Jangarai invited the author (P. Y. L.) and his wife back from Gowlapalli to attend a special service of the baptism of some Bandela families. Those Christians in the congregation who have the traditional duty of beating drums at village festivals were supposed to be taking part in the *Ugadi* procession at the very time of the Christian service. They went to the village officials and said, 'Our Guru is coming. First we must receive him and take him through the village. After that we will come and beat the drums in your procession.' The officials agreed, and the time of the Hindu procession was changed!

The Church has made considerable use of the characteristically Indian practice of the *jatra* (religious fair) to gather the scattered Christians of the pastorate. It has been an effective means of creating a corporate sense of belonging to the wider Christian fellowship and has provided a valuable occasion for Christian preaching and teaching. It has also been the occasion for one of the larger and more significant offerings by village Christians. One such *jatra* was held at the pastorate headquarters in Wadiaram during the period of survey, in May 1959. This was in the midst of the hot season, when villagers have considerable leisure, since they have no work in the fields until the rains begin in June. The 'pilgrims' arrive one evening and leave after the service of Holy Communion the following afternoon. The main programme of the *jatra* takes place on the first night. The open yard in front of the church hall is decorated with coloured paper and mango leaves, and in the centre a big wooden cross is fixed in the ground. When the thanksgiving service begins, the members of the Women's Fellowship dressed in their best saris carry little oil lamps in their hands and, singing appropriate lyrics, go round the cross and illumine it.

At the end of the service the presbyter distributes to all those present (both Christians and non-Christians) some light refreshments (*palahāram*) over which he has asked God's blessing. This 'consecrated' food is considered a kind of Christian *prasādam* (literally, 'grace.' Some eat it right away, while others take it home with them. Sometimes the association with an integral part of a Hindu *jatra* is made explicit: some presbyters distribute jaggery and pieces of wet coconut, and call this food *Yesuswami's prasādam*.

At Hindu *jatras* the general distribution of light refreshments blessed by one of the Hindu deities is sometimes done by the temple priests and sometimes by an individual after he has visited a shrine of that deity, especially if he has brought a thank-offering for being healed or for some other blessing. Such *prasādam* is sometimes distributed outside one's own family or even outside one's own religious community. Villagers are usually glad to accept the *prasādam* of any deity, and Christians often accept it from Hindus. At one Christian *jatra*, the non-Christians present were offended because they were not given any *prasādam* by the presbyter.

The custom of distributing Christian *prasādam* began at the 'caste summer schools' of the 1920s and 1930s. (See p. 24.) It not only provided a familiar religious feature for Hindus from the Sudra castes, but it also continued the Methodist tradition of the 'Love Feast'. It was intended as a symbol of fellowship in the name of Christ. The custom soon became a regular part of the annual *jatra* in each pastorate. At the present time the practice is widespread, but there is little reflection on its theological significance, in particular on its relation to the Lord's Supper. Each presbyter has his own interpretation of Christian *prasādam*, but he does not explain its significance to those to whom he distributes the 'consecrated food'. For many presbyters, this is only a substitute for Hindu *prasādam*, taken over along with other features of a Hindu *jatra*, in order to provide a popular and indigenous means of strengthening the Church. While this practice was introduced on the analogy of the Love Feast or Agape Meal, for most it now has more of the village Hindu meaning of *prasādam*; that is, it generally signifies a blessing *from* God more than fellowship *with* God, and it seems to convey very little of the idea of the fellowship of all the participants—both Christian and non-Christian—with one another.

After the service ending with the distribution of Christian *prasādam*, there is usually a programme of religious films, dramas or *burrakathas* lasting long into the night. These *burrakathas* are stories (*kathas*) narrated in lyrical form by a leader playing on an instrument called a *burra*, with the help of two assistants who stand on either side of him. On the death anniversary of the retired evangelist in Jangarai, the superintending evangelist of another section of the pastorate used this method to get across the message of Christian hope to an audience of both Christians and non-Christians. A similar method of presenting the Gospel is called *kālakshepam*, which literally means 'whiling away the time'. Here the leader sings for a little while, accompanied by a drum and one or two other instruments, and then explains in dramatic form, with the help of a few assistants, the story he has sung. He goes on like this until he has finished the whole story, now and then giving some piquant illustrations to keep his audience attentive.

After the Easter Sunday night service in Jangarai, the men and women separately performed folk dances, the men doing the *kolātum* (stick dance) and the women the *kummi* (group dance). The *kolātum* is performed by two concentric circles of men, who leap and dance with the greatest vigour, and each dancer turns around on his own axis at the same time both circles are revolving in opposite directions. Every dancer strikes the sticks of all the other dancers within his reach in a rhythmical pattern which fits the song that they are all singing. Periodically the men in the two circles change places. Christian words have been fitted to the traditional tunes, and in this way a real element of village culture is being 'baptized' into the Church. In the *kummi* dance, the women also dance around in circles, clapping or holding hands and singing songs the tunes of which are very appealing to the villager.

The most remarkable and spontaneous adaptation of a traditional dance was done in Ambojipet. There is a dance which has become very popular among the young men, called *Chirutala Rāmāyanam* (stories from the Hindu epic, the Ramayana), which is more or less like the stick dance except that wooden cymbals (*chirutalu*) are used instead of sticks. This was adapted to the Christmas story by the Hindu leader of the dance group because of the three Christian members of the group, two of them new converts (see p. 157).

The Christian women in Jangarai came to the special baptismal service on *Ugādi* with their oil saucer lamps. While the non-Christian villagers were going in a big procession to the shrine of the goddess Poshamma carrying lighted *bonālu* (pots containing oil lamps), these Christian women illumined the cross with their little lamps before the service began. A large wooden cross was fixed in the ground with little flat wooden plates sticking out of it. The leader first lit one lamp and placed it on the plate sticking out from the centre of the cross. The women came singing lyrics and lit their lamps from the cross and then placed them on the other wooden plates attached to the cross, thus symbolizing that they take the light from Jesus who is the light of the world and then pass this light on to others. After this the baptismal service was conducted. Both the lamp-lighting ceremony and the special service in which new converts were baptized made a deep impression on these Christians and kept them away from the non-Christian procession. This form of lighted cross service has been in general use in the Diocese for many years, and is performed as part of Christian worship on special festival days and at *jātras*.

In this particular instance, this adaptation of the use of lights was used in conjunction with a service which provided a direct alternative to joining in the village religious ceremonies. The provision of such imaginative alternatives is relatively rare in these congregations. No cycle of Christian festivals at different times from the other village festivals has yet been developed, nor has any Christian adaptation or reinterpretation of the traditional festivals been worked out, e.g. no use of the Methodist New Year's Day Covenant Service on the Telugu New Year's Day.

An incorporation of a traditional custom in a Christian service is seen in the use of the *tāli* (chain) instead of a ring in the Christian marriage service, and the optional ceremony of the seven steps which is adapted from high-caste Hindu weddings. So few Christian marriage services are celebrated in these congregations, however, that these adaptations have at present little significance for the Christians in these villages. Some evangelists try to make a Christian naming ceremony on the twenty-first day after birth replace the traditional *purudu* ceremony. The rites associated with a girl's becoming mature do not seem ever to include a special Christian prayer meeting for the family and relatives like that which is held elsewhere in South India. Occasionally there is a Christian service on the occasion of a funeral or a death anniversary, but here again there has been less general adaptation than in some other parts of South India, because the original non-Christian rites continue to be practised by so many Christians.

It is in the use of the traditional rites marking the various turning points in the life cycle that village Christians themselves are most likely to make significant adaptations. It is these rites which are among the most persistent even among those Christians who have lost their fear of the village deities and demons, because Christians feel that these significant events in a person's life ought to be marked with appropriate ceremonies, not only to ward off evil influences, but to promote the person's general well-being in the following stage of life. The introduction of the Bible and the Cross into the traditional ceremonies indicates some thought or feeling in this direction.

The adaptations spontaneously conceived by village Christians are not so much the indigenizing of Western Christian forms as the Christianizing—even if sometimes only to a very limited degree—of traditional ceremonies used in village festivals or in family rituals at various stages of the life cycle. So far, however, for most Christians in these villages, the appropriate times are largely under the control of the traditional divine powers. It is only as the rituals of appropriateness are felt to belong to the God and Father of Jesus Christ that profound adaptation can occur.

The Church needs to consider how village Christians can come to see, and themselves work out in due response, the lordship of Christ over the 'times' and 'spaces' of their village experience. That experience itself is rapidly changing, however, as the Western secular notion of undifferentiated time and space gradually invades the village. The Church has generally regarded Western education as an ally, because it weakens or even destroys the villagers' fear of the village deities and demonic spirits. It makes a great deal of difference, however, whether village Christians experience Christ's victory over the gods of village space and time, or whether their confidence in the old order is simply eroded by the new rationalism—a rationalism sceptical of the powers of nature but supremely confident of the powers of man. Unless the authority of Christ over the concrete divisions of space and time is acknowledged before the secular mind creates the illusion that they no longer matter to man, it will become even more difficult to realize the fact of Christ's lordship over the many small things that make up daily life.

CHAPTER 9

The Distinctiveness of the Christian Community

A. *Christian and Hindu Names*

One of our objectives in this 'situation study' was to discover as much as possible what it means to be a Christian in these villages of Telengana. Part of this meaning is expressed in distinctive beliefs and part in distinctive actions, but much of the meaning of being a Christian is expressed and experienced in belonging to a particular community within the larger society of the village. The Christian community in many urban settings in India is not only quite distinct in character, but quite separate in its existence from other religious and social groupings. We have already seen that the situation of the Christian community in these villages is quite different. At many points where educated urban Christians are clearly distinct and separate, these village Christians seem to blend into the general village landscape. The physical separation of a field or a cart-track between the Christians and the main part of the village is not a matter of the Christians' own choosing, nor does it have anything to do with their being Christians. The physical separation and the social distance are the result of their separate and inferior status in the traditional social system—belonging to two distinct castes (*kulams*), they are outside or below the system of the four main 'castes' (*varnas*), and therefore are 'outcastes'.

In spite of the social separation, Christians have much in common with villagers of other castes. Their distinctiveness is not something obvious; what they are as Christians appears closely linked to what they are as participants in village society. Like the other distinctive groups in the village, their community existence has two sides: one is separate and distinctive; the other is at one with the rest of the village. As we noted in the last chapter, their existence as Christians consists both of what we recognize as an expression of Christian faith and of what seems to us a continuation of traditional village religion.

One important instance of this dual character, with its 'both-and' attitude, is the fact that most Christians have two names. Even before they received a Christian name at baptism, they had a non-Christian (usually Hindu) name given them on the twenty-first day after birth (*purudu*), and it is this earlier name that most of them use, except when in the presence of the evangelist or presbyter. The Hindu name is often the name of a deity, either the one whose blessing is regarded as responsible for the child's conception or the one whose name was uttered at the instant the child was born. In either case giving the name of a deity to one's child entails a yearly thank-offering to that deity by the parents (see pp. 180–181). A girl may also have another name given by a Brahmin at the time of her marriage to accord better with her horoscope, and she uses this name in her husband's home.

Some of these Christians, especially in congregations without a resident evangelist, when asked their Christian names answer, 'I do not know; the evangelist knows', or 'Which name? Is it the name in your religion, or the name which my parents gave me?' The higher caste Hindus regard the Christian names as foreign and insist on calling Christians by their old names, and it is these names which the village officials like to enter in Government records and census lists, sometimes saying that they cannot be expected to pronounce or spell their 'foreign names'. It is very difficult for Christians to get their new names entered in the important land records. When applying for land or other concessions to 'Harijans' there is a special advantage in giving Hindu names. The Christians do not, in general, think of such an action as a denial of their faith, since they are simply using their common everyday names to obtain rights which they consider their just due. It is more remarkable that some Christians who also use their Hindu names in common parlance refuse to give them to the Government in order to secure concessions reserved by the officials for Hindu outcastes (see pp. 68–69).

The Medak Diocese objects to the use of Hindu names, especially those associated with Hindu gods or goddesses, but it allows as baptismal names the Telugu or Sanskrit names for virtues, colours, jewels, flowers, etc., in order to encourage the 'naturalization' of Christianity in its Indian setting. The neighbouring Methodist Church in Southern Asia allows converts to be baptized with their old Hindu names, and this difference in practice causes some confusion to Christians in the Medak Diocese living near the area of the other Church. Whichever practice is followed, it needs to be recognized that the Hindu names usually still retain a certain religious significance, though the ritual obligations involved in the name are discharged not by the bearer of the name, but by his parents. It might be thought that since the old names have a religious significance, the new Christian name would signify that its bearer was bound to his new Lord Jesus Christ. This may occasionally be true, but in general the significance of the new Christian name is not thus understood. If an old Hindu name has already been given, it tends to be used for the rest of the convert's life after baptism, whatever attitude the Church officially adopts towards it. It might be better to follow the practice of the Early Church and baptize converts with their old names, possibly giving a Christian name as well.

There is far less reason to permit the children of Christian parents to be given a Hindu name which they use in preference to their baptismal name. If the child is given a 'Christian name', of one of the permissible kinds mentioned above, on the twenty-first day after birth (*purudu*) (which only rarely could be the date when the presbyter is visiting the villages and could baptize the child), and if the same name is later used when the child is baptized, it is very likely that the child will never receive the name of a Hindu deity, and will use his Christian name all his life. In the Achampet congregation this practice is now generally followed, and most of the children under fifteen have only a Christian name.

B. *Marriage*

According to both Indian law and the rules of the Church of South India, the minimum age for marriage is fifteen for women, and eighteen for men. Marriages should be solemnized only by ordained ministers or by those holding a licence under Section 9 of the Indian Christian Marriage Act, and no evangelist or Christian elder of the congregation should ever be present at any irregular marriage. In Christian marriages no Hindu rites or idolatrous practices should precede or follow the marriage ceremony, and a marriage of a Christian with a non-Christian has to have special authorization from the bishop (usually granted only when the non-Christian partner is under instruction for baptism). The time, place and date of the marriage should be arranged by the parties concerned, in consultation with the presbyter who solemnizes the marriage. A regular Christian marriage is to be solemnized by an ordained minister after three banns have been published on three consecutive Sundays in the home congregations of both parties and (if different) in the congregation where the marriage ceremony is to take place. If any Christian contravenes the above rules, he is liable to the discipline of the Church.[1]

Most of the marriages arranged by the village Christians do not conform to the above rules, and consequently very few regular Christian marriages are being solemnized by the presbyter in the villages. In 1958 no marriages were solemnized by the presbyter in the whole of Wadiaram Pastorate and only three during 1959 (of which two were of village Christians and one between educated Christians).

Most of these Christians, especially the girls, are married below the minimum legal age. Like other villagers, Christian parents try to have their daughters married before they reach puberty. Even in the few cases where the children are old enough to meet the Church's require-ments, the parents usually prefer to have a marriage performed according to the traditional rites, because they believe that misfortune would plague the married couple if they were omitted. A Pastorate Committee member from another village in the Pastorate reported, 'We married a couple whose parents did not make them use *bashingalu* (see p. 47), but the boy died after the marriage, so our Christians hesitate to allow marriages to be performed without *bashingalu*.' Christians almost always consult a Brahmin, and pay him a fee to set an auspicious day and hour. Though they will not walk to Wadiaram to ask the presbyter to arrange a date, they will walk several miles to consult a Brahmin, if there is none in their own village, and meticulously follow his instructions.

Sometimes when the evangelist protests against irregular marriages, the Christians say, '*Pantulu*, please do not interfere with our marriage but allow us to practise these traditional rites. We shall give you your wedding collection all right!' The evangelists often acquiesce.

In addition to the very few regular marriages performed by the presbyter in accordance with the rules of Church and State, Christians are married in a number of ways that are all regarded as irregular. We have divided these irregular wedding ceremonies into five categories, all but the first of which contain some Christian elements:

(1) The marriage ceremonies are conducted by the caste headman or some non-Christian priest, using all the traditional rites, without the presence or knowledge of the evangelist.

(2) Either before or after the traditional ceremonies, the evangelist prays for the couple, and receives a wedding 'collection'.

(3) Only a few traditional customs are observed, such as the wearing of *bashingalu* by the couple and *bottu* by all the participants, and the evangelist's prayer is an important part of the ceremony.

(4) A few devoted Christians omit all the non-Christian rites, and the marriage is solemnized simply by the evangelist's prayer. This may occur in cases where the girl or boy is too young for the presbyter to marry them, or where there is not enough time after the date is set for the publishing of banns.

(5) Recently a few Voluntary Church Workers in other pastorates have been misusing their 'bishop's licences' by reading the entire marriage service, thus usurping the sole right of ordained presbyters and deacons to solemnize a Christian marriage. These V.C.W.s sometimes keep the collection they receive at such weddings, but sometimes turn it over to the evangelist or presbyter.

If the marriage is between a Christian and a non-Christian, the non-Christian family insists on the traditional ceremonies, whether the Christian family wants them or not, and in any case the presbyter may not solemnize such marriages unless the non-Christian partner is first baptized, which in these villages is rarely considered. The following table shows what a large proportion of marriages between Christian and non-Christians have taken place in the six congregations of the section which have had resident evangelists.

Only a few Christians make a deliberate effort to find Christian partners for their children. The criteria of most Christians are the wealth and health and purity of caste of the prospective husband's or wife's family, and the closeness of the relationship on the mother's side, since first cousin relatives have the first rights and are considered the most desirable partners. Following these criteria sometimes leads to the choice of a Christian partner, but since the Christians make up only a small proportion of the Mala and Madiga castes, it is not surprising that more than half the marriages are with non-Christians. (If the unbaptized daughters of Christian parents, about whom there are no statistics, were included, the proportion might be about three in four.[2])

One reason why the Church has not been very concerned about the high proportion of Christian–Hindu marriages is because such marriages have sometimes proved a means for the spread of the Gospel. The

Villages	Jan-garai	Acham-pet	Bandapo-sani-palla	Kondapu-ram	Ambo-jipet	Gowla-palli	Total
Christians marrying into the congregation	13	9	14	26	6	13	81
Christians marrying out to Christians	12	7	10	9	11	2	51
Total marriages between Christians	25	16	24	35	17	15	132
Hindus marrying into the congregation	21	24	30	29	11	36	151
Christians marrying out to Hindus	13	20	13	17	24	7	94
Total Christian–Hindu marriages	34	44	43	46	35	43	245
Total marriages	59	60	67	81	52	58	377
Percentage of Christian–Hindu marriages	57%	73%	65%	67%	74%	74%	65%[2]

Ambojipet congregation started this way fifty years ago, but in that instance the Christian father insisted on his son-in-law being baptized before the marriage (see p. 64 and, for a recent parallel, p. 194). However, there has been no direct repetition of this experience in the section in the past fifty years, though there may have been a few wives from Christian families in other villages who had some influence on the group decision for baptism in the more recent congregations. In any case, at the present time the girls who are married out into Hindu families are completely absorbed by the traditional religion and pass out of the Christian community. They usually make frequent visits to their Christian parents, but many of these are for their family's observance of the non-Christian calendar festivals. Neither before their marriage nor during such visits home do the evangelists make any effort to strengthen them for living as Christians in a non-Christian village. Nor do the evangelists or their wives ever visit these daughters of the congregation in their new non-Christian homes in other villages. It was discovered that about a dozen Christian girls from several of these congregations had been married into the large non-Christian Madiga community in the nearby village of Madur, but no evangelist or presbyter seems to have been aware of this fact, or has visited Madur, and these girls are gradually losing all traces of having been Christians.

The congregation is certainly not losing numerically by these inter-marriages, but the girls coming into the Christian community constitute a problem as well as an opportunity. They are willing to accept their husband's religion, though this does not imply for them that they should give up any of their traditional religious practices, either in their husband's home or in their parents' home when they return during the festivals. These girls are eventually baptized some months or even years after their marriage. It was observed in the congregations studied that no instruction is given to these girls before baptism; they are simply brought for baptism when the presbyter visits that congregation. Nor is any special instruction given to them after baptism; some of them attend prayers and occasionally take part in other activities of the congregation. The girls so initiated into the Christian community become the mothers of a majority of the children in the congregation. Without adequate training, they tend to bring up their children in all the non-Christian traditions in which they themselves have been raised, although if they were given teaching by their new family and the evangelist which awakened their own faith in Christ, they could in their turn teach their children the Gospel and the traditions of the Church. That this is possible we saw in the case of a devoted Christian woman in Gowlapalli who came from a Hindu home. Likewise the girls from Christian homes married to non-Christians could become effective witnesses for Christ in their new villages, but only if they received proper preparation for such a difficult task and the continued support of the evangelist and the congregation in their home villages.

Not only is little or no teaching on Christian marriage given to these congregations, but the requirements for Christian marriage do not fit the present situation of these Telengana villagers. Both the minimum age limit for Christians set by the Government at the suggestion of educated Christians and the Government's even higher age limit for Hindu marriages are the embodiment of modern Western conceptions. They go against not only the practice of these villagers but also their experience and conviction that girls should be married before they reach puberty. Modern conceptions of marriage have already spread widely among educated Indians of all religions and are beginning to make an impact on the villages, but the fact remains that the traditional conception of marriage is still held in these Telengana villages. It seems to us highly questionable for the Church to maintain that a higher age for marriage is a necessary and essential implication of the Christian faith and that the traditional view and practice of child marriage is 'un-Christian'.

The same is true of the older Western Christian requirement of publishing banns on the three Sundays before the wedding, which was adapted from the practice of the Church of England and included in the constitution of the Church of South India. The original purpose of discovering impediments to the marriage is rarely if ever served in these village congregations. If village Christians were to observe this requirement, it would mean that they would have to change their present practice of celebrating the marriage as soon as possible after the marriage negotiations are completed and would have to give up the consultation of a Brahmin priest concerning an auspicious day and hour, which he rarely sets more than a week in advance. Since they are very seldom prepared to make such changes, the requirements of banns on three Sundays before the wedding prevents the presbyter from marrying most of the relatively few couples who meet the minimum age requirements.

Before the Hyderabad Methodist District was merged with the Church of South India and the semi-independent rule of the Nizam in Hyderabad State came to an end, the minimum age limit for girls was twelve, and even this was not strictly observed. Christian marriages could then be performed by the superintending evangelist of the section. The Church insisted that marriages should be performed according to Christian rites, and a considerable proportion of the marriages were thus solemnized by the S.E. or the presbyter. The introduction of the new requirement of a higher minimum age (after puberty), publishing of banns, and withdrawal of marriage licences from the (un-ordained) superintending evangelists who are closer at hand than the presbyter, have all made it more difficult for village Christians to have their marriages solemnized with an authorized Christian service. They have therefore turned to the various forms of irregular marriages described above.

There has thus been a sharp decrease in the number of Christian marriages in the rural pastorates of the Medak Diocese. In the thirty-six pastorates of the two rural District Church Councils, 160 Christian marriages were reported in 1958 (about 6% of the total number of births reported), whereas in the nine city pastorates in and around Hyderabad there were thirty-three marriages (19% of the number of births). Since many of the Christian marriages in the rural pastorates were between educated Christians, the number of village Christians married by a presbyter was very small indeed. That year there were ten rural pastorates (of which Wadiaram was one) in which there were no Christian marriages, and another fourteen in which there were five or less. The Diocese is very much aware of this fact and has asked the C.S.I. Synod to recommend a lowering of the legal marriage age for Christian marriages. The Synod has not only refused to do this, but has urged that an even higher age limit be adhered to by the Church.

A somewhat similar situation exists with regard to divorce. In the old Hyderabad Methodist District, all cases of divorce were dealt with by a minister in a church panchayat, and the proceedings were communicated to the Chairman of the District, who on the recommendation of the minister could grant a divorce. The Church was vested by the Nizam's government with the authority to issue divorces to Christians, and the Church's own rules permitted it to remarry such divorced persons. Now after Church Union and the end of the Nizam's rule, marriage difficulties are supposed to be brought before the presbyter or the pastorate court, who should make every effort to bring about a reconciliation. If this proves impossible, the findings of the court may be sent to the bishop, and if he approves, the parties seeking a divorce may go to the civil court, which alone can grant a divorce. Village Christians, however, find the civil courts both bewildering and costly, and have therefore returned to the traditional village practice of seeking divorces from a panchayat of their own caste. Such divorces are not recognized either by State or Church, and presbyters may not marry such divorced persons. The second marriages of these divorced persons must therefore necessarily also be according to the traditional rites. On this issue the Synod has been more amenable to the Diocese's repeated requests to seek a change in the law, and the suggestion that the Church itself should have the power to grant divorce to Christians is being considered by a committee of the National Christian Council which is to recommend changes in the Indian Christian Marriage Act.[3]

The Diocese feels frustrated by the present situation, in which it can neither enforce the new marriage rules nor secure their alteration or relaxation. Perhaps some further reflection on the theological significance of marriage might lead to practical steps being taken even in this present frustrating situation, as well as to the asking of basic questions for the whole of the C.S.I. to ponder. The Church should consider any marriage (whether Christian or not) as an ordinance in God's creative providence, and as a symbol of the fellowship with His own people which He has accomplished in Christ. The present marriages according to non-Christian rites are therefore *valid* in the sight of God, although they are irregular in the eyes of the Government and the Synod. Should not the presbyter or the evangelist be encouraged to pray for God's blessing on such a marriage, that it may truly fulfil His purpose in Creation and mirror His achievement in Redemption? Should not such a marriage by traditional rites be regarded by the Church in the same way as a civil marriage: valid, but incomplete for the Christian, for whom and with whom the Church ought also to ask God's blessing on the marriage? Since the children of a marriage initiated with traditional rites are assumed by the Church to be legitimate, the validity of such a marriage seems to be tacitly accepted. Its validity is also accepted when a question of divorce arises. Is not a marriage solemnized by traditional rites, like a marriage begun with a Christian marriage service, a 'great mystery' or 'sacrament' (Greek *mysterion*)? 'For this reason a man shall leave his father and mother and be joined to his wife, and the two shall become one': the deeper meaning of this 'mystery' is the union of Christ with the Church (Eph. 5: 31–32, Gen. 2: 24).

Granted that idolatry and magic are involved in the traditional marriage rites and that the system of child marriage contains great evils, should not the Church be more concerned with the blessing of such a marriage, even long afterwards, until such time as the original marriage ceremonies can be completely centred around this blessing, which is itself a prayer for God's blessing? Child marriage as a system can only be compared to another system, such as that of 'love marriage' in the West, which has its own attendant evils. In both cases the Church's function should be to remind the man and woman—in whose relationship there may be many kinds of individual and social sin—of what God intends their marriage to be, and to pray to God that He may enable them to develop their marriage according to His will. If every marriage between Christians is accompanied with such admonishment and blessing by the Church, whether or not it has been attended with traditional rites and whether or not it is considered legal by the national Government, then a much firmer basis is laid for more extensive admonition concerning the commandment 'You shall not commit adultery', which is not a Western cultural requirement but an essential requisite of all marriages and an echo of the fundamental commandment to God's People, 'You shall have no other gods besides Me!' (Ex. 20: 3).

C. *Moral Standards and Practices*

Christians share the general moral standards of the village (*loka-niti*), according to which lying, cheating, sexual immorality, drunkenness and quarrelsomeness are looked upon as wrong, and helping one another in times of difficulty is considered a positive virtue. Women are expected to be modest and submissive to their husbands. A 'good person' is one who keeps calm, minds his own business, does not quarrel, is kind and loving to others, works hard and deals honestly with those with whom or for whom he works, and fulfils his obligations to his family and community.

These theoretical virtues, however, often seem to the villagers to be quite remote from their daily life. They often say, 'There are just two or three good people in the whole of this village'. Drunkenness is very common, especially among the lower castes. Adultery is fairly common in all castes. There is frequent stealing of crops, poultry and other belongings, and housebreaking and murder are on the increase. Deceitfulness is quite common in the villagers' day-to-day dealings with one another. The traders say, 'We cannot get along in the world without cheating'. Village officials and political party leaders frequently take bribes. According to village people, hatred, jealousy and bitterness are on the increase, and most people now perjure themselves on oath without any fear of the consequences—telling lies has become second nature.

The ideal of a good Christian is one who observes the *loka-niti* and in addition the ritual obligations of the congregation: attendance at worship and giving 'collections'. There seem to be no specifically Christian moral standards, nor any distinctively Christian content given to the general village standards. Moreover, with a few exceptions, Christians seem to be no more successful than Hindus in living up to the village standards, and they are equally involved in the gradual breakdown of the traditional morality.

People say, 'Things were better in the old days of the Nizam. Morals have depreciated like the currency. Nowadays everyone considers himself a raja'. The unfavourable comparison of the present with the past is known in many parts of the world, and an assertion of individual rights and rejection of traditional authority does not necessarily indicate a moral decline. Nevertheless, there are disquieting signs that this particular social transition is leading to an increase of such crimes as robbery and murder, and to a further weakening of the already loose obligations concerning marital fidelity and pre-marital sexual behaviour. It is said, for example, that even marrying a girl before puberty no longer guarantees that she goes to her husband as a virgin, so widespread has sexual promiscuity become in pre-adolescents. Village Christians are involved in every aspect of this breakdown of traditional morality—if it is that—or in any case, in the continual failure to live up to the moral standards of the village.

Such a period of social transition and moral uncertainty can provide great opportunities for witness to a Church whose members have the strength of character to live up to and beyond the traditional standards, because they derive their highest ideals and their deepest motivation from another source than that of the world around them. The Christian community may then become, as it did in the disintegrating Roman Empire, a centre for a new integration of values and a new pattern of behaviour for the entire society. But if Christians are relying solely on the traditional standards and sanctions of morality in an era when the sanctions are crumbling and the standards are becoming blurred, then the Church faces a crisis which may mean a terrible judgment indeed.

D. *The Distinctiveness of the 'Average' Christian*

It is difficult to measure the differences which conversion to Christianity has made in the lives of these village Christians. Their caste neighbours look for signs of economic, hygienic and moral improvement. The Hindu officials in Jangarai said, 'There is no change in them at all; they have the same Madiga mentality. They have no morality (*niti*). You have been spending so much money on these fellows. You have kept an evangelist here for so many years. But they still live in the same huts. In spite of all your continued efforts there is no change. They are very ungrateful to the Mission and to God'. In some other villages Hindus say, 'Through your efforts, Christians have got a bit of education, but nothing else'. In another section of the pastorate, a village official said, 'It is sixty years since Christianity has come to the village. Has even one Christian learned to read? Is there any change in that *basti* (outcaste section of the village)? Has even one of them bettered himself?'

These negative assessments may be coloured by the caste people's reaction to the self-assertiveness of the outcastes in the last fifteen years. It is also true that they apply a higher standard in judging Christian outcastes than in judging non-Christian outcastes. Nevertheless, it is significant that they do not find (or at least admit to finding) the sort of changes which Christian teaching and preaching have stated would come in the lives of Christians.

The evangelists define a 'good Christian' as one who lives up to the general village moral standards, and in addition regularly attends worship services, gives regularly for the support of the Church, and forsakes practices inconsistent with Christian teaching. At the interviews with evangelists held in Wadiaram and four other pastorates in the Diocese, the evangelists repeatedly said that there were not more than four or five out of a hundred Christians who were living good Christian lives; these few form the dependable nucleus of each congregation. The other 95%, in their opinion, 'are neither here nor there, but somewhere in the middle'. They are 'on the surface' or 'on the edge' of the Christian religion, and might 'at any time fall off into Hinduism'.

Here again this judgment tells us something about the evangelists as well as about the congregations under their charge. The evangelists continue to hold up a theoretical standard which they do not believe will be generally followed; there is little expectation that their teaching will be used by God to produce a real transformation of character, and little vision as to what the Holy Spirit might inspire a 'good Christian' to be and to do in these villages.

However this may be, in four of the five villages, with the exception of a few families, there seems little outwardly to distinguish Christians from Hindus of the same outcaste background. They have the same personal habits, share the same attitudes, have the same vocabulary of abuse, and join in the same ceremonies, both at the calendar festivals and at the sacrifices to the village goddesses.

In Achampet, as we have already noted, there is more of a distinctive Christian style of living, shared in some measure by all the Christians. These Christians, who are Madigas, are readily distinguishable from their outcaste neighbours, the Malas, who in this village have not become Christians, by their cleanliness, dress, cleaner language, and greater education. Although many of them still share a large number of beliefs in common with the rest of the villagers, there are some of the calendar festivals (e.g. Holi) in which none of them participate, and only the Madiga headman (*Pedda Methar*), who has the duty of officiating at the buffalo sacrifices, takes part in the sacrifices to the village goddesses. As was noted above, a fairly large proportion of the Christians here refrain from participating in any of the calendar festivals. This distinctiveness of the Achampet congregation is partly a greater conformity to the standards of educated Christians and partly an expression of Madiga community self-consciousness against the Malas. But it is also in part a real feeding on the Word of God and a responding to the leading of the Spirit of God in its present situation, as is indicated by its development of effective lay leadership after its evangelist left.

The few exceptional families in each of the other four villages (between two and five in each congregation) stand out in their congregations in the same ways in which the Achampet congregation distinguishes itself from the other Christian congregations as a whole. (The evangelists from the southern section of the Wadiaram Pastorate, who in general have been giving their congregations better pastoral care than the evangelists in the Jangarai section, gave a similar report on the number of 'good Christian' families: 'two or three in each congregation', they said.) These 'devout' families are much more regular about giving to the Church and attending Christian worship and have to some extent abandoned non-Christian beliefs and practices. There are also instances when otherwise 'average' Christians make a responsible Christian decision in a difficult situation (some of these will be related in section E, below). Such decisions, especially when they are arrived at by a group, may be at least as significant a Christian witness to the village as the distinctive pattern of living of a few faithful families.

The Christians as a whole are distinguished from the entire village not so much by their customs or attitudes, as by the fact that they form a distinct religious community, with a distinctive time and manner of worship and with their own religious leaders (the evangelists and the presbyter). Christians have their own word for 'worship', *ārādhana*, a Sanskritic Telugu word not used by most village Hindus, who use the general term *puja*, which especially denotes worship before an idol or consecrated image. Christian worship is distinctive, though not unique, in not being directed to a material image. It is also unusual in the village in being a congregational rather than an individual act. However, the congregation considers its participation in worship to be rather passive, comparable to listening to a Brahmin chant Sanskrit *mantras*. Few Christians join in the responses, but even if they do, they do not consider congregational speaking and singing during the service the same kind of active participation that they sense in some village Hindu rites, for there is virtually nothing *happening*, no physical *action*, in their Christian worship.

Christians are not the only ones in the village to belong to a distinctive religious community. There are the Muslims (especially in the larger villages), the Baljis (Saivites), the Visva Brahmas (Vaishnavas), and also the Lambadis (Gypsies), who have their own distinct gods and rites and, like the Muslims, maintain their own language. The members of all of these groups join to some extent in the general religious ceremonies of the village or take part in one another's festivals, and some of them occasionally present offerings to one another's religious leaders or unusual religious personalities.

Christians in these villages constitute a self-conscious religious community with pride in their religious leaders. When the evangelist left Achampet to go to the Divinity School in Medak, the congregation complained. When asked what it was the evangelist did they could not do themselves, they replied, 'But a congregation without an evangelist is like a *jatra* without a god!' An evangelist is a symbol of the Church by his very presence, even if he is not doing very much. There is a similar attitude towards the presbyter, who is respectfully greeted and sometimes proudly 'displayed' to the rest of the village during his brief and infrequent visits.

Very few Christians in this area are inclined at present formally to renounce Christianity and return to Hinduism, in spite of the occasional pressures in this direction exerted by Hindu landlords and Arya

Samajists. In only one village in another section of the Pastorate did several Christian families thus revert to Hinduism, and this was a generation ago. The using of Hindu names to secure land and other benefits for 'Harijans' is not felt by those who do it to signify a renunciation of their Christian communal allegiance. Since the Christians value their membership in their own district religious community, and in general see no conflict between that membership and their participation in the general religious and social fabric of the village, they are little affected by the rationalistic arguments of educated Hindus. At the present time they are more inclined to become angry and stubborn than to be intimidated by the threats or actual measures of persecution by high-caste Hindus.

The *object* of the average Christian's belief is more distinctive than his own conduct. As we saw in the last chapter, the Lord Jesus is accepted by villagers in general as being one of many '*Swamis*' (divine lords) and no distinction in quality is made between *Yesuswami* and any of the other Swamis, including the Muslim saints. Jesus is one among many such powerful 'Lords'. Yet even the 'average' Christian, whose ideas about the Christian God are very vague and considerably influenced by Hindu beliefs, feels that through his membership in the Christian community he is specially related to this particular Swami, Jesus Christ, and many Christians feel that their 'Lord', above the village goddesses and yet closer at hand than the vague supreme deity Narayana, is a powerful helper in time of trouble and a source of blessing. Neither the village Christian nor his non-Christian neighbours see much that is 'distinctive' in his personal Christian name, but both of them recognize a very real and distinctive power in 'the name of Jesus'.

E. *Testing Points of Faith and Loyalty*

A woman who had recently died in Kondapuram was regarded by Christians there as an example of piety or devotion (*bhakti*). She used to pray continually while performing her household duties, uttering the name of Jesus over and over again, in the way that some devout Vaishnavas repeat the name Narayana or Rama. One daughter-in-law was particularly impressed with her late mother-in-law's piety. 'As a result of her prayers, our family received the Lord's blessing and prospered, but since she died we have missed her prayers very much, and our family has begun to decline.' This 'decline' was particularly evidenced in the fact that the young woman's husband (one of the devout woman's sons) had taken to housebreaking and robbery. Eventually he was caught and put in prison. The young woman despairs of ever being able to pray the way her mother-in-law did, with a devotion that surely brings the Lord's blessing.

The piety and good works of the widow of the retired evangelist in Jangarai are also highly regarded by both Christians and non-Christians in that village. Her husband was a miserly and unscrupulous money-lender, who neither attended worship nor contributed to the church, once he had retired from active service as an evangelist. His wife followed his example, but now that he has died, her life shows a great change. She attends Christian worship regularly, helps the evangelist's wife in all her activities, and gives an example to the other Christians by refraining from participation in non-Christian rites. She brings some Hindu caste people along to the worship service, and testifies to all concerning the power of Christ in her life. She has contributed quite large sums to the congregation, and is planning to construct a regular church building for the congregation at her own expense.[4]

Many of the other instances of devotion to Christ and loyalty to the Christian community do not conform so closely to the popular village stereotype of remarkable piety (*bhakti*). What stands out in many of the other cases that came to our attention is not so much a reputation for 'good works' or unusual powers of prayer, as a costly decision to take a stand on some particular issue, even by a person or group whose life is in other respects far from exemplary.

Two other women in the Jangarai congregation stand out by their regular attendance at night prayers and at the occasional pastorate-wide women's meetings held in Wadiaram, from which they return singing, in the presence of Hindus and Christians, the Christian lyrics they have learned. They refrain from taking part in the Hindu calendar festivals of Holi and Ugadi, when most of the other Christians freely join in them. These two women fast on Good Friday and celebrate Easter reverently and enthusiastically. One of these women is a widow; the other has been deserted by her husband and is now living openly with another man in the congregation.

Another woman in this congregation lost her first child and two years later was blessed with another son, but he became seriously ill when he was three weeks old. The neighbouring Christian women suggested that the mother should sacrifice to the local goddesses to avert their wrath, but the mother refused to do this. Instead she asked the evangelist and the author (P. Y. L.) to come and pray for her child. After that the child recovered, and the parents' faith in the power of Christ was greatly strengthened. At the worship service on the following Sunday, the parents brought a thank-offering to God.

Closer to the piety of the women first mentioned is the religious life of some of the lay leaders mentioned in Chapter 6, but the devotion of these men is generally less ecstatic and more practically oriented. The Achampet congregation elected Luke as the leader of their panchayat committee for several reasons. They considered him to be patient, loving, and not easily provoked, and they recognized his regular participation in Christian worship and his non-participation in village rites (see p. 134). Luke has contributed regularly out of his very small income, but his conception of dedication and stewardship goes far beyond the 'collections'. 'I am guided by our Lord from within,' he said, 'to dedicate my youngest son and my grandson for the service of Christ in His Church, and God willing, I am going to educate these two boys and offer them to the Church.'

Devadass of Gowlapalli is already carrying out a similar resolve about his youngest son, Anandam, who has become the first young man in the section to complete the first stage of his V.C.W. training and receive a 'bishop's licence'. Devadass sent his son to take a number of short courses and to three or four two-week courses in Medak, sacrificing his son's wages for the time that he was away. Devadass is eager to have his son continue with this training and is also happy to have him regularly spend some of his time helping the evangelist.

Devadass considered marrying Anandam to a non-Christian first cousin, but after the author (P. Y. L.) had talked with him, he gave up the idea and decided to wait until he could find a suitable Christian girl for him. He opened negotiations with a Christian family in another village, but broke them off when he discovered that that family belonged to the other subcaste among the Madigas. Later Devadass arranged for Anandam to marry a girl from a non-Christian family of the same sub-caste, but he insisted that she first be baptized, and then he arranged a marriage performed by the presbyter using the Christian marriage service.

For a number of years before our study, the most active layman in the Ambojipet congregation was a man named Yesuratnam, but he had had little or no official recognition of his informal leadership. When the congregation elected a chairman of their new panchayat committee, he persuaded the others not to vote for him, but to elect a rather inactive Christian named Philip, who belonged to the other major caste group in the congregation. (Yesuratnam is a Mala, while Philip is a Madiga.) Yesuratnam felt that Philip had leadership potential that would be realized only if he were elected chairman. Yesuratnam's judgment was astute, and to his great satisfaction, Philip responded to the challenge. 'Saul,' Yesuratnam reported, 'has become Paul!' Yesuratnam's action was remarkably shrewd, but it also testified to a level of humility rarely attained in any Christian community: the willingness to withdraw from an official position of leadership in the interest of the community, and to continue to serve without recognition. While less spectacular than some of the incidents still to be described, this, too, may have been a costly sacrifice (cf. p. 135).

The head of the other strong family in Gowlapalli is named Nathaniel. His family, like that of Devadass, is regular in attending Christian worship, contributes far more to the evangelist than do the other Christian families, and has given up all its non-Christian practices. Nathaniel is an illiterate, but he follows the Christian way with considerable comprehension. Christians in this area have generally not attended the village celebrations on national holidays, but after Nathaniel had learned that there was nothing wrong in Christians sharing in these celebrations and, indeed, that it was their duty to attend, he and another Christian attended the Independence Day celebration in Gowlapalli. The high-caste Hindus who organized the celebration tried to force the two Christians to have *bottu* on their foreheads, but in spite of all the urging and threatening, they refused. They wanted to participate in the national celebration, but to do so as

Christians, without wearing the Hindu symbol of divine blessing. Devadass had a somewhat similar experience several years before when he went to his second son's engagement ceremony in Hyderabad. He bluntly refused to have *bottu* put on his forehead, and paid the twenty-five rupee fine levied on him by the non-Christian relatives for defying the traditional custom.

During the time when the author (P. Y. L.) and his wife were living in Gowlapalli, Nathaniel and his family were passing through severe trials. Nathaniel owns some land, which he works himself, and he derives most of his income from farming. That hot season his male buffaloes died, so that he had no draft animals to plough the fields, and then his wife and his only daughter fell seriously ill. He was greatly troubled in spirit by these misfortunes, the more so because some of his fellow-Christians came to him scoffing, bidding him curse God and give up his faith in Christ. 'You worship so regularly and pray to Christ on your knees, but what benefit did you get out of it? You have lost all your male buffaloes and your wife is ill. Why do you suffer all these hardships in spite of your devotion and prayers to Christ?' They urged him to worship the village deities, but Nathaniel remained firm in his Christian prayers and invited the author to come to his house and pray for his family. In such trying circumstances, that was itself a striking witness, but even more significant was his answer to his critics. Both Christians and non-Christians in these villages believe that devotion and Divine blessing inevitably go together, and many have been led to faith in Christ because of some miraculous healing or good fortune which they believe they have received from Christ. But this illiterate Christian, who was baptized at the same time nine years before and in the same group to which those who were taunting him belonged, penetrated to a deeper level of Christian experience in his answer to his Christian neighbours: 'Not my will, but His will be done. These troubles do not last long, and Jesus will help me to bear them.'

The efforts of some Hindus to cause village Christians to deny or obscure their membership in the Christian Church presents another important area of witness. Usually this is a different type of test from the question of participation in non-Christian rites, for whereas the latter involves the inner pull of traditional beliefs and attitudes that may conflict with Christian teaching, the former involves primarily an external pressure from some higher caste Hindus.

There are some Arya Samajists in this area who try to persuade Christians formally to renounce their religion and by a purificatory rite (*śuddhi*) to be readmitted to the Hindu community. Only rarely do the Arya Samajists try to argue with evangelists or presbyters. They generally accost village Christians individually, ask them puzzling questions and sometimes threaten to beat them with a sandal (more an insult than a painful punishment).

A Christian from Gowlapalli was travelling by train to Nizamabad when an educated Arya Samajist asked him the following questions: How could Jesus be born without a father? Are you not worshipping a *śakti* (demonic spirit) of a man who died violently? He did not rise again but became a demon. Don't we have our own gods? They are quite sufficient for us. Why do you go in for foreign gods? You have the name given by your forefathers. Why do you change your name in the middle of life?

Then the Arya Samajist asked him to give some explanation of Jesus Christ. When the Christian remained silent, he asked, 'Why do you profess to be a Christian when you do not know anything about Christianity?' The Christian replied, 'I cannot explain, yet I want to be a Christian,' whereupon the Arya Samajist stood up in the train, took his sandal in hand and threatened to beat him. Later the same Christian went to his wife's village, where there were no Christians at all, in order to bring home his wife, who had been visiting her (non-Christian) parents. There he had an encounter with another Arya Samajist who asked him similar questions. The Christian was thoroughly frightened by these experiences; a doubt was created in his mind about the Christian faith, which he had previously accepted unquestioningly. When he returned home to Gowlapalli, he continued to attend worship with the congregation, but the doubts that had been raised were worrying him, so on his own initiative he sought out the author (P. Y. L.) and asked him to answer the questions that the Arya Samajists had put to him.

In Kondapuram another member of the Arya Samaj similarly argued with one of the Christians. The Hindu said, 'You are born here; your houses and lands are here, and your living is in our hands. Why then do you accept the white men's religion? They are working to gain a majority. They are trying to come back to India and take our country out of our hands again. Do not believe them!' This same kind of attitude towards Christianity is found among many of the local Congress Party leaders and influential village officials.

Although these Christians have not been able to answer the Arya Samajists, they are by no means inclined to renounce their membership in the Christian community because of what they regard as one more effort on the part of high-caste Hindus to intimidate them and destroy their new social status as Christians. As we have seen, however, many Christians are prepared to deny or obscure their membership in the Christian Church temporarily, in order to secure some of the benefits which the Government is now offering to Harijans.

It is in the Gowlapalli congregation that this question has been posed by the Christians themselves as a test of Christian loyalty. Because the Gowlapalli congregation only began in 1950 (see pp. 66–67), there has probably been more pressure upon these Christians to revert to Hinduism than members of the older congregations have experienced in the last two decades. Certainly the Hindu landowners of Gowlapalli bitterly resent the fact that a large group of their outcaste labourers have become Christians. Yet though this issue may not everywhere else have been so openly felt and discussed, the same situation found in Gowlapalli is present in most of the other rural congregations throughout the Diocese.

We noted in Chapter 4 that in 1954 twelve of the older men in the congregation, led by the ex-leper Konka Yesudas, who had persuaded them to become Christians four years previously, had given their Hindu names to the Tehsildar in order to be granted Government lands available for Harijans. A number of younger men in the congregation, however, refused to use their Hindu names to secure lands, even though they used these traditional names every day in talking to one another, and the young men even reprimanded their elders for doing so.

The men who gave their Hindu names in 1954, and considered doing it again in 1958 and 1959, to be eligible for some other Harijan benefits were asked whether they had struck off their own Christian names from the church roll at the time that they denied that they were Christians and gave their Hindu names to the Government. They would not dare to do that, they replied, for then they would die, since only the names of persons who have died are struck off from the church roll.

Whatever their reasoning may be, it is fairly clear that the older men regard their membership in the Christian Church as something permanent, however lightly its obligations may rest upon them. They considered their denial that they were Christians before the Tehsildar, not as a permanent renunciation of their church membership, but as a bit of temporary deception that had to be practised to secure the land to which they were rightfully entitled.

In some other congregations, Christians have simply given their Hindu names to officials who have been willing to accept those names without inquiring too closely whether they were Christians, and these Christians regard their action as a necessary measure to get their rightful due from a Hindu-dominated Government, not as a denial of their faith in Christ or their membership in the Church. (In Mallupalle, several families delayed their final decision for baptism until the lands they had been cultivating were formally registered in their names.)

Wherever the officials inquire more closely, however, and insist on a virtual or even an open denial of their membership in the Christian Church, these Christians are forced to choose; may they temporarily deny their religion for the sake of securing what they regard as their just rights? That is a question which Christians elsewhere should be wary of trying to answer for them. It is in any case significant that when the issue was thus clearly put, a number of rather 'ordinary' young Christians in Gowlapalli felt in good conscience impelled, not only to forgo the material benefits, but also to reject the opinion of the older men in the congregation. Similar instances have been reported from various parts of the Diocese. Up to a generation ago, the hope of economic gain through education and the removal of the landowners' oppression was one of the chief motives for these outcastes accepting Christianity. Today, however, there are more disabilities than material advantages in outcastes becoming or remaining Christians. It is in this situation that these Christians, most of them very poor and few of them well instructed in the Christian faith, face a test of faith and loyalty—and of practical wisdom—the outcome of which may have momentous consequences for the whole Church.

CHAPTER 10

Baptism and Communicant Membership

In all the congregations studied there are a large number of baptized adults who are not communicant members. In only one congregation Achampet) are more than half the adults communicants. The average for the six congregations in the section where there is or recently has been a resident evangelist is 41·1%, but the average for the other three congregations without an evangelist is only 4·7%, bringing the average for the section to 32·6%. This is slightly better than the figure for the Pastorate as a whole—28·1%—and only a little less than the average for the whole Diocese: 33·8%. Since this last figure includes some urban pastorates with a much higher percentage of communicants, the percentage in the Jangarai section is evidently about the same as the average for all rural pastorates in the Diocese.

There is also a large proportion of non-communicant adults in a number of other dioceses of the Church of South India, particularly in the rural 'mass movement' areas (see Table 1 in the Appendix). Table 2 shows that the percentage of communicants in the Medak Diocese has gradually risen since the height of the mass movement in 1930, and a similar rise has taken place in other dioceses. However, the situation in the congregations studied indicates that the very gradual increase in the proportion of communicant members is not solving the fundamental problems behind these figures.

Since only communicant members may participate in the Lord's Supper and take part in the government of the Church, the majority of baptized adults in these village congregations are excluded both from the central act of Christian worship and from sharing in the management of the Church's affairs. In those places in South India where Christians consciously accept a distinction between communicants and non-communicants, the congregation tends to think of itself as an inner circle, the Church proper, surrounded by a larger circle, the 'Christian community'. The members of the inner circle, who alone share in Holy Communion, feel themselves responsible for the spiritual guidance of the whole Christian community and the management of its temporal affairs. They can encourage those who belong only to the outer circle and whose decision thus far has been only to belong to the Christian community, to make a decision for Christ, to believe in Him and accept His lordship.

In the five congregations specially studied and in a number of others that we visited briefly, we asked, 'What is the difference between the life and character of communicant members and those of non-communicant members?' The evangelists generally replied, 'We select people for confirmation who regularly come to prayers and give collections'. In addition, many evangelists look for such signs of progress in Christian living as not drinking toddy, not worshipping idols, not celebrating Hindu festivals, and having marriages solemnized with Christian rites. There is also the additional practical qualification that the Christian who is to be confirmed should be able to memorize the answers to the questions in the confirmation service. (In the new order of service, these answers are short.) Some evangelists explain the difference confirmation makes as follows: 'Members on trial are like people sitting on the veranda, but full communicant members are like those who have entered the house'.

In none of the congregations in which we asked the above question did the village Christians themselves make any reply. They do not understand the basis of the distinction between two kinds of Christians or grasp its significance; many of them are scarcely aware that there is such a distinction. Sometimes the evangelist must go round during the service and whisper to some in the congregation that they are communicants and should therefore go forward to receive Communion from the presbyter.

The communicants do not regard themselves as a smaller congregation or 'saving remnant' within the larger Christian community, and they therefore feel no responsibility to exercise by themselves, without the other adult baptized Christians, the powers of church government. In the congregations studied, representatives on the pastorate committee were either selected by the evangelist without consulting the communicant members, or they were elected at an informal meeting after evening prayers at which no distinction was made between communicants and non-communicants. If the 'limited electorate' of communicants were strictly observed, it would cut right across the family, clan and caste structures through which community decisions have usually been reached. In the congregations studied, the dividing line is not observed in the matter of elections, if elections are held, but it is adhered to in admittance to Communion. Certainly in these congregations, as well as in many others nearby, the group of communicant members has thus far not become a meaningful new 'community' superseding the traditional ties of family and caste within the larger community of Christians.

The Medak Diocese, like the other dioceses of the Church of South India, has been concerned about the large number of non-communicant adult members, perhaps particularly with the consequent deprivation of the means of grace to so many baptized Christians. At every Diocesan Council the discrepancy between the number of baptized adults and the number of communicant members is noted by the diocesan statistician, and presbyters are urged to make a deliberate effort to increase their emphasis on securing communicant members during the coming year.

Presbyters then return to their pastorates and once again encourage their evangelists to bring more people for confirmation. Many evangelists try to persuade at least a few of the non-communicants and tend to take

H

any who will come, but they often bring them to the pastorate head-quarters for the confirmation service without proper instruction. The 'deliberate effort' urged by the Diocesan Council is often interpreted to mean nothing more than this.

The policy of the Diocese has had some numerical success, as the figures in Table 2 indicate. It is expected by the Diocese that this progress will continue, but that it will be slow, because of the low spiritual state of so many village Christians and the related lack of proper teaching in many village congregations. We doubt seriously, however, whether the progress is sufficiently rapid to remove the present obstacles to the spiritual health of these village congregations within the foreseeable future. We question, moreover, whether the increase in the proportion of communicant members has not often been achieved in such mechanical fashion as further to complicate the life of the congregation and to becloud the theological issues at stake.

The evangelists who bring in as many candidates as possible for confirmation still retain in theory the 'veranda and house' distinction mentioned above. They say that there should be a higher level of spiritual attainment, and they know that they should not select people at random, but they cannot find Christians in their congregations of an obviously higher spiritual level, so in order to avoid their presbyter's displeasure, they tend to take anyone who will come. The presbyter, too, expects higher standards of Christians if they are to be confirmed, but he usually realizes that if he is to meet the expectations of the Diocesan Council, he will have to be 'realistic'. Over a period of years, therefore, there is a growth in number and proportion of communicants but it is doubtful whether their understanding correspondingly increases as to why they are communicant members but others are not.

Many Christians in the villages studied are more or less indifferent as to whether or not they become communicant members. In rare cases the bishop may suspend a communicant from Holy Communion, on the recommendation of the presbyter in charge of his pastorate. Such a step may be taken on account of such serious offences as persistent working against an evangelist, committing adultery, or marrying a second wife. It appears that few of those suspended feel the burden of this punishment; they do not care whether they are permitted to receive Communion or not. It is only very rarely that a village Christian comes to plead that his suspension be removed.

Some Christians, however, do not wish to be confirmed, because they would then be expected to receive Communion, which is a holy thing. 'They must live righteously and be truthful; otherwise Communion becomes a curse to them'. Here is evidence that some teaching con-cerning the special status of communicants has been understood by some members of these congregations, but it is the teaching, not of the present presbyter or evangelists, but of those of a generation ago!

The old designations 'M' and 'T' are still used in the church rolls: 'M' stands for 'full' or 'communicant member'; 'T' signifies 'member on trial'. This terminology implies that the baptized convert has to go through a trial period in which he should show evidence, not only of some increase in his Christian knowledge, but also of the reality of his Christian experience, and of his growth in grace as measured by moral conduct. Only after the successful completion of such a trial period would the convert be worthy of admittance to the Lord's Table. If a baptized Christian shows insufficient evidence of consecrated Christian living, he is considered not yet to be ready to become a 'full member'. Most of the earlier 'mass movement' converts remained 'on trial' all their lives and never became 'full members'. The children of converts are generally baptized as infants, and when they become fourteen, they automatically become 'members on trial'. They are then old enough to be eligible, after instruction by the evangelist, to be brought for confirmation. However, since they grow up in an atmosphere where communicant membership has little meaning, they have little desire to be confirmed when they become fourteen. Often this is true even when their parents happen to be communicant members.

This situation of having only a small proportion of baptized adults who are communicants has arisen in many mission areas in Asia and Africa, particularly in those missions which, while practising infant baptism, put the major emphasis on the evidence of spiritual regeneration as a condition of admittance to Holy Communion. Instead of the largely Christian populations of their home countries, many or all of whom were baptized as infants but few of whom had a personal experience of salvation, these missionaries with such a Pietist understanding faced an entirely non-Christian population, some of whom were deciding by groups to become Christians. In most mass movement areas, irrespective of denominational tradition, the standards for baptism were not held very high. However, those with a Pietist theology could easily interpret this baptism of mass movement converts as analogous to infant baptism—a rite of admission to the Christian community which could later be followed by the more significant rite of admission to communicant membership as soon as the individual showed that he was truly a 'regenerate Christian'.

This apparently convenient solution was not open to Baptists and others who rejected infant baptism. Equally influenced by the Evangelical and Pietist tradition, they were in the embarrassing position of baptizing large numbers who showed little or nothing of the Christian experience which they normally expected of those who were 'born again', and which in their home countries they had insisted upon as a prerequisite for 'believers' baptism'. Yet the apparently convenient solution which the analogy with infant baptism provided for most Protestant missions in South India led to a serious problem, for most of those baptized did not 'grow in grace' to the point where it was thought justifiable to admit them as 'full members'. Having administered 'infant baptism' to adults, these churches found themselves made up largely of adults who had to continue to be treated as spiritual 'babes'.[1]

The Pietist theology which seems to be the basis of the present practice is now much less influential in the Church of South India, in so far as the tests of Christian experience and morality, as conditions for confirmation, are much less stringently interpreted. Many church leaders hold that in the case of individual converts who show evidence of faith in Christ and who are carefully instructed, admission to communicant membership may follow immediately after baptism, and provision for this is made in the new C.S.I. orders of service.[2] In the case of 'mass movement' converts, however, they believe that there should continue to be a period for additional instruction and spiritual growth after baptism and before confirmation, though that second step should be more effectively and systematically encouraged than was the case a generation ago.

Many leaders of the Church of South India thus continue to believe that before a Christian is confirmed, he should come to a fuller understanding of what his baptism has meant; then in the confirmation service he publicly accepts God's promise sealed by his baptism and dedicates himself to Christ. He is then also in a better position than he was before baptism to understand the other two elements in the act of confirmation: the prayer for the gift of the Holy Spirit and the reception into the full fellowship of the Church, which includes the fellowship of the Lord's Table. Moreover, in the confirmation service the Christian accepts more explicit and far-reaching obligations towards the Church than he accepted at baptism.

There are some in the Church, however, who are beginning to ask whether it is ever justified to treat the baptism of an adult as if it were 'infant baptism' or the introduction to a kind of 'catechumenate' prior to full membership in the Church. Some of the wording of the explanation of the structure of the baptismal service would seem to raise the question. It is stated that 'where baptism is administered to an infant, the understanding of the gift of God and of the reception by the Church comes gradually and is personally accepted later.'[3] Is this true *only* of infant baptism? If so, the understanding and the personal acceptance should not be postponed in the case of an adult convert, though it is certainly true that 'this understanding is never completed within this life'. This interpretation would seem to be supported by the statement about *Preparation for Baptism:*

> Candidates able to answer for themselves must be well instructed in the Christian faith and way of life and approved by the Minister and the representatives of the congregation before they are brought to baptism. It is recommended that at the beginning of their preparation they should be publicly received as catechumens, according to the service appointed, and commended to the prayers of the congregation.[4]

A similar implication might be drawn from the statement about the structure of the service:

> In the ancient Church candidates were baptized, confirmed and given their first Communion in one continuous rite, as is still done in some churches today. With us, those baptized in infancy are later by Confirmation received into the full fellowship of the Church; but we must remember that the two rites are part of one process of entry into the Church.[5]

The drafters presumably did not intend this to mean that *only* in the case of infant baptism should baptism be separated from confirmation, but the logic of the whole statement almost requires such a conclusion. At the very least it would seem to encourage the combination of the two services in the case of candidates for baptism 'able to answer for themselves'. There is in fact provision for a combined service of baptism and confirmation, 'if the candidates have been specially prepared to be baptized and confirmed at the same time'. 'In this case the Vows of Confirmation (p. 24) are transferred to the Baptism Service to take the place of the Vows of Baptism (p. 8).'[6]

If the baptism of 'candidates able to answer for themselves' may not properly be treated as 'infant baptism' or as a service for their reception as catechumens (which should have preceded their baptism), on what grounds may *additional* spiritual growth or intellectual comprehension of the Christian faith be required of a baptized adult Christian before he is recognized as a 'full member' of the Church? The first of the three necessary elements in the new C.S.I. Confirmation Service is that 'Each candidate accepts for himself in public God's promise, of which baptism is the effective sign, and dedicates himself to Christ as his Lord and Saviour'.[7] If the baptismal candidate is old enough to undertake the baptismal vows himself, is it meaningful to require him to repeat substantially the same vows at a later ceremony, and is it right to withhold from him the privileges and duties of communicant membership, once he has been baptized?

The C.S.I. dioceses may be too large for the bishop of the diocese to be present at all adult baptisms, but, since confirmation may be administered by a presbyter, there is no practical reason why the services of baptism and confirmation cannot be combined. However, if it is desired to have confirmation by the bishop as often as possible, it would be possible for newly baptized adult converts to gather at some central place, within a few weeks of their baptism, for confirmation by the bishop. What is at issue here is not a brief gap in time, but a spiritual 'space' between baptism and admittance to full membership with the Church.

In the Medak Diocese, combined services of baptism and confirmation now occasionally take place in the case of some well-prepared adult converts. The problem for the Church, however, in this Diocese, as in many other 'mass movement' areas, is that baptism of adults who have made personal and sometimes costly decisions to follow Christ and join His Church represents only a minority of the baptisms of 'candidates able to answer for themselves'. The majority of adult baptisms are now of the following two kinds.

First, there are wives (occasionally husbands by *illutam*) from non-Christian families in other villages who have been married to Christian husbands (or wives) in the congregation. Some months or years after their marriage they are persuaded to be baptized. (In a slightly different category are the girls from Christian families who themselves have not been baptized, usually because the family feared that their baptism would hinder their marriage into a non-Christian family, if that should prove advantageous. Those who finally do marry Christians are baptized like the girls from non-Christian families, some time after their marriage.) Most of these girls adopt the religion of the Christian families into which they enter as a matter of course, but they feel complete freedom to join in their old religious practices on their frequent visits home during the Hindu festivals.

Second, there is still occasionally a village caste group, usually one of the two main 'outcaste' *kulams*, the Madigas or Malas, which has made a group decision to become Christian. Although the other adults express their opinion and share to some extent in the preliminary discussion, the final decision is often made largely by the caste elders and heads of families. The solidarity of the *kulam* has been decreasing in recent years, as the recent events in Mallupalle show (see p. 160), and the moving spirits in the decision may be others than the hereditary caste leaders. It is still true, however, that many of the group coming for baptism have only passively acquiesced in the group's decision to become Christian.

In both these cases there is the same evident lack of individual decision and inward conversion which made the earlier evangelical Protestant missionary so reluctant to baptize 'mass movement' converts, and led to his separating the baptism of such converts from their admission to communicant membership. The Church in this area thus still confronts all the theological problems connected with 'mass movement' baptisms and is still trying to solve these problems in the same way, though it is trying to narrow the gap between baptism and confirmation by encouraging more intensive pre-baptismal instruction. In practice, though certainly not in the official policy of the Diocese, the gap is being narrowed by the evangelists' and presbyters' lessened expectations of spiritual growth in candidates for confirmation. Yet it is precisely in these two difficult 'test cases', we suggest, that it is highly advisable not to separate confirmation from baptism, for the church membership into which these converts enter after baptism ought to be understood and experienced by them as nothing less than the whole range of privileges and responsibilities which are theirs after confirmation.

In the village congregations studied, the non-Christian girls (and the few boys) married into the congregation are usually baptized any time from several months to several years *after* their marriage, often with little or no pre-baptismal instruction. In part this is a consequence of the lack of acceptance of the Christian marriage ceremony. If Christian families were regularly in the habit of asking the presbyter to marry their sons and daughters, it would be the presbyter's duty to prepare the non-Christian partner for baptism before the wedding was celebrated. There are other causes as well: the unbaptized partner's indifference and resistance to thorough instruction, the evangelist's negligence in giving such instruction and in regular pastoral care, and the lack of proper examination of candidates by presbyter and evangelist before baptism is administered. All of these causes are themselves strongly influenced by the understanding of baptism shared by the congregation and the evangelist, and perhaps to some extent by the presbyter: baptism is considered a naming ceremony like *Purudu* and the formal rite of entrance into Christian community which does not require any personal response of faith in Christ—in a word, 'infant baptism'.

But however young and immature these girls may be, they are not infants, and they will have soon (or have already had to) assume the responsibilities of motherhood. In spite of the theoretical supremacy of the husband in the new family, the wife must take a leading part in managing the family's affairs. Even in a joint family, her role is not so negligible as it might seem to be, and many of these young wives now move after a few years into their own houses. Whatever their degree of subordination to husband or mother-in-law, these wives exercise the most formative influence on their children, who will grow up in the congregation and should become its active nucleus in the next generation. The fact that these girls are married into the Christian community does not, it seems to us, make it legitimate to baptize them under the same conditions as the infant children born of Christian parents, allowing them to defer their own personal response of faith and their acceptance of the baptismal vows into the indefinite future. These non-Christians ought to be baptized before their marriage to Christian members of the congregation, as occurs in most other areas in South India, but the present situation in these villages is that they are married to Christians in a non-Christian ceremony without (with a few exceptions) the question of baptism having been raised. It is in this situation that the proclamation and demonstration of the Gospel to these non-Christians married into the congregation should take place, by the congregation as well as by its ministers. When these wives (or husbands), after a period of instruction and reflection, have shown their sincere desire to be baptized into the death and resurrection of Jesus Christ, they ought at the time of their baptism to receive the Church's prayer for their strengthening by the Holy Spirit (a prayer which according to the new C.S.I. Confirmation Service is essentially the prayer of the congregation, though spoken by the bishop or presbyter)[8] and should be admitted to the fellowship of the broken body and shed blood of the same Lord Jesus into whom they have been baptized.

These young wives are now baptized, with little more will in the matter than as if they were infants, at a time when they should and could accept for themselves God's promise and dedicate themselves to Christ. It is little wonder that both the newly baptized wives and the rest of the congregation look upon their baptism as a ceremony in which the girl receives a new, additional name, but a name which is used only in the presence of the evangelist or presbyter. Neither the teaching of the evangelist nor the general spiritual life of the congregation is usually sufficient impetus to lead the girl to take the further step of seeking confirmation. Not having understood the significance of her baptism, she finds it even more difficult to grasp the meaning of confirmation and communicant membership.

With the slowing down of the 'mass movement' to Christianity, these non-Christian wives (and a few husbands who live in the wife's village) now constitute a large proportion of the adults who come for baptism. However, there are still occasional group decisions for baptism in this area on the part of a whole (or a substantial part of a) caste group in a village. It is in such instances that the most serious difficulty has been felt in admitting newly baptized persons immediately to communicant membership. It is felt legitimate to baptize the whole group at the same time, after a suitable period of instruction, even though it is known that the decision to become Christians was made largely by a few leaders of the community. Confirmation, however, is considered to be an act which should await the individual's spiritual maturity and individual decision, and the body of communicant members is expected to be a real 'gathered church' in the midst of the larger nominally Christian community.

Sometimes the same evangelist who has been quite diligent in preparing a new congregation for baptism does not continue with systematic instruction after baptism. Laziness does not provide the entire explanation for this; the evangelist often does not understand the relation of his teaching, either to baptism or to the life of the Christian community after baptism. Before baptism catechumens are supposed to be taught to pray and to sing Christian lyrics, to have some experience of Christian worship, and to study the life of Christ. However, in practice, the evangelist seems to be engaged in teaching as many as possible in the future congregation to memorize the Ten Commandments, the Lord's Prayer, and if possible even the Apostles' Creed. Those who memorize these things are generally the children and younger adults, but neither they nor the older men and women are taught very much about the meaning of the words they are supposed to memorize. If there is any explanation, it is likely to be of the meaning of the Commandments, rather than any explanation of the theological terms which are meant to convey how God has saved His people.

As long as the evangelist conceives his teaching ministry as a process of coaching candidates for an examination, it is quite understandable that when the examination is over the teaching ceases. Even if the evangelist feels a continuing obligation to teach the new Christian law, it is still primarily the *Law* with which he is concerned in his systematic instruction. The Gospel does come into the sermons of the evangelist, but usually in a rather truncated form, since the same simple lesson about the power of *Yesu Swami* to heal diseases and bring material blessings is drawn from every parable. It seems to be very little understood that if the faith of the community is to be deepened and continually reawakened, the congregation must keep on feeding on the word of Scripture as it is illuminated and brought home to its experience by the evangelist, the presbyter and its own lay ministry.

The consequences of the community's corporate decision for baptism are felt by almost every member of the group, and the teaching before baptism is meant to ensure that the entire group measures up to the minimum standards of Christian knowledge though, curiously enough, the least teaching is given to the older men who are directly responsible for the community's decision. The presbyter and the evangelist in charge of the new congregation know that a further step is necessary after baptism if members of the congregation are to become full members. The new Christians, however, begin by thinking of themselves simply as 'Christians', not as 'members on trial'. It is extremely difficult for them to appreciate the significance of a further step for which no corporate decision is possible and for which no corporate instruction is offered. The distinction between a *corporate* decision for baptism and an *individual* decision to seek confirmation was an understandable adjustment of the individualistic theology of many Western missions to the realities of the situation in a culture where many (though not all) important decisions are made, not by individuals, but by groups. The Church needs now to consider, however, whether such a distinction is theologically justified.

Those who support this distinction argue that the Christian community is everywhere larger than the Church. By recognizing this fact, the Church can take steps to persuade those who have joined only the Christian community to make the further decision to accept Christ and become part of His Church. It is clearly desirable, they maintain, to work for a community of fully committed Christians within the larger Christian community; there are many cases where such a nucleus of committed members has had a beneficial effect on the whole cause of Christianity in the villages.

There are fundamental questions involved here that will need to be discussed by Christians for some time to come. It is obviously difficult to determine the limits of the Church, even as a visible human institution, yet some practical delimitation of church membership has to be attempted. There is also good reason for a group of Christians to strive for a greater measure of conscious commitment to Christ. We question, however, whether either the definition of church membership or the encouragement of greater commitment are served by the *present* distinction between baptism and communicant membership in many Churches in South India. In their statistics, Baptists in Andhra Pradesh include a very large number under 'Christian community', by which they mean the children and other (often many other) unbaptized members of Christian families. We question whether the baptized children and adults who are not communicants in the Church of South India can similarly be considered as only in the penumbra of the Church, in the so-called 'Christian community'. The C.S.I. Constitution states that 'Baptized children are members of the Church, and share in the privileges and obligations of membership so far as they are capable of doing so'. It then goes on to describe a more restricted category of 'full membership':

The full privileges and obligations of membership in the Church of South India belong to those who, having attained to years of discretion and having gained some measure of experience in the Christian life, and having received due instruction in Christian truth and in the duties of their Christian calling, make public profession of their faith and of their purpose, with God's help, to serve and to follow Christ as members of His Church.[9]

I

The crucial point, it seems to us, is the inclusion of 'some measure of experience in the Christian life' *before* the public profession of faith, the prayer for strengthening by the Holy Spirit, and admittance to 'full membership in the Church', thereby becoming 'eligible to partake of the Holy Communion in the Church'.[10] Is the 'experience in the Christian life' not markedly impoverished *until* one shares 'the full privileges and obligations of membership'?

Apart from the question of doctrine, should not the Church face the fact that the present distinction does not correspond at all accurately to the observable distinctions between Christians in many village congregations? Nor does the present policy by itself encourage more and more Christians to progress in their Christian knowledge and experience. In each of the congregations studied, there is a nucleus of 'good Christians', ranging in size from a few individuals to five families, but not all of these are communicant members. Moreover, there are many communicant members who are part of the majority involved in a combination of—or compromise between—Christian discipleship and participation in village *mores*. The minority of more fully committed Christians do not presently think of themselves as the 'saved' among a large body of 'nominal Christians', and we do not believe that they should. They feel a part of one congregation, which is both 'church' and 'community'. For that very reason, if they become sufficiently aroused, they are capable of influencing the entire 'Christian community'—and many beyond it—in a remarkable way.

Whatever policy the Church adopts towards the relation of baptism and communicant membership, there is no doubt of the need of much better instruction about their meaning. What we are here suggesting is that the present practice of preparing prospective church members for a 'compulsory first examination' (baptism) and an 'optional second examination' (confirmation) greatly adds to the congregation's difficulties in understanding the significance of their membership in the Church and the relation of both preaching and the two sacraments to that membership.

The Church of South India has been much concerned in recent years with increasing the opportunities for rural Christians to participate in Holy Communion. The significance of more frequent celebrations in the villages is considerably lessened, however, if more than half the adults in the congregation are, in actual fact, excluded from participating. Likewise there has recently been increased concern with developing responsible lay participation in the Church. It is a sound principle that the same group which gathers at the Lord's Table and shares in the breaking of bread should share also in the spiritual and temporal responsibilities of Christ's People.

Village Christians can hardly be expected to take these responsibilities seriously when only a fraction of the entire adult membership is entitled to share in the government of the Church, and when neither the inner circle nor the rest of the congregation understands what the significance of this particular fraction might be.

Although these villagers are used to making important decisions corporately, they do know what an individual decision means, and the incidents related in this book show some of the situations in which individuals or small family units have made significant responses of obedience to God's will in the face of indifference or opposition from their community. However, if the Church considers that a community's decision to become Christian is a genuine corporate response to God's call which justifies the baptism of all its members, should it not consider that same corporate response as sufficient grounds for confirming all the adult members of the community without any additional requirements of Christian knowledge or moral behaviour? This is the primary question which the Church must face, but the question of timing, though secondary, is also important. Should not even such 'mass movement' converts be confirmed at the same time that they are baptized? To do so doubtless places an awesome responsibility upon these new Christians and upon the ministers who are to guide them. but is not this precisely the responsibility to which God is calling them and which He wills them to undertake together as a community?

We ought not, we believe, so to separate baptism and confirmation as to make of the first a corporate act and of the second a step resulting from an individual process of spiritual growth and decision; we surely ought not to distinguish between the faith and spiritual maturity required of adult candidates for baptism and that required of candidates for confirmation. The two sacraments belong together in the congregation, and they belong together with the Gospel, of which they are the visible and effective demonstrations in the world.

The Church is constituted by the Holy Spirit as men respond to the proclamation of the Good News of God's Salvation in Christ. They thus become 'full members' of Christ's Body, the Church, though always 'on trial' before their Lord. Their faith must continue to be reawakened and deepened within the Church, but they can now be appealed to live out in their individual and corporate life what they already are in Christ. The Church's great need in these villages is for such proclamation and explanation of the Gospel, and for exhortation addressed to a community of Christians who know that they *are* in Christ and *are* members of His Church; therefore they are to witness as His own People in the world of the village.

APPENDIX: PERCENTAGE OF BAPTIZED ADULTS
WHO ARE COMMUNICANT MEMBERS

TABLE I.   STATISTICS IN 1958 OR 1958–59

	Number of Communicants	Percentage
Jangarai section	*252*	*32·6*
Six congregations with a resident evangelist	244	41·1
Jangarai	40	40
Gowlapalli	39	37
S. Kondapuram	46	42
Achampet	52	63
Ambojipet	31	44
Bandaposanipalli	36	29
Three congregations without a resident evangelist	8	41·7
Edulapalli	5	11
Chettipalli	0	0
Mirzapalli	3	5
Wadiaram Pastorate	*929*	*28·1*
The Four C.S.I. Dioceses in Andhra Pradesh	*106,970*	*37·8*
Medak	*28,791*	*33·8*
Dornakal	28,025	36
Krishna–Godavari	37,744	45
Rayalaseema	12,410	35
Other C.S.I. Dioceses		
Mysore (Mysore State)	19,312	64
Madras (Madras State)	36,315	68
Tiruchi-Tanjore (Madras State)	19,199	43
Madurai-Ramnad (Madras State)	26,306	79
Tirunelveli (Madras State)	70,328	70
Kanyakumari (Madras State)	19,499	31
North Kerala (Kerala State)	13,029	78
Central Travancore (Kerala State)	42,284	71
South Kerala (Kerala State)	14,209	33
Jaffna (Ceylon)	3,488	90
All Fifteen Dioceses of the Church of South India	*382,233*	*51*

TABLE 2.   HISTORICAL SURVEY IN THE HYDERABAD METHODIST DISTRICT
AND THE MEDAK DIOCESE

		Baptized Adults	Full Members	Percentage
Hyderabad Methodist	1880	25	17	68
District	1885	171	147	86
	1890	743	283	38
	1895	2,600	672	26
	1900	4,867	1,449	30
	1905	6,060	2,034	34
	1910	9,161	2,862	31
	1915	13,954	3,965	28
	1920	26,406	4,923	18·6
	1925	35,386	6,695	18·9
	1930	54,985	8,875	16·1
	1935	69,444	13,045	19·4
	1940	86,532	19,429	22
	1945	98,355	23,580	24
	1947	101,609	25,780	25
Church of South India,	1948	70,463	20,033	28·4
Medak Diocese	1950	75,784	21,882	28·9
	1952	79,618	24,393	30·6
	1954	—	—	—
	1956	80,802	26,057	32·2
	1957–58	82,601	27,137	32·9
	1958–59	85,113	28,791	33·8

Acknowledgements:

This information is obtained from:

(a) the village church rolls in the Jangarai section and the pastorate rolls of the Wadiaram Pastorate;

(b) the statistics included in the Minutes of the C.S.I. Synod and the Medak Diocesan Council;

(c) 'Growth of the Hyderabad Church', in *Our Hyderabad Bulletin* (January–March 1948, Vol. X, No. 1) p. 12—for figures prior to Church Union.

N.B. Cf. also the Appendix to Chapter 2: 'Growth of the Hyderabad Methodist District, and Progress of the Medak Diocese, C.S.I.'

CHAPTER 11

The Crisis and Opportunity of the Church

A. *Challenges from the Church's Environment*

Our directive for this study, which we quoted at some length in the preface, states:

> the aim of the studies in the Life and Growth of Younger Churches is to try to see the local church as it really is and to understand the distinctive insights which it may be gaining into the meaning of the Gospel and the Will of God. The point at which this distinctiveness of Younger Churches begins to develop is to be found in the Church's *encounter* with its environment.[1]

We shall begin this concluding chapter by attempting to summarize what we have said about some of the significant challenges to the Church in these villages and the response of Christians to those challenges.

1. *The Challenge of Inferior Social Status*

At the beginning of our study, all the Christians in the Jangarai Section belonged to one of the two 'outcaste' *kulams*. Like most Protestant Christians in Andhra Pradesh, they are either Madigas or Malas. While they are thoroughly involved in village life, they have not had all the privileges of membership in village society. They have been regarded as servants and as inferior creatures, forced to perform the menial and 'unclean' tasks, and despised because they do so. They are kept outside, and apart from much that the village values, especially the 'higher' aspects of Hindu religion and culture that are directed by the Brahmins. The outcastes are despised for their lack of culture by the very people who have kept it from them.

In the past, education has been the Christians' chief response to this inferior status. Very often it has meant the acquiring of the means to *escape* from the village and to secure in urban life both a higher social status and a larger income than they have known in the village. There are only a few now in these village congregations who have even learned to read; most Christians who have received more education have left the village.

This situation, however, is now beginning to change. The place of the evangelist's class is being taken by the government school, and the aim of the government programme of free education in the villages is to educate children for better life in the village. Christian children of outcaste background are allowed to attend these schools, but in some of them they are forced to sit at a distance from the children of higher castes. If this discrimination continues, it may encourage the continuing exodus of Christians from the village, for they can hardly find it attractive to stay as part of a society in which all are educated, yet they remain at the bottom of the social ladder. The coming of universal education, however, also provides Christians with an opportunity to raise their own economic and cultural level, and to achieve a dignity in the eyes of the rest of the village that will make it unnecessary to escape to the city. If Christians do not seize this opportunity, they will probably remain at the bottom of a more dynamic village society in which every caste and family seek to advance. Furthermore, they will have neither the better educated leaders nor the literate members who are needed to establish the Church in the changing village of the future.

The desire for *dignity* is very strong among these Christians, even when they have not tried to secure any education. It is one of the powerful motives in their accepting Christianity and perhaps the most important reason why they want an evangelist stationed in their midst, however little he may actually be doing. This desire for dignity or enhanced social status is a powerful motive and is likely to become even more so as the caste system becomes less rigid, and more and more opportunities develop for changing the status of one's family and improving its lot. This motive force can be used in building up the congregation, but if it is not guided, it can lead to an uncritical imitation of the culture of the higher castes or a competition between individuals or families that can destroy the unity of the congregation. Such developments are already discernible among urban Christians in Telengana and among the few village Christian congregations of higher caste background near the Godavari.

An alternative response to the challenge of inferior social status is that implied in the Apostle Paul's injunction, 'Slaves, be obedient to those who are your earthly masters, with fear and trembling, in single-ness of heart, as to Christ; not in the way of eyeservice, as men-pleasers, but as slaves of Christ . . .' (Eph. 6: 5–6a). These Christians have never been 'slaves' in the Roman sense, but most of them have been more or less the serfs of large landowners, and all of them have been to some extent in servitude to the village as a whole. Now, due largely to Christian influence, *yetti* (forced labour to the village) has ceased, and only a few Christians still remain the serfs of landowners. The Diocesan Young Men's Organization, the *Yavana Samaj*, has the development of a spirit of service as one of its principal aims. The Hindu landowners in the villages studied claimed to see nothing distinctive in the service Christians rendered, but it may be that there has been a silent and unnoticed witness that has influenced caste Hindus in their present openness to the Gospel. Christians outside the village should clearly recognize the great difficulty of achieving this spirit of service: to be willing to continue to serve higher caste Hindus as Christian neighbours when it is no longer necessary to serve as outcaste serfs. Yet if the village Christian is to develop a Christian sense of his vocation, he needs to be challenged to such a spirit of service, both in his daily work as an agricultural labourer and in the new type of voluntary service—voluntary '*yetti*'—in which all the villagers must learn to participate, if the village is to seize the opportunities in the Community Development programme.

2. *The Challenge of Poverty*

Poverty and economic insecurity present a severe challenge to village Christians. We found some individual responses to this challenge, but no concerted action by the whole congregation. All wish to improve their economic position and believe that the best way to do this is to obtain the government benefits for Harijans. However, they are generally ignorant of the provision of the laws and the prescribed methods of application, and they are depressed and frustrated by the refusal of village leaders and government officials to help them, on the ground that they are no longer Harijans, but Christians.

While some Christians see the only hope of improving their lot in moving to a town or city, most of them have some hope of overcoming or at least lessening their poverty while remaining in the village, especially since the government aid programmes for the rural areas have begun. What they prize most is land. Not only does owning land and working one's own land increase one's income, it also gives a man more dignity and more economic independence; he is no longer dependent on a landowner to give him work from day to day.

There seems to have been a slight improvement in the income received by many Christian families during the past several years, but this has been accompanied by an increased cost of living and a rising standard of living. Villagers now buy such articles as soap, face powder, mill yarn, cloth shirts, and petticoats and some of them now spend more on weddings and other special occasions. Increased income, therefore, does not free these village Christians from the burden of debt at very high rates of interest. Those who earn more generally also spend more on toddy and tobacco and are equally heavily in debt.

From the beginning of Christian work in this area, the Church has been keenly aware of the extreme poverty of most of its members and has taken various steps to improve the economic level of Christian families. Much of the educational programme has had this as one of its aims, and some schools have been specifically designed to train Christians more effectively in village occupations. At conferences and training institutes, there have been repeated efforts to encourage and assist village Christians to take whatever steps lay within their power to improve their earnings and their living conditions. During the period of our study, in April 1959, a conference for the whole Diocese was held in Medak, attended by about one hundred and twenty delegates from all the pastorates. Its main theme was 'building up the total life of village congregations to ensure their spiritual vitality and economic stability, so that they may become spontaneously expanding churches'. Leaders in the Diocese are certainly very much concerned with 'economic evangelism'.

Some congregations within the Diocese have been specifically included in a Diocesan programme of economic uplift. These happened to include two in the Jangarai section: Achampet and Gowlapalli. At the time of our study, however, virtually no improvement had been effected. A few families in Gowlapalli have the 'smokeless *chula*', an inexpensive stove built of clay that is vastly superior to an open fire within a hut.[2] Four young men in Achampet have taken a course at the tannery in Ramayampet.

The Christians in the Jangarai section are only beginning to be affected by the various government programmes of economic uplift. Like the other villagers, they are now using chemical fertilizer (ammonium sulphate), but at the time of our study they had had little opportunity to improve their technique of agriculture or animal husbandry. In previous chapters we have noted the difficulties Christians have encountered in their applications for land or financial aid for new homes, wells or cattle. As the government programmes increase in scope, there will be opportunities for village Christians to benefit from them, especially in putting improved agricultural techniques into practice, even when they are discriminated against in more direct grants of financial aid.[3] Participation in co-operative credit societies will be more difficult for Christians, because most of them have little or nothing to invest, are likely to have little voice in the management, and could only take loans if they had land as security. In spite of the problems, it is essential that the efforts of the Diocese in economic uplift be geared as closely as possible with the new government programmes. This is a practical necessity for village Christians, but it is also a moral imperative for the Church: the future of Christians is bound to the future of the village as a whole.

The permanent indebtedness of most Christian families points to what is more than an economic problem: the high expenditure on items that are not essential to life and health, but that seem quite essential to most villagers, including Christians. The nightly drink at the toddy shop, the entertainment of relatives, the celebration of weddings and religious festivals, the bangles and the ornaments for the women—all of these add colour and variety to what is otherwise a very drab existence. There is no doubt that more attention needs to be given to the virtues of frugality and sobriety, but these Christians can hardly be expected to change their habits unless they find alternative ways of reducing the drabness of their existence, new ways of appreciating and enjoying the dimensions of life that are hard to discern in the dull and grinding routine of the daily round.

3. *The Challenge of Village Religion*

At a number of points in the previous chapters we have discussed the challenge to village Christians presented by village Hinduism, and, to a lesser extent, popular Islam. To a very large extent, Christians in the congregations we studied share the beliefs of village Hindus, perform many of the same rites and join with them in their celebration of various festivals. The rest of the village requires certain Christians to perform their traditional duties in ceremonies common to the whole village. Moreover, all the *kulams*, including those outcaste *kulams* whose members are all Christians, are assessed a share in the expenses of building or renovating a village shrine. Christians are not forced to believe in the deity or deities of that particular shrine. The 'compulsion' is partly a matter of social prudence, but even more a consequence of their sharing, to a greater or lesser extent, the belief of other villagers in the power of the village deities and spirits and in the efficacy of the rites directed to them. If they were to stop performing the Hindu rites and ceremonies, most Christians fear that deities would send some calamity upon them. So far only a few Christians regard the service and worship of Christ as an *alternative* to non-Christian worship. Most participate in the worship of Christ in addition to their worship of various local deities. Since non-Christian worship remains for most Christians in a different but still vital cultic sphere, it is not surprising that there is relatively little incorporation of traditional means of worship into the worship of the Christians' new and foreign deity, 'Lord Jesus'. In the realm of ideas, there is a strong tendency to comprehend the Christian message in familiar village terms, but in the realm of ritual practice, Christians start to 'borrow' significantly from traditional rites only when they have begun to sense the total and exclusive claims of their 'Lord Jesus'.

Our experiences during the study suggests that even a little better instruction by evangelists and presbyters on the implications of belonging to Christ would markedly change the response of village Christians. This may well mean quite specific and emphatic instruction in 'Do's' and 'Don'ts', but far more is needed than the more effective inculcation of a series of prohibitions. At present the village beliefs and practices in which most Christians share provide a great deal of the meaning and, more especially, the excitement, in their lives. Unless the various cycles of life—the daily round, the yearly cycle of seasons and the human span—can be filled with Christian meaning and punctuated by occasions which express that meaning, Christian prohibitions will simply aid in the process of secularization which is already beginning to affect these villages, undermining the meanings which the villagers find in life without substituting any new meanings in their stead. Too often the ministers of the Gospel teach only a Christian 'law', which they hardly expect village Christians to be able to follow. Occasionally, however, whether through formal preaching of the Gospel, the informal witness in a helpful word or deed, or the apparently more direct Divine agency of a dream or a miraculous healing, a village Christian makes some new discovery about the Gospel, about the lordship and liberating power of Jesus Christ, the Son of the Most High. When he makes such a discovery, it often has far-reaching effects, not only on his fellow-Christians, but on many others in the village, and beyond.

4. *The Challenge of Aggressive Hindu Nationalism*

A quite different challenge is presented to village Christians by the activities of the Arya Samaj and the attitudes of a considerable number of conservative Hindus, many of them high in the ranks of the local and district branches of the dominant Congress Party. In the congregations studied, this challenge is at present less important than the pervasive presence of popular Hinduism, but it is sharply defined, so that Christians are more aware of it and more inclined to make some immediate response.

We noted above (pp. 205–206) a few efforts by Arya Samajists to interrogate and embarrass village Christians. Christians were unable to answer the questions that were put to them, and the evangelists were unable to help them. Both village laymen and their evangelist-teacher need the help of their presbyter in reaching a more reasoned understanding of the Christian faith, in order to answer the criticisms of the Arya Samaj. While the questions of the Samajists are extremely embarrassing and sometimes raise doubts in the minds of Christians about some Christian beliefs, they have not proved generally disturbing to the congregation. There are three reasons for the lack of success of the Arya Samajists, in spite of their 'unanswerable' questions. First, the Arya Samaj is a nineteenth-century Reform Movement which intended to defend the ancient Hindu community against the 'foreign' religions of Christianity and Islam, but the new apologetic was influenced profoundly by Western rationalism in its emphasis on the monotheistic, non-idolatrous, and thoroughly scientific character of the original Vedic faith and in its rejection of much of the polytheism, image worship, and social customs of nineteenth-century popular Hinduism. Both Christians and Hindus in the village studied still live very largely in the non-rationalist apprehension of life consciously or unconsciously rejected in Arya Samaj apologetic, even though its aim may be to 'defend' Hinduism. So far, therefore, the force of the Arya Samaj critique of Christian faith, largely based on rationalistic arguments, has hardly been felt. However, as urban patterns of thinking increase their influence in these villages, the arguments and objections of the Arya Samajists may make much more sense to Christians than they do now.

Secondly, it has been clear to Christians that many of the Arya Samajists they meet are less concerned with giving a reasoned defence of Hindu beliefs than with insisting that Christians remain in their subservient role in the village and not upset the *status quo*. This is also true of the efforts of some higher caste Hindus, especially the landowners, to keep outcastes from becoming Christians, or to force those who have to renounce Christianity. Such attempts at coercion, whether subtle or direct, worry Christians much more than the arguments against Christianity propounded by the Arya Samaj, especially since the Hindus with this attitude towards them are often in a position to prevent Christians from obtaining the various government benefits for Harijans. This deliberate pressure sometimes causes non-Christian outcastes to give up the idea of becoming Christians, and influences Christians to give their non-Christian names in applying for government benefits. Whether or not Christians make such applications with a bad conscience, they do not consider it to be a radical renunciation of their membership in the Christian community. Coercion can sometimes compel a grudging compliance or result in an apparent duplicity, but it cannot produce among outcastes, whether Christians or not, the *conviction* to be loyal members of Hindu society. The heavy reliance on coercion, even if it is a subtle coercion, robs the Arya Samajist arguments of much of their persuasive power.

Finally, the positive side of the Arya Samajist message to Christians is quite ambiguous. The logic of the invitation to rejoin the Hindu community requires a community able to receive outcastes, and the Arya Samaj has tacitly reconceived the Hindu social system, so that the outcastes are no longer 'outside' but 'inside'. Precisely because the Arya Samaj draws so much of its support from conservative Hindus interested in preserving the *status quo*, however, its invitation to return, to come back inside the fold, implies 'underneath' as well as 'inside'. Moreover, it usually has the spirit, not of an invitation to outcastes to join a community from which they have perviously been excluded, but of a command to remain in their present subservient status. More and more Harijans, whether Christians or not, are reacting to such commands with sullen silence or even insolent defiance. The term 'Harijans', which means 'child of God (Vishnu)', was coined, not by the Arya Samaj, but by Gandhi. Gandhi's attitude towards outcastes was quite different, but in the villages studied, neither Gandhi's programme nor his conception of village society as a co-operative striving for the 'increasing welfare for all' (*sarvodaya*) is at all in evidence, except for its indirect effect on some of the government programmes of 'Community Development'.

The attitude of many higher caste Hindus towards Christians in the village calls for a concerted response from the whole Church. Interested and informed presbyters and evangelists could do a great deal to help village Christians in applying for the aid to which they are certainly entitled legally, and the aid which they might receive if the officials would consider them as Harijans. There is also a need for a spiritual response to discrimination, on the one hand a witness of patience and forbearance in the face of provocation, but on the other hand a demonstration to the village as a whole that Christians can be loyal to their God and at the same time more truly devoted to the ideals of the Indian nation than are the religious nationalists among the Hindus. Such a response is obviously very difficult, but we believe that many Christians, if given some guidance, could convince their Hindu neighbours that they are not simply withdrawing from Hindu society, but are also contributing to an expanded conception of the village community in which they, who are also 'children of God', will join in working for the 'increasing welfare of all'.

5. *The Challenge of Democracy*

The period of our study happened to coincide with the first democratic elections on the local level in the villages of the Jangarai section: the election of panchayat boards for large villages and groups of adjacent smaller villages (see pp. 95–97). In most of the local elections in this area, the Congress Party candidates were elected, and these were conservative Hindu landowners or represented their point of view. The immediate effect of democracy at the village and taluq level, therefore, was to give increased political power to the very people who in the past have kept the Malas and Madigas as 'serfs'. That this should be the 'first-fruits' of village democracy is naturally rather discouraging to many Christians. The challenge which confronts them is to see beyond the increased difficulties of the present, and to grasp the opportunities that are potentially available in the new democratic system. Awakening of political consciousness may tempt the congregation to affiliate too closely with one political party, but this future danger is less acute than the present one of Christians simply being used as pawns in a political chess game. Our observations during the study indicate that some congregations are responding to this challenge; they are beginning to regard the new democratically elected government as 'ours' and they are joining with other groups in the village to establish responsible government. They very much need the guidance of evangelists and presbyters and of educated Christian laymen from the towns and cities. At the time of our study, however, the official organization of the Church had done little to help these village congregations meet the new situation of local democracy in the village.

One valuable aid to Christian participation in democratic government would be the experience of such democracy within the congregation and the pastorate. Such government by the laity is thus far only present in theory, the theory of government by the communicant members. This means that the Christians in the Jangarai section saw local democracy on the basis of universal adult suffrage for the first time, not in the Church but in the sphere of secular politics. The experiment of electing an informal 'panchayat committee' for the Achampet congregation at the same time that elections were being held for the government 'panchayat board' for two or three adjacent villages, was generally successful. This is not surprising, since we were simply reclaiming for the Church the democratic government which in large part has been the contribution of the 'Free Churches' of the West to the political life of their own and other Western countries.

6. *The Challenge of Urbanization and Secularization*

Political democracy is only one of many features of twentieth-century civilization that have been influenced in their development both by Christianity and by the revolt of Western man against the authority of the Church, a revolt often called 'humanism' or 'secularism'. The secularist component in Western civilization has often been conveyed through Western education, including Christian education. To some extent this has been unwitting, but to a considerable extent it has been the deliberate emphasis of much Protestant teaching against the control of all human life by any human religious institution, including the Church. In particular, there has been strong objection to the State's being controlled by any religious institution, and this view has been influential in India's acceptance of a secular State.

Western 'secularism', whether in a Christian or an anti-Christian form, has probably been less influential than the technological revolution which has brought about the rapid expansion of industry and urban life. This revolution may be called 'secularization'; it is not the deliberate spreading of a philosophy of secularism or humanism, but the changing of the conditions of man's life in such a way that the traditional religious setting, especially in its explanation of what lies beyond man's power and understanding, comes to appear uncertain or even downright ridiculous. When the Tamil Separatist Movement uses the arguments of Robert Ingersoll to denounce Brahmin religious leadership, we see the influence of Western 'secularism', but when quite orthodox Hindu vaccinators put an end to the scourge of smallpox in a village and make belief in the goddess of smallpox superfluous for those villagers, we clearly confront an example of secularization.

'Secularism' and 'secularization' can thus be distinguished, but in practice they are both present in the general change from predominantly rural to predominantly urban patterns of life and thought. Whatever may be the precise relation of cause and effect, this 'urbanization' brings with it a host of new ideas about the meaning of life, and new attitudes towards working and living which we sum up in the terms 'rationalism' and 'individualism'.

It is becoming apparent that these new patterns of living and ideas about life are increasingly affecting India's city dwellers. Our study would indicate that they are also beginning to affect life in the village, even in what has often been considered a remote and backward section of India. Whether we include them all under the term 'secularization' or divide them into a number of distinct categories, they constitute collectively another major challenge to village Christians. If this challenge is at present 'a cloud no bigger than a man's hand', its implications are so revolutionary that the Church would do well to begin its response now, while there is still time to seize the opportunity in the coming crisis.

The two types of reaction among the Christian young men who have returned to the villages after some time in the cities indicate two possible responses to this challenge, either one of which might become the response of most village Christians in the next generation. Both groups of men have lost their fear of village deities, but one group continues to join in the community festivals for their excitement value; the other group does not join in and has become more self-consciously and thoughtfully Christian. Both groups represent quite different positions from that of the rest of the Christians in these villages, who largely share the fears and hopes of their non-Christian neighbours about life and about the powers that both support and threaten it.

The bonds of shared conceptions and attitudes are joined to the bonds of blood and to the traditional network of rights and obligations linking villagers from the outcaste *kulams* to the other castes in the village. Christians have largely shared the common village values and moral standards, as well as the practices that often do not measure up to those standards. Now, however, the traditional authorities supporting these values and standards are respected less and less, and the few who have spent some time outside the village are beginning to question the traditional supernatural sanctions. This incipient secularism can be an ally of the Church in combating traditional ideas and practices, but it is a most uncertain ally, or perhaps we should say, a two-edged sword, for it undercuts confidence in Christian 'religion' as well as in non-Christian 'religion'. Furthermore, it does not by itself furnish any new basis for the life of the village, though it may be accompanied by some new ideology that does, whether the secularized Judaeo-Christian ideal of Communism or the Westernized Hindu ideal of Sarvodaya. By itself, however, this negative secularism leads to an irresponsible individualism and a disintegration of community, both within the caste group (the *kulam*) and in the village as a whole.

Christians who are not to be estranged by any of the forms of secularism that arise during the process of secularization will have to reason through their faith far more than they have done before, and they will have to find, as some of the Christian young men returning to these villages have done, a framework for their lives within the structure of the Christian fellowship itself. They must for the first time develop a morality based on Christian standards, to replace the crumbling *lokaniti* (moral standards accepted by all religious communities in the village). So far most Christians have not been able to develop and sustain such a morality, and both Christians and Hindus say that the morality of all communities in the village is now declining. It would be possible for Christians to try to separate themselves more sharply from the other villagers and to attempt to build up a stable community life for themselves while the rest of the village disintegrates, but it is extremely doubtful whether these Christians could break the bonds that tie them to their non-Christian kinsmen and neighbours before the process of secularization had proceeded so far that they would be even less committed than they are at present to the Christian fellowship and to its Lord.

Even if such separation from the 'world' were possible it would certainly not be a truly Christian response to the challenge of secularization. Christians dare not separate their efforts to build up their own life in the congregation from their continuing attempt to reach and keep friendships with their non-Christian neighbours. The bonds of neighbourliness are an obligation in themselves, but they may also result in opportunities for witnessing to the Gospel, and provide means for inviting others to join a fellowship of those who try to live in the power of that Gospel. The church in the village needs to combine an untiring effort to enter a village-wide community of service with a persistent invitation to the rest of the village to join this narrower community which worships the true Lord of creation and redemption. To undertake such a double task at a time of radical change in the village is tremendously difficult, and if village Christians are to respond creatively, they need help from the ministry of the wider Church. Some leaders of the Diocese have long seen this challenge of secularization approaching, but many church workers are barely aware of the problem, and few seem able to help village Christians begin to prepare their response.

Of all the challenges facing village Christians, the challenge of secularization is perhaps the least obvious, but it may in the long run prove the most significant. Like the other challenges, this one contains both threat and opportunity. The threat may prove greater than the present danger of dissolution in a sea of syncretistic Hinduism, but the opportunity is likewise staggering: to build a community which, as the village irrevocably enters the modern world, can preserve the traditional village sense of the diverse powers of the cosmos and of the concrete meanings of the various aspects of life—being able to do so because of the hidden rule of One who is Lord both of the changing seasons and of the modern secular age.

B. *Internal Obstacles to the Church's Response*

There are many factors that impede the response of the village congregations in the Jangarai section to the various challenges presented by their environment. The outside observer is likely to be struck with what seem to be evident weaknesses in their Christian faith and Christian life. There appears to be a persistence of the more material or worldly motives which influenced them, or their parents or grandparents, to become Christians. One important reason for this situation is the lack of effective preaching and teaching, even in villages where an evangelist has regularly been stationed, as well as the almost total lack of Christian teaching or pastoral care in congregations that have no resident evangelist. To this must be added the failure of some evangelists to give a Christian witness through their lives. It has often been all too clear to these village Christians how much evangelists (and sometimes presbyters) have been motivated by considerations of financial gain, prestige or power.

Christian in the villages we studied are not accustomed to accept responsibility for the management of their own congregation; they have grown to expect that the mission would pay their evangelist's salary. In part their attitude is a reflection of their general spiritual weaknesses, but in part it is a consequence of the assumptions that the leaders of the mission and the Church have made about the village congregations, and the fact that responsibility has been offered them in a form that is difficult if not impossible for them actually to exercise: the Leaders' Meeting limited to communicant members, who in most cases constitute less than half the adults in the congregation but have little to distinguish them from the rest of the congregation. While the pastorate committee has more appearance of functioning than the

Leaders' Meetings in the congregations, it is affected by the same fundamental difficulty. The election of the representatives is seldom taken seriously by the village congregations, and in some cases the evangelist simply appoints the representatives. Moreover, both evangelists and presbyters find it difficult to accept the idea that a pastorate committee composed of village lay leaders should really be the responsible body for managing the church's affairs in the pastorate. The presbyter often does not try to encourage expressions of opinion by village Christians or to be guided by their opinion. Frequently he prefers to have both village lay leaders and evangelists approve decisions that he has already formulated.

The administrative structure of both the pastorate and the diocese seems to us to constitute in many respects an obstacle to the village church's response to the challenges confronting it. The presbyter's tendency to command rather than guide makes it difficult for him to establish real partnership with the evangelists in a programme of evangelism and pastoral care. The presbyter's visits to his village congregations with resident evangelists are infrequent; one in three months is considered a good average. His visits to so-called 'second village' congregations are still less frequent. The presbyter usually arrives in a village one evening and leaves the next morning. The chief function of his visit is the conducting of the Communion Service. He has little time to visit in the homes of the congregation, little opportunity to observe the evangelist's work, and no occasion apart from his sermon for instruction of those brought for baptism during the service, let alone those already baptized who should be preparing for confirmation.

During such a brief visit, the presbyter does not have time even to perform all his formal duties. Perhaps still more important, he does not really get to know his people; to *listen* to them relate the problems of their day-to-day living, to *see* how they live among the pressures and attractions and hard realities of village life. The only village Christians he gets to know are the relatively few who come to the meetings at the pastorate headquarters. It is difficult for a shepherd with such a large flock to know all his sheep by name, but the presbyter of a pastorate like Wadiaram should really learn to know each member of his flock by both his names, his Christian name and his Hindu name, and learn what both of these names imply about his life as a Christian in the village.

The work of the presbyter and the evangelists is affected by the administrative structure of the whole diocese. The changes that have been made since a large part of the Hyderabad Methodist District became the Medak Diocese of the C.S.I. in 1947 have not lessened the Western character of this administration, and they have increased its complexity. Instead of an annual Synod meeting, for two weeks, during which time most committee work was transacted, there are now briefer biennial meetings of the District Church Council, the Medak Diocese Council, and the Synod of the Church of South India, in addition to more frequent meetings of many large diocesan boards and standing committees. The centralized financial system and administrative machinery require a large office staff, which adds to the financial burden of the Church. The system is still more costly in terms of the time it consumes, especially that of the bishop and the senior presbyters. There is considerable awareness of the need for some simplification and decentralization of the administrative machinery, but no agreement on precisely what should be done. A subdivision of the diocese into two or three smaller dioceses might remove the need for District Church Councils within a diocese. Within such smaller dioceses an annual session might take the place of most of the committee meetings.

Whatever might be done in improving the assistance which the wider Church can offer to the local congregations, it is these local congregations, we believe, that should be at the centre of the Church's planning. To a large extent, village Christians will have to struggle by themselves; they can no longer be dependent on their evangelist or their presbyter. We should expect the Holy Spirit to work in and through these village congregations, through the awakening of evangelistic concern, the awakening of responsibility for the management of the congregation's affairs, and the contributing of their evangelist for new work. Nevertheless, new acts of faith on the part of village Christians need to be stimulated and sustained by a more intensive teaching programme on the part of the evangelists. This teaching needs to be guided by the presbyter, not only through specific instruction to the evangelists but by demonstration of his teaching in the villages and observation of the teaching and preaching done by the evangelists. Such teaching will require teamwork between evangelists and their presbyters, which can only proceed in an atmosphere of mutual confidence. There are also other educated Christians who need to be more effectively involved in helping village Christians respond creatively to their environment: both retired evangelists who are still in good health and the few educated Christian laymen who live in the villages, particularly the teachers in the government schools.

C. Crisis and Opportunity

The internal weakness affecting the Church are more than minor obstacles to rapid growth. They make it extremely difficult for village Christians to respond to the various challenges that they face. The failure to respond to, or in some cases even to discern, some of these challenges constitutes a crisis in the life of these congregations, for without some significant response it is doubtful whether there will be a continued presence of the Christian Church in the villages of the Wadiaram Pastorate, and many others like them. Moreover, the decline in the number of evangelists and the spirit of depression among them threatens a destruction of the traditional system of pastoral care before there is an adequate substitute through the effective training of village Christian leaders and the increase in the number of ordained ministers.

The depression among the evangelists is a symptom of a spirit that affects many church leaders. It was perhaps inevitable that the optimism of a generation ago, the sense of being part of a great forward-moving enterprise, should be severely shaken by the realities of the situation in independent India. Our own study certainly indicates that there is sufficient cause for concern, not only about the more dramatic attacks on Christianity by aggressive Hindu groups, but also about influences that are less immediately threatening: the pervasive Hinduism of traditional village culture, on the one hand, and the potentially radical changes being introduced by urbanization and secularization, on the other.

At the same time, however, that the life of village Christians appears to be anything but a persuasive Christian witness and that many educated Christians are making sobering appraisals of the Church's continuing status as a tiny minority in an overwhelmingly Hindu nation, there is evidence of a remarkable evangelistic opportunity. It appears that the Holy Spirit has powerfully used the courageous witness of a few individual Christians and has worked by means often unknown to us in villagers who are still outside the organized Christian Church.

When we look at the situation more closely, we see that the *crisis* and the *opportunity* are closely linked. This is quite obviously the case from the standpoint of human relationships. Both the crisis and the opportunity are largely determined by the Christians' thorough involvement in the inter-caste society of the village and in the inter-village community within a particular caste. In their relations with non-Christian neighbours of different castes and with non-Christian relatives of the same caste, Christians are in a position both to be influenced and to influence. They must either discover and express to their neighbours the distinctive meaning of the Gospel in their village situation, or become less and less distinguishable in the general amalgam of popular Hinduism and Islam. They must either offer a new basis for family and community morality to the whole village, or see their own fragile community structures crumble under the mounting pressures of urban ways of life and thought.

The most striking instance of such involvement with non-Christians lies in the marriage relationships. An average of 65% of the sons and daughters of members of the congregations studied are married to non-Christians. There is not a single Christian in these villages who does not have many Hindu blood relations and 'in-laws' in nearby villages. At present there seem to be more Hindu influences on Christians than vice versa, but in one non-Christian village where the wives who had been baptized and grown up in Christian congregations had even forgotten their Christian names, the entire Mala community had considered the possibility of becoming Christian.

If there were even a slight deepening of the faith of the Christian congregation as a whole and some real enthusiasm for the Christian life on the part of at least a few Christians, the basis would be laid for an evangelistic campaign planned by evangelists and presbyters to follow the existing relationships of kinship and marriage. Such an evangelistic effort, we believe, might well tip the balance of influence the other way. If this happened, it would mean not only that within a few years large groups would be asking for baptism, but also that the

Christian Gospel would have many more channels through which to influence the life of the whole village.

Because the Christians have such a low wall of protective Christian 'culture' around them, Hindu influence easily penetrates the Christian community, but the same absence of a protective wall makes it relatively easy for the Christian Gospel to be conveyed to a non-Christian. Crisis and opportunity are both present in the Christian's involvement in village life, and we may well ask whether this is not more than a sociological fact, whether it is not an indication of the way God deals with His Church. The other challenges of the village Christians' environment likewise combine a real threat to the continued existence or integrity of the Church with a magnificent opportunity for a creative and faithful response. In the face of each of these challenges, the Church must either move forwards or be driven backwards; there is no possibility of standing still.

The Church's chief task in the present situation in the Telengana villages is neither to seek frantically to expand its membership nor consciously to apply the brake, cautiously retrenching in the interest of economy or of good relations with the much larger Hindu community. The Church's task is to acknowledge in word and deed the Creator of the Universe and to proclaim His redemption of the world in Jesus Christ. We believe that where Christians faithfully witness to their Lord, some who observe that witness will respond in faith. There are signs at present in Telengana, certainly in the villages we studied, that God is using the witness of faithful and courageous Christians to draw men to His Church, and that He is speaking to non-Christians in strange ways where His Church is absent or asleep.

The very evidence of God's activity in the midst of an apparently unpromising and even desperate situation is itself a call to the Church to awake, in order to participate in the Divine work of salvation in whatever way God intends. But there is no possibility of revival or renewal or advance without beginning with repentance. Many of the weaknesses in the rural congregations and the pastorate can be attributed to the lack of material or intellectual resources, or to the pressure of past tradition, or to some other external force. There can be no doubt, however, that the root of the Church's difficulty, here as anywhere in the world, is its own sin. The presbyter and evangelist must be aware of the special sins of their people, but they must, first of all, as they try to start new programmes of advance, be aware of their own special sins, particularly those which have contributed so heavily to the weaknesses among their people.

One of the prominent features of the present situation is the self-deception present among presbyters and evangelists, which may be regarded both as sin and as the consequence of sin. Most of the covering up of the weaknesses and exaggeration of 'encouraging features' in the reports which evangelists and presbyters submit is not a deliberate effort to mislead, but the result of long habit which now has led to a striking degree of self-deception. There is an unconscious effort to avoid facing unpleasant facts, and a large amount of wishful thinking which imagines that as soon as a new plan is put on paper, it is as good as realized. This spiritual blindness, even more than the occasional deliberate misrepresentation of facts, has two very serious consequences for the Church. The more obvious of these is the unawareness of the grave dangers to the Church which are now very close at hand, but the second consequence is equally serious, and perhaps even more tragic. Once our sensitivities have been dulled by this kind of self-deception, we do not see the real signs of the Church's life and growth which abound in our midst; we fail to recognize the tremendous opportunities which the Holy Spirit is creating at our very door-step. Repentance, therefore, for those whose task is to guide these village congregations, must certainly include an acknowledgement of this self-deception.

Repentance, however, is more than a painful awareness of mistakes. It is a fundamental change of heart and mind which produces 'fruits worthy of repentance'. Many of the steps we have proposed on the basis of our findings[4] are not very different from the proposals of the New Pattern, and the New Pattern was not so 'new', for many of the same proposals had been made years before. Some, indeed, have been urged repeatedly since the church was founded. The New Pattern, however, like previous efforts at reform, has so far largely failed because there has not been any fundamental change of heart on the part of both the congregations and their leaders. The steps we have proposed will likewise never be taken, or will amount to no more than some new tinkering with the machinery of administration, unless there is a real spiritual renewal within, which includes a confession of our sin, a real desire to change, a willingness to sacrifice, an openness to new leading, and the courage to act.

Even in our disobedience, we see the miracles that God is working at the edge of the organized church, but it is only as we obey that we can expect God to work His miracles through us. If only the church awakes, there are immense possibilities before it. The number of congregations might be doubled in five years, while at the same time the life of both old and new congregations could be greatly deepened. Throughout the history of this church, revival has come in a time of crisis. This should teach us a hopeful expectancy and the wisdom to discern the signs of the times. There is no excuse for complacency, however, for there have been crises to which the Church has not responded, and then God's judgment has descended upon it, sometimes more terribly than upon the world at large. All the outward pressures upon the Church will not bind the Word of God. We need not fear them if we repent and obey, but we do well to fear them as the judgment of God upon a disobedient Church.

This is the time for decision, for repentance, and for obedience. The day of judgment is at hand, 'the axe is being laid to the root of the trees' (Matt. 3: 10)—that is the message of the prophets and of John the Baptist. Yet there is the still more important word, the Gospel word, 'Now is the acceptable time, now is the day of salvation' (2 Cor. 6: 2)—not for us alone, but for the world, a world that includes the villagers of Telengana.

NOTES

CHAPTER 1. THE POLITICAL AND SOCIAL BACKGROUND OF THE TELENGANA VILLAGE

1. *Gazette of India*, 'Hyderabad State', 1909.
2. 'Hyderabad 1952', *Best Foot Forward*, issued by the Hyderabad State Government.
3. In the writing of this brief account of Telengana history, use has been made of the section 'History: the Andhras' in the feature article in Andhra Pradesh in the November 29, 1959, issue of the Indian News magazine *Link* (vol. 2, No. 16, p. 17).
4. *India, a Reference Annual, 1959*; *Andhra Pradesh*, January 1959, Vol. III, No. 3; and *Andhra Pradesh at a Glance*, published by the Andhra Pradesh Government.
5. Cf. S. C. Dube, *Indian Village*, London, Routledge and Kegan Paul Ltd., 1955. His account of 'Caste in the Village Community' (pp. 32–44) gives more details but is remarkably sketchy about the 'untouchable' groups, and his account diverges at that point from the composition of the outcastes in the Jangaria section.
6. Dube confirms our view that the villagers regard the Malas as slightly higher than the Madigas, and that the Madiga tacitly admits this by accepting food from a Mala. Elsewhere in Andhra Pradesh, Madigas sometimes do not admit the higher caste rank of the Malas (*ibid.*, p. 38).
7. Note that there are several differences from the picture Dube gives of the Malas and Madigas in Shamirpet (*ibid.*, pp. 41–42).
8. Dube has analysed the economic activities of the various castes in considerable detail (*ibid.*, pp. 57–69).

CHAPTER 2. THE HISTORY OF THE CHURCH IN THE MEDAK DIOCESE

1. A statement attributed to John Wesley, *Methodist Conference Minutes, 1744*, p. 15, quoted in F. C. Sackett, *Posnett of Medak*, p. 5.
2. *Report of the 1918 Mass Movement Commission* of the Wesleyan Methodist Provincial Synod of South India.
3. "Annual Report on the work of God in the Hyderabad District 1950", *Our Hyderabad Bulletin* (October 1951, Vol. XIV, No. 1), p. 7.
4. *Diocesan Paid Lay Workers' Committee*, Minutes 1959, p. 12.
5. This information on the "New Pattern of the Church" is a summary taken from the *Methodist Diocesan Council Minutes*, October 1955, p. 77.
6. The Statistics prior to Church Union are taken from "Growth of the Hyderabad Church", *Our Hyderabad Bulletin* (January–March 1948, Vol. X, No. 1), p. 12. The Statistics for the Medak Diocese are taken from the Minutes of the Diocesan Council and the Minutes of the C.S.I. Synod.

CHAPTER 3. HINDUISM AND ISLAM IN THE VILLAGE

1. M. N. Srinivas, *Religion and Society among the Coorgs of South India* (Oxford, Clarendon Press, 1952) especially pp. 212–14.
2. S. C. Dube, *Indian Village*, p. 92. With this entire chapter, compare Chapter Four of Dube's study, entitled 'Ritual Structure', pp. 88–130.
3. On the subject of the meaning of the 'auspicious', and the different degrees or kinds of ritual purity and impurity, compare Srinivas's study, especially Chapters Three and Four on 'The Ritual Idiom of Coorgs', pp. 70–122.

4. Dube, p. 89.
5. *ibid.*, pp. 89–90.
6. *ibid.*, pp. 89, 93.
7. Srinivas, especially pp. 212–14.

CHAPTER 5. THE LIFE OF CHRISTIANS IN VILLAGE SOCIETY

1. Before 1948, Hyderabad State had a special currency called Halli Sicca, of which the rupee was worth slightlv less than the rupee used in the rest of India. After the Police Action, the regular Indian Government currency came into use (a rupee divided into sixteen annas, each equal to twelve pies). Now the annas and pies are gradually being replaced by the naya Paise (one hundred to the rupee).
2. *The Hyderabad Gram Panchayat Act, 1956*, published by the Local Government Department, Hyderabad, Deccan.
3. *Building New Villages: Community Development in Andhra Pradesh*, Andhra Pradesh series 3, Department of Information and Public Relations, Andhra Pradesh, October 1958.
4. Information about co-operatives was secured from one of the Village Level Workers, who lives in Wadiaram.
5. A letter from the Social Service Officer, Sangareddy, dated April 22, 1959 (No. B 694/58/442), sent to Konka Nathaniel of Gowlapalli.

CHAPTER 6. THE MINISTRY AND LAY LEADERSHIP

1. *Minutes of the Medak Diocesan Council, October 1957*, p. 77.
2. *The Constitution, Regulations and Rules of the Diocese of Medak*, December 1958, pp. 72–74.
3. *Minutes of the Medak Diocesan Council, October 1955*, p. 41.
4. F. C. Sackett, *Vision and Venture* (London, 1929), pp. 254–55.
5. *Our Hyderabad Bulletin* (May–July 1942), p. 3.
6. Taken from the Principal's notebook.

CHAPTER 7. NEW CONVERTS AND INQUIRERS

1. The foregoing account is based on the author's (P. Y. L.) personal acquaintance with Sadhu Joseph, and first-hand knowledge of his healing ministry near Alisagar in Bodhan Taluk and at Sathalli in Yellareddy Taluk.

CHAPTER 8. THE MEETING OF THE GOSPEL WITH THE VILLAGE MIND

1. The Diocesan Advisory Committee for our study believes that this degree of ignorance of basic Christian teachings is not characteristic of most village Christians in the Diocese.

CHAPTER 9. THE DISTINCTIVENESS OF THE CHRISTIAN COMMUNITY

1. This summary is made from the 'Rules Concerning Marriage' in the *Constitution, Regulation and Rules of the Diocese of Medak, 1958*, Chapter XXII, pp. 83–85.
2. How does it happen that the total number marrying out of these six congregations (to both Christians and Hindus) is only 145, whereas the total number marrying in is 232? In five of the six congregations the proportion is one to two, though in Ambojipet it is just the reverse. The discrepancy is too large to be due only to the plurality of boys over girls in the families of five congregations and the reverse phenomenon in the sixth. For two of the congregations we have more detailed data which provide part of the answer.

In Kondapuram seven non-Christian men came into the congregation as *illutam* (the husband coming to live with the wife's family where her parents have no sons), but no young men went to other villages as *illutam*. In Achampet, two boys went out of the village, one by adoption and one as *illutam*, but five boys came into the congregation, three by adoption and two as *illutam*. Presumably in the Ambojipet congregation, the balance was just the other way. Another cause in the over-all discrepancy in favour of the number coming in is the fact that a number of children (chiefly girls) are not baptized as infants, or up to the time they are married out of the village, and therefore are not included in the figures above, which are only for baptized Christians whose names are on the church rolls. Since many of the unbaptized children are daughters who are deliberately not presented for baptism so that the evangelist will have no right to object to their marriage to Hindus, the actual percentage of daughters of Christian parents married to non-Christians, and thus also of all marriages between Christians and Hindus, is even higher than the figures above indicate. The proportion of 57% shown for Jangarai would be much higher if the statistics covered the large number of unbaptized children there in the last two generations, whereas the 73% for Achampet, where there are fewer unbaptized children in the congregation, gives a good indication of the actual proportion. The Gowlapalli figures look peculiar because the congregation only began in 1950. All children (mainly girls) married out to other villages before 1950 do not enter into these figures, whereas Hindus married into the community before 1950 are included (21 of the 36), because they were baptized with the rest of the group in 1950; the other 15 Hindus have come in since then.

3. There are a few cases of Christian men having two wives at the same time. In one of the congregations studied, five such families are accepted as regular members of the congregation, but such a large number is exceptional. No church discipline is being exercised. Excommunication is generally not possible, since most of those involved in such bigamous marriages are not communicant members. (There are some cases in other pastorates of men with two wives who are communicant members and even members of the pastorate committee.) Each presbyter is left to deal with this situation as he sees fit. The children of such second wives are tacitly accepted as legitimate.

There are a few illegitimate children in some congregations, though this is rarer in the villages than in the towns, because divorced or widowed women with children are usually married again, and almost every child therefore has a legal father. There are some abortions and some abandonments of illegitimate children. Presbyters are permitted to baptize illegitimate children, but some feel uncertain whether they should.

4. This was the situation at the time of our study in 1959. About two years later, however, this widow's son returned from Hyderabad with his family, quarrelled with his mother and forced her to leave the village. The son himself then took over the house and the management of the other family property.

CHAPTER 10. BAPTISM AND COMMUNICANT MEMBERSHIP

1. The only two mass movement areas within the Church of South India where most baptized adults are communicants are those where there have been missions of the Anglicans and the American Congregationalists. The former, especially those of the more Catholic wing, also separated the baptism and confirmation of adult converts as two independent acts of the Church, but they did not impose a test of Christian experience or moral growth on the candidates for confirmation; they therefore expected that all baptized Christians would after proper instruction be confirmed at a time chosen by the bishop. The American Congregationalists, for their part, have unhappy memories of the 'Half-Way Covenant' of eighteenth-century New England Puritanism, whereby the majority of baptized church members were excluded from Holy Communion, because they had not had the requisite conversion experience.

The American Congregationalists have reacted sharply against 'fencing in' the Lord's Table, and have made admittance to Communion more or less automatic for all baptized Christians above a certain age.

2. *The Church of South India: Baptism and Confirmation. A Draft Presented to the Synod, January 1960*, p. 21, par. 3.

3. *ibid.*, p. 1. par. 3.

4. *ibid.*, p. 2, par. 7.

5. *ibid.*

6. *ibid.*, p. 21, par. 3.

7. *ibid.*, p. 20, par. 1.

8. 'All pray that God may increase in the candidates the gift of the Holy Spirit by whom He makes us His own unto the day of redemption and enables us to live in God' (*ibid.*, p. 20, par. 2.).

9. *The Constitution of the Church of South India*, II–4, p. 4, and III–2, p. 18.

10. *ibid.*

CHAPTER 11. THE CRISIS AND OPPORTUNITY OF THE CHURCH

1. 'Studies in the Life and Growth of Younger Churches: under the auspices of The International Missionary Council: Aspect Studies' (Mimeographed Statement, revised January 1959), p. 3.

2. It was invented by Dr. P. T. Raju, an engineer who is a lay member of the Medak Diocese and for many years its honorary Treasurer.

3. Christians contend that the subordinate officials are wrong in interpreting the term 'Harijan' to apply only to non-Christian members of Scheduled Castles, since 'Harijan' is intended to include Christians as well, when the benefits are offered from the secular State and not from a Hindu religious trust or organization. However, the major area in which benefits for Christians have been officially approved is one in which the term 'Harijan' has been avoided. Educational grants to Christians of outcaste background have been approved by using the term 'backward classes', rather than 'Harijan', to designate the groups to which grants may be made.

4. The concluding chapter of the first draft of our report was a series of recommendations entitled 'Steps to Renewal'. In consultation with our various advisers, we later decided not to include this chapter in the published book, but to present a copy to the Bishop in Medak, the Rt. Rev. Eber Priestly. Some of these recommendations are alluded to briefly in the course of this chapter, or in one of the previous chapters.

INDEX